The SPIRIT of PLACE

A WORKBOOK FOR SACRED ALIGNMENT

The **SPIRIT** *of* **PLACE**

A WORKBOOK FOR SACRED ALIGNMENT

Ceremonies and Visualizations for
Cultivating Your Relationship with the Earth

LOREN CRUDEN

Destiny Books
Rochester, Vermont

Destiny Books
One Park Street
Rochester, Vermont 05767
www.gotoit.com

LIBRARY OF CONGRESS CATALOGING-IN-PUBLICATION DATA

Cruden, Loren, 1952–
    The spirit of place : a workbook for sacred alignment / Loren Cruden.
      p.   cm.
    ISBN 0-89281-511-6
    1. Spiritual life. 2. Spiritual exercises. 3. Shamanism—North America.
    4. Cruden, Loren, 1952–   I. Title.
    BL624.C78 1995
    291.4'3—dc20   94-35159
                                                CIP

Printed and bound in the United States

10 9 8 7 6 5 4 3 2

Destiny books is a division of Inner Traditions International

Distributed to the book trade in Canada by Publishers Group West (PGW), Toronto, Ontario
Distributed to the book trade in the United Kingdom by Deep Books, London
Distributed to the book trade in Australia by Millennium Books, Newtown, N. S. W.
Distributed to the book trade in New Zealand by Tandem Press, Auckland
Distributed to the book trade in South Africa by Alternative Books, Ferndale

Gratitude to all whose love has been a pure well from which my spirit drinks, and to my teachers, whose patience and belief in me were perhaps the greatest teaching of all.

CONTENTS

INTRODUCTION

ALL OF EARTH'S LIFE IS INTERCONNECTED AND SACRED. AN AWARENESS of that sacred relationship opens a direct path to spiritual understanding—a path that all living beings have a right to tread. Prayer—the ceremonial remembrance of "all my relations"—is a vital recognition of kinship. We are all interdependent.

The context that informs this book, and my spiritual path, is the natural world, not culture or religion. It is the world in which I live and have raised my son. There is a wilderness-dwelling heritage in the blood of all peoples, a legacy that can serve as a resource to any who choose to receive it, whether they live in an urban or rural environment.

From a place of daily intercourse with whatever in your habitat is elemental and wild, you can forge an alignment with the primal nativity of the sacred Earth.

This book is not about Native American spiritual practices. I am not a Native American, and regardless of associations with friends, students, and teachers, my experience of life in human society is that of a white person.

Nor is it about becoming a shaman—something that cannot be learned from a book or workshop. It is about a way of life offering connection to the natural forces of healing and power in the universe. It is a voice toward awakening to love. It is a response to the imperative of the medicine in my life and to the raising of a child in a world reeling from violence.

This book is personal, with the intention of touching the personal in the reader and the recognition that we are of one blood, sharing the cycles of realization and enactment. I speak from where I am now and try to sort the voice of wisdom from the static of personality.

People ask, how did I learn the teachings I share with others? It is important to honor the giveaway of guides and associates and to name the streams that feed the rivers of understanding. It is also important to realize that all life teaches, and what is shared in this book is part of an ongoing culmination of beliefs formulated by perception and experience, not a parroting of instruction. My path in particular is one that seeks understanding through direct involvement with spiritual practice.

My parents were my first teachers, and they raised their children to respect, attend to, and exalt in nature as a living, intelligent matrix of beauty. They taught us to be participants, not consumers, and my mother insisted that we transform fear into love in every encounter and attitude, with all species.

Sri Sant Ji Maharaj was my second teacher, from whom I learned to practice meditation and service starting in 1973, while traveling and living in Europe, Africa, and Asia, and spending time as housemother of ashrams in Germany and the United States.

Following those experiences, I became a householder, living with my son on eighty acres in northern Michigan. The land and my work as midwife and herbalist became profound teachers in those years. In 1981 I began a six-year association with Lewis Sawaquat, a Potawatomie medicine man who introduced me to the ceremonial forms of the sacred pipe, the sweat lodge, and the vision quest. His personal medicine was Grizzly Bear, so he specialized in dreaming, and he continues to appear as a bear in my medicine dreams.

This teacher, although a full-blooded Native, was unorthodox in his attitudes about women. He made no division between "women's" and "men's" spirituality or medicine ways—something that now makes me an oddity in terms of training and practice. Lewis was also well versed in European shamanic magic and taught me to read tarot and observe the pagan holy days that are part of my Scots heritage. He encouraged me to learn directly from the medicine, to develop my inherent capacities rather than to imitate Native tradition, and to abide in the integrity of what flows from personal relationship with the Mystery.

Six years after I first offered tobacco to Lewis, he came to my cabin with a pouch of ceremonial herbs and asked me to conduct a healing sweat for him. It seemed to be his way of saying that I was suited for the work.

In teaching others and in conducting medicine work, I am mindful of what is Native and what is native (of the land). I try to urge a native spirituality as an appropriate basis for practice.

The counsel that Lewis gave to me in the first sweat I entered returns to me again and again: he said that I must participate in life. From that commitment to participate have arisen many questions that awaken awareness: In what ways is participation best embodied? What guides relationships? What beliefs are at the core of desire? What is the dream that participation fulfills?

To participate is to be a willing part of the dance, to risk, to learn, to touch. On the deepest level, it is to realize wholeness, the end of separation's illusion. It is to affirm love, not fear.

One of the doorways for participation is through the mandala of the seasons, the path that attunes to the natural pace of rhythmic change. Wherever you live, there is that underlying presence of indigenous change—the shifting balances of light and dark, heat and cold, dry and wet, growth and rest. There are moon cycles, weather cycles, seasonal cycles. Within your own body there is constant change and interlocking patterns of function and consciousness: hormonal cycles; biorhythms; responses to light, temperature, activity, and so on.

The teachings in this book draw attention to pattern and matrix and to processes of transformation within those living webs. The lessons are meant to be applicable to the variety of belief systems and spiritual paths in current use in our world, with the intention of promoting an integration of spiritual vision with daily life and of human destiny with planetary well-being.

On this journey of consciousness, I use the medicine wheel as a map. It has counterparts in the mandalic systems of such paths as Kabbalism, Tantric Buddhism, and Taoism; but for me, living on this North American continent, it is the medicine wheel that is resonant with experience.

There is a spirituality indigenous to every land. When you move in harmony with that spirit of place, you are practicing native (not Native) spirituality. Ceremony and tradition have origin with and connection to particular peoples, but spirituality itself is a direct experience available to all.

If you are from a race or culture that isn't Native American, you can still feel a soul connection to the spirit and form of this land. What seems to be emerging in North America is a path derived from the same spirit of place that the Natives tuned to, but that expresses itself through a marriage of ancestry and place.

Ancestry gives form and continuity to spiritual practices; place gives immediacy and manifestation to power. The similarities and differences in the way medicine is made by people of various heritages should not dishonor or deny validity of the ways of others. It is certainly not a blurring of paths that is desired but a truth of what is present. It takes time, patience, and practice to find the right relationship between ancestry and place. Within that search must abide respect and care for what has come here before us.

I believe there are many walking this path. They are of all colors, all ancestries, and come to this land in one way or another to heal and be healed, to participate in transformation.

I pray that we find good ways of walking this path, ways that do not further rob the Native peoples of their cultural traditions. I pray that we recognize the racism implicit in our assumptions that religious knowledge and Native ceremonies should be accessible to us. I also pray that we clear our minds of the destructive image of white people as spiritually impoverished monsters. White people as well as all the other peoples living on this land must be part of the solution to the ills of our times.

Let there be peace. Let us weave respectful bonds of kinship. Let anger and shame pass from us. In the dawn may we be glad of one another's company. We are not separate, though our pain is the anguish of separation. The bird's flight carries our awareness in its circling, soaring rise of freedom. It carries the truth of child and ancestors, ours, everyone's. We must go forth with this reality.

Let us hear the music that comes in the heart's listening beat, see light through forest green—light that is more than light, more than leaves, light that is the joining of life to life. We must not forget anything, the small or the large, the thunder or the vast desert stillness.

There is little time for awakening, no time for waiting for a leader, only time for love beyond our thoughts of love, reaching past the faces and facades, the bitter past, the old boundaries.

Be now listening and seeing, from the center of love. The dance has begun.

SUGGESTIONS FOR USING THIS BOOK

The cycle of the year carries all aspects of the medicine wheel. By tuning to the rhythms of this dance, you can easily find the corresponding energies within yourself that are characteristic of the seasons and directions. It makes sense, just as the seedling's emergence in spring, growth in summer, fruiting in autumn, and retreat in winter make sense. It is a natural cycle. If our purpose is to reunite with the web of life and to realize our potential within it, then our path of unfolding should align with the natural cycles through which power breathes.

This book is arranged as a round of learning, a wheel where each direction, each season, invokes interrelating knowledge and skills. The lessons of one week build a foundation and open the way for the teachings that follow. The lessons reflect and embody the attributes of the seasons, which give reality and impetus to the teachings.

Working around the wheel of lessons is an experience of weaving the personal path with the larger natural matrix: the seen and unseen, known and unknown dimensions of life in motion. The resulting medicine has a truth that can't be duplicated by a disconnected modern perspective. It has the truth of a living relationship with the Mystery.

For that reason, I strongly suggest you work with this book as a literal year-long commitment that begins, if possible in the spring, just as the book begins. If this seems impractical, the lessons can be accessed through another of the seasonal doors, each of which can serve as a starting place for the year-long cycle of involvement. In our hurry-up society, this may seem an unnecessarily prolonged engagement, but in comparison with traditional approaches to esoteric knowledge, this is a quickie. I urge patience and thoroughness. It is worthwhile to walk the path with respect for the gestational duration that will give birth to something viable.

This book is not about culture, ritual, myth, or religion. It is about freedom of consciousness, love, and beauty. It is about being aware of and in harmony with the essential sacredness of life. The teachings presented here are indigenous to human enlightenment; they can be found in many cultures, many lands. I feel they are relevant to our lives in these times, on this continent. I give thanks for them to my teachers in all realms. My purpose in sharing them is to serve the awakening of consciousness.

The teachings are not final destinations. They are portals, meant to provoke insight—to be used, not collected. It is hoped that they will lead to a richness of personal practice, becoming part of our garden of individual expression. It is hoped that the first year's cycle will not end their use—that in the way of the medicine wheel, one cycle opens to the next, each time around bringing new and deeper insight and more effective application. Each lesson has many levels of practice, many dimensions of understanding. To integrate these teachings with daily life will take more than one cycle's enactment, yet they are not beyond anyone's capacity.

Each lesson concludes with suggested practices for the week, practices that ask for daily commitment in order to be useful. In addition, I recommend the following ongoing practices:

- ∾ Smudge yourself and your working space each day (see part 1, week 7).

- ∾ Keep a journal of your dreams and spiritual experiences.

- ∾ Offer prayer each day for life's blessings.

- ∾ Be patient, compassionate, and nonjudgmental toward yourself within your work. That will open the way for transformation.

The number of lessons is fewer by four than the number of weeks in a year. That gives a week following each season as a transitional rest in preparation for the next quarter. One of the weeks may perhaps be used as a time of vision questing.

I wish you well on your journey. Your feedback and correspondence are welcome; together we learn.

THE MEDICINE WHEEL

A medicine wheel is a mandalic system of correspondences relating to the six Directions: East, South, West, North, Sky, and Earth. Every medicine wheel reflects its specific location; thus there is no one "correct" wheel, only a variety of environmental perspectives true to local experience and understanding of place.

The manifested hoop of creation, expressed through natural life forms— buffalo, pine, rain cloud, hawk, waterfall—is a threshold into sacred relationship, and beyond, to cosmic consciousness. A medicine wheel can be a map of that network.

Work with the medicine wheel is based on the awareness, integration, and honoring of the six Directions, the manifested realms by which creation functions. When you address the Directions, you call into wakefulness those particular aspects of Spirit reflected in yourself. You participate more fully in life.

There is no separation from the whole of consciousness in this kind of prayer—no importuning a severed God. Rather, it is an acknowledging of wholeness, a remembrance.

Traveling the medicine wheel is the journey of the soul exploring all aspects of life. There is no duality on the wheel. The further you go into understanding

A cross-quarter medicine wheel on First Thought Mountain, Washington.

Photo by Gabriel Cruden

the East, for instance, the deeper is your cognition of the West. Balance then is not compromise, it is completeness.

Imbalance comes from boxing yourself into one spot on the wheel and trying to identify yourself with it—like saying, "Oh, I'm a Scorpio. I hold grudges," or, "I'm a South person. I can't deal with responsibility." As soon as you confine your potential you stop learning, and you also risk losing the truth of what you have already discovered. It is not the nature of healthy life to be limited in that manner.

The physical structure of the medicine wheel is often a circle of stones with four spokes, or "roads," oriented to the cardinal directions. It can be a big wheel for large gatherings, a small personal-sized wheel, or a circle on an altar. There is no one correct diameter, since the wheel in its spirit form cannot be measured in conventional terms.

It is a place to focus intentions, to pray. When you construct a medicine wheel, do it in a sacred manner: with right intention, centeredness, and attention. Attention, simple as it sounds, takes practice. Most of the time, attention is fragmented, unrooted, or fleeting. You must center your attention within all levels of function for effective work.

Another essential aspect is gratitude. It is easy to forget your dependence on the rest of creation—the trees, minerals, sun, insects, wind. When you forget your relations you isolate yourself and begin manifesting disharmony. When you forget to honor, you forget to love, and you lose touch with your own soul. Gratitude is a state of grace. It clears and strengthens you. When you live in a sacred way you are open to power and grateful for life.

Traditional medicine ways give specific paths of ceremony, sacred formulas passed down the centuries that weave the patterns of power. The formulas hold the keys, but the keys exist independent of the ceremonies. The ceremonies are a doorway, but they are not the only path. The sacred way is in the heart.

To build a medicine wheel, clear or smudge your selected stones. Also smudge your working space and anyone participating in what you are doing.

Place your center stone and surround it with a circle of seven smaller stones, a little distance away. Next place your four directional stones a good way out from center, perhaps starting with the East and going clockwise.

Now set your roads. Place three stones from the center circle out to the South stone, then three from center to North, three from center to West, and three from center to East.

Finally, connect the directional stones with a curving perimeter, three stones between each pair of directional stones, corresponding to the moons of the year.

You may want to sing or drum as you work. When finished, circle the stones with smudge herbs and then invoke the energies you hope to have present at the wheel. You can do this by making offerings, visualizing the directional spirits in turn, and raising your arms and voice in heartfelt prayer, asking for blessings and giving thanks. When the Directions have been called, then the Earth, Sky, ancestors, children yet to be born, spirits of place, and Great Mystery are asked for blessings, presence, and guidance.

By asking for blessings from the Directions you begin to explore what these realms really mean to you: what things you actually associate with Sky, Earth, and so on. You deepen your understanding of these realms and thus your relationship with the forces of life they embody. When your prayers come from your own sense of relationship, the wheel becomes a true spiritual locus for you.

The wheel can be used for seasonal celebration, healing work, group unity, vision seeking, building medicine, or other ceremonies. It is good to make offerings and smudge yourself each time you work with the wheel. It is an altar both drawing and radiating prayerful power. Working with the wheel is a way of remembering the sacred hoop and making it your precinct of spiritual practice.

Concentrate on places in the wheel that attract or intimidate you at various times. Explore beyond the surface. Use the wheel to strengthen ties with totems. Seek fresh perspective. Feel the dance of diversity at the edges of the wheel and the convergence of view from the center.

Discover which animals, plants, minerals, and attributes of spirit correspond, for you, to the different Directions and moons. Study the medicine wheels of the various peoples who work with them and see how they relate to your own intuitions. Trust that the knowledge you need is present. Because medicine wheels always mirror a specific environment of land and sky, a Zuni's wheel will not have the same correspondences as a Lakota's. Working with your own wheel is a way of becoming familiar with what is present in your own surroundings.

Use of a medicine wheel ranges from intellectual to ceremonial, yet for all its own beauty and complexity, the wheel is also a threshold to still wider realms. The components of the wheel are one language through which truth can begin to be understood.

In the East of the medicine wheel, spiritual vision is revealed—possibility, intention, motivation, inspiration. Something awakens in the dawn and is given an impetus toward expression. East is the power that rises, birdlike, into clarity and perspective.

As the sun travels from morning to midday, so movement to the South on the wheel brings expansion into the experiences of relationship and alliance. Concepts formed in the East find their testing in the fire of the South. Sexuality also comes into play as an animating and transforming medium for conceptual energies, a creative channel within alliance.

The setting sun in the West carries Spirit's vision into the realms of mystery. These depths encourage introspection, reflection, nonordinary states of mind, and acceptance of self. The West is a place of sorting and letting go and of conscious participation in acts of power. The vision that was perceived in the East and engaged with in the South now becomes multidimensional, and its broader and more subtle implications are made apparent.

In the North, the vision is manifested, enacted, embodied in fullness, and set free. North is where wisdom is attained and knowledge released, healing fulfilled and strength offered to others. Then the wheel turns and again the dawn brings new vision.

The wheel can also be seen to resemble the cycle of a butterfly. In the East, the egg: mind looking at the world (awareness). In the South, the caterpillar: mind experiencing relationship (alignment). In the West, the chrysalis: mind entering multidimensional consciousness (acceptance). And in the North, the butterfly: mind embodied (actualization).

In the knowing of the matrix—the web of life—is the knowing of sacred self, because all aspects of the matrix are interwoven expressions of the Mystery. That is the core of what is being said in the Native ceremonial phrase "all my relations." It is an acknowledgment and honoring of universal kinship.

Bisecting the sphere of the medicine wheel are two "roads," the East-West axis and South-North axis. The East-West road is the interplay of inward and outward sight. It is the cyclic path of understanding and acceptance. In the East, concepts are formed, and their arrangements in consciousness become charged with energy. These thought patterns, when charged with emotion, become the ego's belief system; emotional and intellectual energy, bound into specific formations, determines the paradigm guiding individual life experiences.

When energy is emptied from belief, the thought patterns can shift, just as molecules form new structures when heat or stress is applied. When energy is routed through the altered thought structures, perception and experience change. When beliefs are utterly transformed or disrupted, or are let go of so thoroughly that their attendant thought patterns lose the stability of their structure, the experience is that of either madness or liberation.

The West is where belief goes through its changes. The fluidity of this realm, which is associated with nonordinary states of mind, enables conceptual reorganization. Working with dreams and trance helps the mind release fixated beliefs and learn to apply thought patterns flexibly in ways supportive of spiritual intention.

Resources and alliances can be invoked to create or strengthen applicable mental structures. Beliefs that do not serve a perceived good are dismantled, and their energy rerouted. That is one way of describing the act of "making medicine." Energy, through established spiritual alignment, is called into a pattern, and the manifestation of energy-within-pattern is brought through the realms.

The South-North path is the road of fulfillment, of spirit within body, just as the East-West axis is the path of heart within mind. The South-North journey is a lesson in balance and purposefulness. Belief must find reference in spiritual adjustment, which guides action and relationship. If the East-West road is the understanding of being, then the South-North road is actualization through doing. The truth of Spirit is carried into physical expression: Heaven and Earth unite. Most modern spiritual seekers are oriented to the East-West path, whereas most "primitive" peoples traditionally focused on the South-North path. For today's spiritual explorer to go beyond self-involvement into an integrated expression of spiritual truth within daily life, he or she needs to make a shift of axis.

The South-North and East-West roads are as important as the directional stations. Those two axial paths, of capacity (South-North) and intention (East-West), become precincts of transformation when a wholeness of spiritual practice and understanding has been awakened.

The associations for the medicine wheel in the accompanying table are an example of one mandala of manifestation.

When the wheel and its roads become familiar ground, something deeper begins to emerge, like consciousness within breath. The mandala of the wheel becomes a passage into the folding and unfolding cosmos, where delineating consciousness loses boundaries and anchors of form, belief, and ego, and enters the mind of the Mystery.

The thought of the matrix, the forms and dimensions of life's manifestation, emanates from here—the sacred dream—in its vastness of potential and realization. When the mandala is entered, Spirit is invigorated by love—the medium of the sacred dream—and by beauty, which is the truth of its expression. Spirit glimpses home, mirrored in the matrix, in light, in grace, in the blossom of a rose. From form to essence to cosmic mind, the resonance of love guides the journeyer home, whether that journey begins in the cry of an eagle, the coils of a snake, or the silence of snow.

There are infinite doors into the wheel's center, a place without measure or location. A Tibetan Buddhist may enter using meditation on the form of a particular deity; a North American shaman may, in trance, align with the medicine of a

THE FOUR DIRECTIONS OF THE MEDICINE WHEEL

Spring/East	Summer/South	Autumn/West	Winter/North
mind/awareness	identity/ego	heart/emotion	embodiment
wind	fire	water	earth
morning	afternoon	evening	night
childhood	youth	adulthood	elderhood
beginnings	growth	transition	fulfillment/renewal
trust	idealism	introspection	wisdom
acceptance	relationship	maturation	knowing
fourth chakra	third chakra	second chakra	first chakra
thought	action	intuition	being
hope	grace	power	strength
vision	sexuality	dreaming	livelihood
guidance	freedom	metamorphosis	justice
illumination	courage	beauty	healing
innocence	transformation	protection	endurance
communication	experience	prayer	purification
speech	music/dance	creativity	rest
leadership	searching	sacrifice	guardianship
truthfulness	generosity	humility	perseverance
joy	passion	compassion	peace
belief	testing	karma	detachment
concentration	desire	psychic skill	actualization
spontaneity	loyalty	self-acceptance	prosperity
clarity	sensitivity	clairvoyance	evaluation
quickness	vigor	patience	organization
intelligence	will	perception	balance
seeing	touching	hearing	counsel

THE ROADS

East path	South path	West path	North path
clarifying lessons	lessons of growth	karmic lessons	purifying lessons

East-West axis: path of cycles; integration of vision into your life

South-North axis: spirit path; integrating your life with vision

totem. All mystic practices are ways of freeing consciousness from limiting beliefs about self and reality. Success in these practices allows truth to be experienced, in the realization of healing, peace of mind, and right relationship with others.

Work with the medicine wheel does not necessitate complicated ritual or extensive knowledge. It begins in the heart, with prayer. It begins in the heart because that is love's compass—love, the breath of the Mystery—and so the heart knows where to turn to find home.

East, gate of the morning, I come here in prayer.

Thank you for this new day; for the light, for the moving airs, for the awakening of life.

May my eyes lift to see the freedom of the birds; may my thoughts be in awareness of the gifts of each moment.

South, sacred fire of creativity, I seek your vitality in healthy alliance. Thank you for the teachings of relationship. I pray that my life may unfold in harmony with my kin in all realms.

Thank you for humor, music, dance; those things that carry joy and communion.

West, power of the places between the worlds, I turn to you seeking passage into the depths of knowing.

Thank you for the lightning and the cleansing rain, for the experiences that teach compassion and nourish understanding.

Thank you, Panther, for the medicine of solitude, and of the patient stalking for truth.

North, Spirit's mountaintop, I look to you for wisdom. In the place free of shadow I seek perspective and a path of service.

Thank you for the gifts of lodge and sustenance. I pray to live upon this gracious Earth with remembrance of gratitude, and with respect for my elders in all realms.

Thank you for the times of renewal and healing.

Great Mystery, Spirit in all, I give thanks for my life on this good day.

All my relations.

THE SPIRIT OF SHAMANISM IN NORTH AMERICA

Many of the people who tell me of their interest in a shamanistic path have had their inspiration come from reading Lynn Andrews's or Carlos Casteneda's books, or similar tales of power. These books have brought aspects of shamanism into the popular culture, for better or worse, but their translation into practical terms is problematic.

Psychic battles, guarding and stealing power, sorcery on the mountaintops, and wise old teachers in wilderness cabins are not the essential elements of a spiritual path, though in some cases they might be experiences encountered along the way. They fire the imagination far more than do the simple practices that are the basis of a spiritual life, but it is misleading to characterize shamanism as a life of Hollywood special effects.

One of the clearest indications of the shaman's changing role and position in society is the glamorizing of the image of the shaman. In the past, public admiration of prominent medicine people was due to their deeds, not their office. Celebrity status in today's world has little to do with substantial contribution. Modern society tends to lavish its attention on those who stimulate and entertain it—and to starve its true workers.

Ironically, fame invokes envy and criticism as easily as it invokes adoration and awe. Either response can impede effective medicine work. In such a shadowed, divisive framework, money issues have become the focus of considerable controversy.

These days, both Natives and non-Natives often express indignation over the "selling of medicine," as if this were some new (European) scheme. Certainly, there are rip-offs, exorbitant fees, cons, and abuses to be found in the arena of shamanic practice, as in all realms of human interaction. But the selling of medicine is not new. In former times, medicine objects, songs, healings, and other spiritual services were often paid for in one form or another. In most traditional cultures, the shaman's work was part of a web of giving and receiving within the tribe—the shaman supported, and was supported by, the tribe. In contrast, the urban shaman often operates outside the interconnectedness of community, making it easy for the accumulation of money to become a goal that overshadows service to community.

I believe that at the root of the current controversy over the "selling of medicine" is a more fundamental issue: the confusion over who "owns" shamanism and medicine ways. Many traditionalists feel that non-Native use of Native shamanic forms, like selling medicine for money, is inappropriate. Others are concerned that Native spirituality is being misappropriated and exploited by non-Natives. Native spirituality should not be one of the spoils of conquest. Non-Natives cannot in clear conscience presume claim to it. Neither can Natives own what is indigenous to the land, a spirit that requires no particular skin color to access and align with it.

There are many questions waiting to be addressed. Are the powers of the pipe, the lodge, and the vision seeking expanded or diminished through their use and change by non-Natives? Are these forms cultural or universal? Are traditional taboos cultural; what part do they play in an evolving shamanism? By whose authority does anyone approach the sacred? How can we speak together when so many lines have been drawn?

Recently, I have been left with the feeling that shamanism is branching as well as changing: one road leads back to traditional communities that are culturally distinct, indigenously Native; one road goes to the city, where it is seen as a technique, therapy, or path of personal power; and one road meanders across the natural Earth, where it becomes simply native. All those paths may have their gifts to offer, their evolving parts to play.

As we watch and participate in this transformation of shamanism, it is important to consider the nature of tradition. Tradition is associated with historical duration, but actually it mirrors the perspective of a certain people at a particular time. When a society evolves as a harmonious part of the living world, its traditions usually evolve also; thus tradition includes both continuity and change. When a society becomes momentarily stagnant or stalled, the emergence of new patterns—made manifest through the work of visionary individuals—brings vitality and movement to traditional systems. Whether those visionaries are welcome or unwelcome depends on the society.

Oftentimes the agents of change are those individuals on the fringes of tradition. No matter how unorthodox those agents, though, any change that is rooted in the fertile ground of understanding and resonant with wisdom will not be capricious or destructive. It will be as natural and fruitful as an acorn falling from an oak and growing into a new tree.

For a people whose culture is under siege, however, tradition can easily become a symbol of the past. It can become static, dogmatic, a wall rather than a living force. When this happens, people may find it easier to preserve their distinct cultural identity, but their medicine ways can lose touch with Spirit—the source of transformative and healing power. Such societies prefer the stability of tradition to the vagaries of direct interaction with Spirit, and they learn to fear visionary individuals—the shamans and changers.

At the opposite end of the spectrum from those bound to tradition are those shamanic practitioners who try to extract shamanism from the culturally coded, symbolic language of gesture, art, myth, protocol, natural correspondence, and so on. A shamanic practice thus extracted becomes orphaned. It may be able to survive on its own, but it is likely to grow up impoverished—outside of community and context.

When I hear of urban shamans, I must admit I am reminded of urban cowboys, all sexy specialized garb and paraphernalia. Their talk of Bear, Wolf, and the power of the Moon seems incongruous with their city habitat and lifestyle. Admitted bias aside, there seems to be something ungrounded in a shamanism that has no immediate physical correlation. Shamanism arose in and was intimately informed by the shaman's natural setting: the world of plants, animals, stars, rock formations, streams, balances of light and dark, heat and cold, rain and drought. The urban dweller has a habitat to connect with also: city animals, trees and other plants, pets and companions, seasons, weather, rhythms, energy, machines, community, city structures. The Earth is alive in the city too. When urbanites align to this life respectfully, their priorities shift and they can begin to nourish, rather than exploit, the living Earth.

But what I see in urban-suburban shamanism is a focus on techniques severed from either cultural or environmental contexts. When a psychologist invites a client to journey to find a power animal, and the client returns with the image of a bear, is it a power animal or a projection of desire for power? You can read what Bear represents in a New Age book or meditate upon its image depicted on a divination card. In these modes, Bear becomes a two-dimensional symbol or projection of power, but for must urbanites Bear has no correlation in direct experience.

When multilevel relationships with natural and supernatural beings and places are forgotten and are replaced by systems of metaphors and exercises of the imagination, can the resulting practices be honestly called shamanic? Is this truly a new development in shamanism, or is it something else—perhaps a development in psychology? In the past, shamanism included psychology, but in trying to incorporate shamanism, psychology reduces it to a Jungian technique.

The crucial difference here is that between the personal matrix and the transpersonal (cosmic) matrix. The personal matrix is defined in psychological terms. It is the web of beliefs that shapes self-identity and that is separate, limited, and linear in perception. It is like a fearfully fenced-in house. The cosmic matrix is a network within which the self identifies with all aspects of the Mystery, with "all my relations." It is defined in sacred terms and is expansive, inclusive, and multidimensional. This perspective is like a house in the wilds where there is an integration of inner and outer, home and habitat, self and other. Beliefs that constrict identity create a fence past which Bear or Wolf or River cannot go, except as concepts, and as such their power is constrained within psychological parameters.

Traditional shamans and the people they served derived their insights from both spiritual and physical experience. Their understanding of Bear medicine included actual encounters, prolonged observations, direct interactions, and sometimes confrontations with bears. Physical experience informs emotional response, which is translatable into realizations integrating knowledge with feeling. Bear medicine has a different power and application—a deeper relevance and meaning to life—when it is an element of immediate experience, when you are available to it physically as much as it is available to you metaphorically.

Bear is not just representative of a psychological concept. Bear claws and skins come from bears, not stores. Bear is indivisible from its physical manifestation, and a spiritual relationship with Bear is lacking in wholeness if there is not some level of direct involvement. To claim Bear as an ally from the comfort of your apartment—while in the wilderness grizzlies are almost habitatless—would seem to indicate a widening gap in relationship.

Part of traditional medicine work was to mediate—to maintain harmony and good relations—between the tribe and spirit beings. Not only was this service accepted by the people, but it was considered essential to the survival and well-being of the community. Now that society no longer feels threatened by bears or in need of respectful relationship with them—or, as some might have us believe, in need of bears at all—modern shamanic practitioners are seldom called on to mediate with external spirit beings or powers. Instead, they tend to focus almost exclusively on internal processing, working on individual healing, empowerment, and personal growth.

The spirit of shamanism remains one of awareness of the sacred, of service to the web of life, and of bridging the realms. This map includes plenty of room for each individual's dance with power, and with the community. Out of respect for the Native cultural integrity that has been so arrogantly assailed, however, perhaps non-Native visionaries who are inspired to change traditions would do well to create new names for their new paths. Clarity in naming can dispel many of the shadows that cause us to collide and move disharmoniously with one another.

A woman at a workshop I was conducting came to me afterward and said, "When you took out the feathers I suddenly realized that power is a serious thing and not a game. I felt the medicine in the room and needed to sit still for a while."

Toying with shamanism didn't happen much in the days when the path took a certain commitment, effort, realization of risk, public responsibility, and demonstration of competency. If shamanism is ever again to be joined fully to our natural and societal fabrics, it needs to be represented by adept and Spirit-aligned practitioners, and it needs to have relevance to truth, which is at the core of healthy change. Shamans, like artists, lead and reflect society, and so are gauges of both our potentials and our ills.

Recently, when I visited Bear Butte and was told that there is no fee for people who are visiting for religious purposes, regardless of color, I wept with relief. As I climbed the sacred butte, praying as I walked, there was a quiet in the air—contrasting with the lightning storms and tornadoes we had passed in crossing the prairies. I sat for a while beside a pine tree partway up the butte, watching an eagle, a buzzard, and a hawk riding the thermals above a ridge. Feathers fluttered on prayer flags along the path, perhaps stirred as I was by the presence of their relatives. I felt the timelessness of this holy place—knew many others had trodden this same path with intentions of vision or guidance from Spirit. Many other eyes had gazed at those towering rocks, so self-contained beneath the wide sky.

Moving up the trail again, I began to feel a gathering of power, increasingly intense; it was a palpable spirit presence. I took out my tobacco pouch and prayed aloud as I walked. The feeling of presence grew stronger and I stopped. I questioned if it was right for me to be here, but there was no fear, no rejection in that place. The presences I felt resonated in my marrow, lifting me up the trail like the warm thermals beneath the birds.

Then, rounding a curve in the path, I suddenly came upon the flagged precinct of a vision fast. An elderly man—from his regalia apparently a shaman—was deeply in communion with the spirits. The air around him pulsed and shimmered, and I felt as if I were moving through thick honey. I whispered an apology, set down some tobacco, and without pausing removed myself from further intrusion.

Later, after I descended the butte, a bluebird met me at the edge of the parking lot. "Don't fret," it seemed to say, "no harm."

When I remember that experience, I wonder—was that encounter in some way symbolic of the general situation between Native and non-Native shamans? Was I part of something invoked, or was I perhaps not really seen at all?

I remember the vision seeker's eyes, focused on other worlds, turning toward me with neither resentment nor welcome. An acknowledgment of presence, but in which world? An eagle circling, the smell of sage hanging in the glittering air, a tobacco offering left beside the path. No disrespect, only the language of prayer.

The snow has departed,
its justice done for another round.
Spring stirs, sure but unseen within,
beneath. Any pregnant woman
knows the truth of this.
We walk, dog and cat and I,
soft-pawed on the cool earth,
the sun newly confident,
beginning to remember August.
The breeze is infused with life's dreams,
and after a time I must sit, full from
this rich forage.
I have become lean
on the spare voice of Winter wind
and on the silence of night
through which I have so many times
waited for the stars to find me.
One thing I learned—
not to let our offerings
bury what is already here,
shining.

Part 1

EAST/SPRING:
FOCUSING THE MIND
Spring Equinox to Summer Solstice

This journey begins in the East, place of the rising sun, the dawn, the time of beginnings. It commences at Spring Equinox, festival of new life, of balance and hope. The trees are opening their buds. Life is emerging from winter's rest. It is time to move outward from the long dream, to take your gifts into the light.

Because manifestation originates in thought, it is with the mind that you begin the work. It is through consciousness that you experience an awareness of life, explore the potentials of reality, and choose what sort of life in which to participate. The intentions of a spiritual path begin in the mind. It is here that understanding awakens and freedom is realized.

In this season you will focus on opening to awareness, vision and illumination, and alignment with truth.

BEGIN WITH A PRAYER:

Powers of Earth and Sky, powers of all Directions, Great Mystery, I am here with prayer. I am calling for blessings of this work.

Behold me, all you spirits, all you sacred beings—I am here with a heart seeking truth, seeking beauty, longing to be in good relationship with all life. I am asking for help and guidance on my path. I am here to be in alignment with my destiny, with my purpose upon this gracious Earth.

Great Mystery, Sacred Beings, I walk with commitment upon this path of harmony. I call for your blessings, with gratitude for my life. I remember all my relations.

Spirits of Wind, of East, of Spring, I pray with you. In these weeks, I will be walking in your midst. I pray for your support and help. I pray for understanding and insight, for expanded vision.

Light of the morning, gate of dawn, I come before you like a newborn, eager to grow and learn. I come, grateful for the gentle light, the blessing of new beginnings.

O winged ones, I ask for your company, your messages and teachings. I pray for your inspiration and for awakening of spiritual perspective.

Powers of East, I turn to you in the light of sacred intention and give thanks for your presence.

Breath is your most sacred and precious gift as an embodied being. It links you in each moment to Spirit and is also the basis of your physical well-being. Amazing, what little attention is given to this most essential aspect of life.

Breath is the vehicle of power. It is your most effective and ever-present tool for spiritual practice.

To be mindful is to be in awareness of the present moment. The present moment is your doorway to transformation, so to be mindful is to be at a pivot point where conscious movement and change are possible. When you are with your breath in a mindful way, you are with the present moment.

This awareness can take you to your center, a place of clarity because it is not occupied with projection into past or future. It is now, so it sees itself truly. From your center can also be discerned beginnings and endings; here you may be more deliberate with your thoughts, actions, and emotions.

Breath can be used to distribute vitality through the body and aura. It can regulate levels of tension and relaxation, aid shifts into altered states of consciousness, and direct the traffic of energy through the chakras and meridians.

The chakras are intersections in the aura where incoming and outgoing energy flows and circulates through the subtle and material bodies. A later lesson will focus on the chakra system in greater detail. In this lesson you will work with opening and clearing the top four chakras, which are the ones most involved with the East/Spring teachings.

Sit comfortably or lie on your back. Be in present awareness. Feel the presence of the Earth below and the Sky above. Breathe—slowly, deeply, gratefully. Be at home in yourself—you are blessed with the sacred gift of breath.

With each inhalation, feel life's vitality moving through you; with each exhalation, relax and become more peaceful, more clear. Feel the vast universe of which you are part.

Focus your attention on the crown of your head, the very top. Breathe through this, the seventh chakra. Breathe in, breathe out, feel the sensitivity there. Feel your connection to the sky, the cosmos. Breathe in its resources, delight in its beauty, welcome its gifts. Let your chakra open like a flower to the sun. Greet the heavens, embrace a lightness of being. Breathe.

Focus your attention on your brow, the place of the sixth chakra, the third eye. Breathe in through the crown and circulate that vitality through the sixth chakra and out again. Let each breath intensify your awareness and deepen your relaxation. Breathe indigo light. Illumine your inner sight, open your center of spiritual vision, relax your eyes. Breathe. Feel your intuition stir. Feel an awakening of sleeping powers. Let your thoughts float calmly by, without struggle. Breathe and be present.

Move your attention to your throat, the fifth chakra. Breathe blue light. Relax your jaw, your ears, and your shoulders. Feel the light opening the way for breath to flow smoothly, like cooling water, like blue sky. Relax your arms and hands. Breathe deeply, gratefully. Feel the center of your creativity opening. Feel your capacity for communication expanding. Breathe. Allow your inner hearing to open, to awaken, to be aware of messages. Know you are part of a matrix of life, and breathe through that connectedness.

Let vitality flow to your heart, the fourth chakra. Breathe love. Expand your chest and feel your relaxation deepen. Let fear ebb away. Let worry vanish. Let grief turn to healing. Breathe emerald light. Feel the pulsing of life, feel it flowing through you. Breathe compassion, open your heart to love's strength. Feel yourself infused with light. Be luminous, whole.

Feel the breath travel from crown to Earth. Remember your grounding. Sink your awareness to where your body contacts what is closest to the Earth. Extend deeper, into the Earth. Draw upon that stability and nourishment, a reference point for your body's well-being. Breathe awhile more in this safe space, clear and peaceful and energized. Slowly open your eyes and orient yourself to body and place. Be grounded. Thank the universe for its gifts.

During This Week

1. Be attentive to your upper chakras.

2. Remember your breath, as often as possible. Say to yourself things like "I am here in line at the grocery store and I am breathing." Be present with your breath, with yourself. Try to be mindful and to breathe in an unconstricted way. Make sure your clothing allows you to do this. Don't pinch your waist!

3. Several times a day, perhaps when walking or sitting, do eight-count breathing. This technique was shown to me by Lois Barnett, an acupuncturist. It involves counting to seven during an inhalation, counting the number eight as the turnaround pause, and then counting to seven again during the exhalation, with number eight as the pause before the next inhalation, and so on. Use whatever pace is comfortable as long as the counts are all evenly spaced. Note how that pattern makes you feel. It is an Earth rhythm.

4. Count breaths. Try counting at least ten breaths in a row, one for each time you inhale and exhale. If you lose concentration, start again at one. That is a simple and effective way to keep your attention on your breathing, hence in the present moment. It is an important preparation for the next lesson.

5. Practice the following wordless song. It is a Native song, a Swinomish water song taught by the medicine man Johnny Moses to members of the Red Cedar Circle. Use the vowel "Ah" as you practice it. Each line should be done in one breath, slowly! This will deepen and relax your breathing, open your chakras, and bring a positive feeling. The voice can be accompanied by a bell.

MEDITATION

THE PURPOSE OF MEDITATION IS TO BRING YOU AN AWARENESS AND understanding of being that goes beyond attachment or aversion to beliefs. It is to liberate consciousness, resulting in peace of mind, body, and feelings.

Through meditation, you realize that mind is both the subject and the object of consciousness: there is no dichotomy. This realization gives a basis for spiritual work that transcends the limitations falsely imposed on consciousness. It transforms the way life is viewed and experienced. It is a tool for all stages of enlightenment.

In meditation you learn self-discipline, focus, and letting go, all of which can be applied to both mundane and spiritual daily activities. Cultivating capacities for stillness and concentration is important whatever the personal path. Meditation nourishes true vision.

It is recommended that you meditate either in a chair or sitting on the floor, so that your spine is straight. If you have the space, it may be encouraging to have a special meditation nook with an altar and a pleasant place to sit.

I often use incense when I meditate, burning a particular scent that is conducive to that particular state of consciousness. I reserve separate kinds of incense for meditation and for trance, so that the different scents trigger the desired state almost automatically. The burning incense also keeps your space cleared of unwanted influences while you are engaged. Sandalwood, frankincense, and Nag Champa are all traditional allies for meditation. They can be obtained from many food co-ops and meditation supplies stores.

Experiment with what works best for you—it should be something you like to smell! If you keep separate incenses for meditation, trance, or other spiritual work, you will notice how different states of consciousness are more quickly accessed with those catalysts.

Meditation begins with breath awareness, and sometimes it helps to count the breaths as a way of bringing yourself into focus.

There are eight practices taken from Buddhist teachings that I find generally useful in developing mental equilibrium and freedom. They don't need to be practiced in any particular order.

1. Awareness of the breath and the present moment (previous lesson).

2. Observation of the body—focusing attention on each part of the body in turn, with gratitude, and without judgment or analysis.

3. Unity of body and mind—bringing calm to the body through calming the mind.

4. Observation of emotions—noticing each feeling that is present, without separation or struggle, without adversity toward oneself. By seeing, accepting, and understanding with compassion, one can transform unwanted emotions.

5. Observation of thoughts—bringing stillness by allowing thoughts to arise and subside without becoming involved with them.

6. Concentration on an object in mind, becoming one with it, knowing it.

7. Being present with the simple joy of meditation.

8. Awareness of endless transformation—seeing the impermanence of sensations, feelings, thoughts, objects. Realizing your freedom from dogma, from circumstances, from fear of death, from self-image, from neediness, from being caught up in beliefs.

During This Week

Meditate every day, at whatever time is best for you. Early morning is recommended. It helps to establish a rhythm of practice, but more important is to make it a long-term part of your life. The momentum and cumulative effects will be easily discerned if you meditate regularly.

Don't set unreasonable demands on yourself—ten minutes daily is worth more than an hour erratically. Often, sitting in a chair enables you to relax and stay focused longer than if you attempt the classic lotus position on the floor. Meditation should be a kindness to yourself, not a relentless task.

VISUALIZATION SKILLS (Part 1)

IMAGINATION, TOGETHER WITH FOCUSED WILL AND ALIGNMENT WITH power, can invoke, actualize, and shape events in physical life. Visualization is a skill for directing power within consciousness. In its active form, visualization is creative. In its receptive form, it can reveal the inner landscape of the psyche. With the first two parts of this lesson, we will explore the active form, and in part 3, the receptive form.

With the focus, attunement, and directing of power through visualization, you can participate more consciously with your life path. There is power in participation. I see active visualization as useful in seven ways:

1. In training and strengthening the mind and will

2. In understanding the nature of things

3. In making changes or positive outcomes

4. In healing and maintaining healthy states

5. In working with totems and allies

6. In protection and in dissipation of unwanted energies

7. In accessing archetypal presences and energies

This week, practice the first three of those seven. Some examples of each follow:

1. Training and strengthening the mind and will

   Example A.   Visualize a mirror. See yourself in the mirror. Now see yourself seeing yourself in the mirror.

   Example B.   Visualize the color red. Add each of the colors of the rainbow to your visualization one at a time—orange, yellow, green, blue, indigo, violet. Hold them all in your mind's eyes simultaneously. This may take practice! Then subtract one color at a time, starting with red, ending with violet.

2. Understanding the nature of things (this overlaps with number six in your meditation practices)

   Example A.   Visualize the symbol for infinity. Hold it in your concentration for five minutes the first time; after that, hold the symbol for ten or more minutes. Don't think about it, just meditate with it until you resonate with its essence.

Example B.   Visualize a waterfall, from any angle or series of views. Again, try to extend your duration of focus each time you practice. You will probably find that it is much easier to hold this elemental type of visualization than the abstract infinity symbol. This elemental form has added the factors of texture, sound, and emotional connotations from memory.

3. Making changes or positive outcomes

Example.   Visualize a situation in your life about which you have anxieties or difficulties. See yourself working through the situation in a productive, joyful way. Use details of sight, sound, smell, touch, and taste to create a strong and realistic progression of images. Be thorough, but be sure that your visualization does not violate the free will of others in any way. Always do these visualization in the present tense, otherwise you may not be able to actualize what you want in physical reality.

During This Week

Practice these three uses of visualization. Make note of how each feels to you, and what happens in your mind when you work with it. See which ones are easiest or most difficult. Like an athlete, gauge your current level of fitness and endurance, and don't push yourself too strenuously all at once. Have fun with the exercises— explore your mental muscles. Get a sense of possibility, within right use of power and mind.

THE FOLLOWING EXAMPLES OF VISUALIZATION CAN BE EMPLOYED OR CAN serve as springboards for your own ideas:

4. Healing and maintaining healthy states

Example A. Visualize light entering through your crown chakra and systematically filling your entire body. Do this very slowly. Fill your head with light; then fill your hair, ears, brain, every cranny. Then move down to your neck and throat. Go slowly down the right side of your body, filling each part with light. When you reach your toes on the right foot, move over to the left foot and go up the left side of your body; fill each part completely with light until you are once again at your head. Visualize yourself in wholeness, full of light. (I learned this technique from Lois Barnett.)

Example B. Focus your attention on a part of your body that feels painful or stressed. Visualize it. Ask that body part what is going on and listen nonjudgmentally to the answer. Thank that part of you for the specific work it does and for its gifts to your well-being. Breathe vitality and healing into that part of you, or through the chakra that is associated with that area of the body. Visualize a harmonious balance, energy flowing freely as needed to all parts of you, without constriction or pain.

In using visualization for healing, many people choose images that relate to specific physical outcomes or that deal with physical symptoms and manifestations. I suggest, instead, that you approach the situation in a more inquiring way—to seek the roots of manifestation within the subtle levels of causation and to understand what is going on behind the scenes.

It doesn't really further your purposes to merely pacify symptoms or even to "cure" a disease or injury if you are only substituting a cultural belief about what constitutes health for a belief or behavior pattern that caused illness. It is like giving a crying child a cookie and calling the resulting quiet happiness.

Maybe the crying is what the child needed. Maybe it is more valuable to look beyond the superficial cause of the tears, and beyond your own discomfort with the crying, to what is really being communicated. All this takes perceptive attention, compassion, and willingness to let go of reflexive beliefs, emotions, and responses.

5. Working with totems and allies

Example A.   Visualize an animal you feel an alliance with. See yourself with the animal. Note your response to it, and its to you. See yourself and the animal doing something together. Have a conversation—ask some questions.

Example B.   Visualize yourself as being an animal you feel an alliance with. See yourself shape-shift to that animal's form and then have an experience within that form. Make note of how this feels to you and what aspects of the shape-shifting reveal gaps in your factual knowledge about the animal's form and behavior. This visualization work will prepare you for deeper levels of totem alliance, which will be discussed in later lessons. The visualization exercise can give some insight into your feelings about a totem and what you know about that animal.

6. Protection and dissipation of unwanted energies

Example A.   Create a protective zone around your house or room by visualizing columns of light surrounding the area. Charge them with power from the universal matrix to avert harmful intrusion. To draw on universal power, release your belief in a limited self and allow your consciousness to expand into an awareness of cosmic resonance. Use focused intention to direct light, as a specific expression of this resource, into your protective zone. Check on these columns from time to time and renew as needed.

Example B.   Visualize the air around you becoming infused with charged molecules of loving power. Breathe this air, move within its safety. Feel it all around you. Rather than a barrier or shield, it is a permeable aura transforming any ill wishes that you encounter.

7. Accessing archetypal presences and energies

Example.   Visualize dancers coming toward you. See them as corn maidens, young women with faces rubbed with corn pollen. Their skirts and ponchos are white; their sashes have corn husks tucked in them; their headbands are yellow. They carry in one hand baskets of corn meal and in the other, fans of turkey feathers. Hear the deer-toe rattles and the drums as the dancers come closer and circle you. Feel their medicine. Silently make a prayer to them and thank them for coming. See them dancing away into the distance and disappearing.

During This Week

Practice visualization with the examples given here or with others of your own invention. Notice the differences between meditation and visualization. Which is easier for you? There are overlaps in various states of altered consciousness such as meditation, visualization, trance, dreaming; there are also distinct differences.

Sometimes semantics make communication about these states difficult to sort out, particularly because of the overlaps. Practice, study, and experience will help you clarify these distinctions and will guide your use of these states. Understanding the distinctions will enable you to work more effectively. Later lessons will re-address this subject.

When doing visualization, always first relax, ground, and center yourself. Make a safe zone for doing this work. Be warm and comfortable. For visualization directed at change or at establishment of new patterns, be persistent and repetitive.

Work in positive modes, using affirmative words, images, and thought forms. Never interfere with the will or destiny of others. Be conscious of the consequences and possibilities attached to what you are invoking into your life. It is easy to fixate narrowly on an intention or desire without mindfully examining its full implications. It is also easy to visualize change in terms of getting rid of what you don't want, which then leaves a vacuum. In making choice a conscious process, you take on responsibility for applying as much wisdom as possible to the choosing.

IN THE LAST TWO LESSONS YOU WORKED WITH THE ACTIVE APPROACH TO visualization. In this lesson, it is the receptive mode that is explored. In this, the inner landscape of the psyche is revealed, showing a flow of images that can later be decoded or meditated upon.

This type of visualization is usually guided by a sort of fill-in-the-blanks script of your own or someone else's invention. It is always in the present tense and includes sensory details that open the doors of imagination and memory.

With guided visualization, as with other types of visualization, begin by relaxing, grounding, and centering yourself. Use your breath to relax and center in present awareness. Feel your orientation to Earth and Sky. Send your psychic roots down into the Earth with your relaxed exhalations, feeling your body become heavy with gravity. Trust your body to the Earth's care. Create a safe space around you by visualizing a medicine wheel or protective circle.

You may have a script read to you by someone, listen to a recorded script, or have one in mind to follow. Begin by seeing yourself in a certain setting that invokes feelings of safety. This can also help you move more easily into the visualization mode.

Many people use drumming or other trance inducers when doing visualization. I feel that this is generally not useful. The trance state and the visualization modes are not the same. If trance is induced for visualization, a confusion about what aspect of reality has been experienced often results. These trancelike visualization practices cause people to question whether images seen during trance are "made up" within their minds.

If visualization and trance are blurred together, then indeed imagination becomes a factor in trance. It is a confusion of our times, when the psychological and the shamanic are one soup, with personality the main ingredient.

I see visualization as a skill of the East on the medicine wheel, and trance as its counterpart of the West. To generalize, guided visualization reveals the psychological or personal matrix, and trance, the cosmic or transpersonal matrix. The two are linked, of course, but that link may not be experienced by one whose awareness is confined by belief and habit. Modern people tend to be self-absorbed, preoccupied with individual experience and personal growth. The mirror of images given by such a mind-set will naturally project emotions and desires generated by individual perspectives. This kind of visualization can be productive, but it should not be confused with shamanistic trance work. Imagination and fantasy are powerful in what they reveal and thus teach, and they can extend belief into new realms of possibility. Visualization is no less than trance; it is just a different mode.

If your personal matrix is well integrated with the cosmic matrix, so that your work in nonordinary realms focuses through a knowledge of larger relationship, then the distinctions between trance and visualization are less definitive of your experience. Your sense of self, definition of reality, and perceptual experience then encompass territory unknown to ordinary consciousness. As long as the house of self is walled in, you may see only what is contained in that space; when consciousness opens beyond that smallness, integration with a larger reality is possible. Your mind's mirror then reflects those wider realms into which ego has no passport.

The following are examples of guided visualization. If you find yourself losing concentration in the midst of your visualizing, shift your attention to your breathing. Through this, deepen your relaxation. It is important to be very relaxed and open for this experience to be effective.

If you are being guided by someone, choose that guide carefully and discuss ahead of time what work you want or don't want to do. Be careful with kundalini, past life, or regression work. Such things can open doors to trauma and need competent handling and follow-up.

After finishing the visualization, be sure to reground yourself, with food, ordinary talk, earthy activity, or focused connection with the ground. Process your experience as needed.

VISUALIZATION ONE

Visualize yourself at the bottom of a staircase. There are ten steps. Go up them slowly: one . . . two . . . three . . . four . . . five . . . six . . . seven . . . eight . . . nine . . . ten.

At the top you see a hallway with closed doors on either side. The hallway is lit by sunlight coming through windows and skylights. It is pleasantly warm. You smell the fragrance of spring flowers coming in the open windows. Birds are singing; it feels like morning.

Each door along the hallway is made of a different wood and has a different handle or knob. You walk toward the one that attracts you most at this time and stand in front of it, noting your feelings about the door and the room beyond it. . . .

You open the door and enter the room, noticing the different parts of it carefully. . . . A question comes to your mind—something you'd like to know. . . . As the question becomes clear, you see something in the room, an object you didn't notice before, and you walk to it and examine it or pick it up. . . .

After being with it for a while, you decide whether or not to take this with you, and then you leave the room. . . . You decide whether or not to shut the door behind you, then return down the hallway to the staircase. Descend slowly to your starting place, counting the steps back to where your body is. Open your eyes and sit up when you are ready.

Visualization is a technique for accessing information of a certain kind. The preceding visualization leads you to the "upper" consciousness. The setting— light, morning, spring—signals guidance into your mental upstairs, where you may access information that is active in consciousness. If you were intending instead to explore your subconscious, for instance, you would perhaps go downstairs, to a basement or cave. The details of the setting and guided action lead your awareness.

VISUALIZATION TWO

Visualize yourself in a recent situation in which you felt comfortable and good. Remember that context and those feelings. Stay with them for a few minutes. . . .

See yourself as a younger adult at some occasion when you were happy. Feel that pleasure now, seeing clearly the situation and yourself within it. . . .

Remember yourself as a teenager at some moment that brought you joy. See what was around you at the time—what was part of that moment. . . .

Visualize a time during your childhood when you felt good. Remember what you looked like; stay with that special memory for a few moments. . . .

See yourself in a place of dense fog. You are not afraid. You stand still, feeling the touch of the mist and letting it drift around you. There is no sense of time or place, just yourself, peaceful in the soft mist. . . .

Gradually there is a brightening in the light that permeates the mist, and your surroundings begin to appear. The mist thins and vanishes. You look around. . . . As you take note of your surroundings, a person comes into view—someone whose energy is familiar to you even if that person's appearance is not. Look closely at this person. . . .

You greet each other, and this person says something that you will remember. . . . You respond, then turn away. In turning, you see the mist; you walk toward it and into it. The mist encloses you, opening again to reveal your present time and place. When you are ready, open your eyes and sit up.

In this type of exercise you move into the past. You can use this technique to access memory relating to any particular time or person. Note that each stage invokes the best feelings associated with that time. In this way, you safeguard your well-being during the inner journey; you tap into memories that are as positive as possible. If you are deliberately seeking remembrance of distress, you can modify this technique.

VISUALIZATION THREE

Visualize yourself floating in a natural pool in the mountains. A warm spring feeds this pool, in which you float gently, supported by the comforting water. Feel your body relaxing completely. Feel your tensions drain away as the waters cleanse and renew your body and aura. . . .

You float effortlessly; above you the sky is vast and calm. The warmth of the water sends its mist into the air, keeping your body comfortable where the water does not cover it. Smell the mineral warmth of the mist and hear the natural sounds of water and birds around you. It is very peaceful. . . .

You are aware of the mountain beneath the pool—its solid strength and protectiveness. All your cares ebb away as you float in this beautiful, relaxing place. . . .

Around the pool is a forest of big trees, fir and cedar. The ground is mossy and green. Through the trees, you see a young naked child walking toward you. The child is luminous and carefree, a joyful magical being. The child comes into the pool; you realize that this child is yourself. The child merges with you, bringing you a deeper sense of joy and well-being as you continue to float in the warm water. You feel very safe here. . . .

An old woman (or man) walks out of the forest wearing a long robe. Her (his) face is serene and wise, with eyes that flash with humor. Her (his) walk is slow but graceful. She (he) comes to the edge of the pool and smiles at you kindly. You realize that you are a reflection of her (him), and as she (he) vanishes, you feel her (his) presence within you. . . .

The moon rises in the evening sky as you float. Its light bathes you from above as the warm waters wash and vitalize you from beneath. You are in balance and wholeness. . . . You will carry this good feeling with you as you return now to your present space. Open your eyes and sit up when you are ready.

What is sought in this kind of visualization is restoration of vitality and calm. The particular elements emphasized in the visualization will influence what aspect of yourself is most attended to. These are "feel good" visualizations—great for times of tension, loneliness, or insomnia. My son used to love them as bedtime rituals when he was little.

SOUND

SOUND IS ONE OF THE OLDEST AND MOST COMMON MEANS OF COMMUNICATION for many species including humans.

Sound has vibratory qualities that affect your emotions and your body, including your blood pressure, cellular activity, and heart rate. Certain feelings can be either locked within or released by specific sounds. A combat veteran can be galvanized into battle readiness through hearing a car backfire. Hearing a particular song can trigger an emotional recall of a moment marked in memory by that song.

The vibratory qualities of sound can also be useful in healing. Traditional and contemporary healers often use songs, chants, rattles, or drums in their work. Certain tones and patterns of sound are known to restore balance and well-being. Part of this healing power is in the arrangement of sounds, part in the alignment of presenter and presentation, and part is in the receptivity of the one desiring wellness.

When you use personal medicine songs, the songs become the vehicle for power because of the singer's relationship with the underlying medicine. With these sorts of songs, power is greatly diluted if the singer does not have this alignment. Traditionally, there are protocols for using other people's songs—sort of spiritual copyright laws. Permission should be sought, and sometimes payment made, before personal songs may rightfully be used by others. It is also proper to offer tobacco or a gift if asking a person to sing. If you have been given permission to use a song, it is good spiritual manners to give credit to that song's origins whenever you use it. In this way, you help the power that came with that song's creation to be present in its current use.

The phrase "words of power" covers a wide range of esoteric uses of sound, including spells, chants, invocations, vows, curses, mantras, and affirmations. All spiritual and magical paths use some form of words of power. Thought is brought into the realm of physical communication and imbued with emotion through the denser vibrations of sound.

Modern people have lost most of their respect for the magic of words. Language is used carelessly. It is drained of its power through use in advertising. Names no longer have the significance that they carried in olden times. Much is said that is not really meant.

One of the most powerful and enduring uses of words is spoken prayer. To use the breath in prayer is to reconnect the sacred with the sacred. Prayer is an acknowledgment, a remembrance of truth. The voicing of gratitude for blessings, for life, for all that is given, puts you into that state of grace wherein life can unfold in accordance with love.

Mindful prayer does not limit Spirit to narrow paths. It does not presume to know what outcomes are best. It seeks alignment with the wisdom that guides right action. Mindful prayer realizes the impetus toward form that is carried in the spoken word, and so it chooses words carefully, with clear intention.

There is no distance in prayer, no far-off deity. You speak to yourself when praying, and you put yourself in the presence of the Mystery. The illusion of separation is dispelled by true prayer.

In prayer you can release unwanted emotions and dismantle the patterns through which those emotions identify themselves with you. In prayer those energies can be freed and transformed.

In prayer you name reality. You gather to yourself your spiritual resources and call forth those attributes that have waited like dormant seeds for spring. You speak the sacred dream. Your voice is the doorway for truth. What is spoken resounds forever in the universe. Prayer is the path of homecoming.

During This Week

1. Work with the tones associated with the chakras. First, relax and focus on each chakra in turn. Breathe through the chakra, feeling it, then allow a spontaneous tone to be sung with your exhalation. Do this with each chakra, making note of what those sounds are, in pitch and expression. A common tone system used with chakras is as follows:

   ◜❧ First: *ohh* (as in *rope*)

   ◜❧ Second: *ooo* (as in *you*)

   ◜❧ Third: *ahhh* (as in *paw*)

   ◜❧ Fourth: *aaa* (as in *pay*)

   ◜❧ Fifth: *eee* (as in *flee*)

   ◜❧ Sixth: *mmm* (as in *om*)

   ◜❧ Seventh: *nng* (as in *ring*)

   Try using these as you work with the chakras. Observe if and how they differ from your spontaneous sounds. Note how high or low and how tight or relaxed your sounds are with each chakra. Hear if these change as you consciously relax and open the chakras. If you find your noises funny, go ahead and laugh—it will probably help loosen the flow.

2. Practice using the voice of your totem. If you don't know your totem, be aware of your own voice: What does it sound like? What are your habitual

speech patterns? What happens to your voice when you are in various emotional states or with different people?

3. Sing or chant. Pay attention to the effects of different organizations of sound.

4. Think about your name: What does it mean to you? How do you feel when you hear it? What sounds does it incorporate?

5. Check your memory for promises or vows that need fulfilling or undoing. Take care of these. In unconscious or unresolved form, they tie up a lot of energy and have an influence on the course of your life. Undoing vows is a matter of spoken release for yourself or others you have bound. If you can recall the specific vow, make a statement such as the following: "I release myself and any others who may be bound or influenced by the vow I made to . . ." Recite the vow. "I take this vow out of the laws of manifestation and send it into the realms of transformation. I ask that its energy be used to nourish the well-being of all. So be it." If you can't remember the exact vow, make a more general statement of release. Visualize the vow as a bundle of energy becoming dissolved into a dispersing field of purifying light. You may need to repeat this a few times or to reinforce with ceremony. Be as specific and emphatic as possible. Some vows may be from childhood or past lives. It may take some exploration to uncover them. The more emotion put into them at their making, the more pervasive their effects. Some vows you may want to keep or to modify.

6. Consider other sounds and what they evoke for you. Become conscious of what sounds attract or bother you and what images or feelings are attached to them. Work with these as you did with vows, releasing energy that is locked into sound memories if they are not serving a beneficial purpose. Transform or ground that energy. Move into a more conscious relationship with words and sound.

DAWN PRAYERS, PRAYER SMOKES, AND SMUDGES

DAWN PRAYERS

DAWN IS THE NEW DAY UNVEILED, THE WAKING OF CONSCIOUSNESS, its light given without prejudice, reminding us to be accepting. Dawn prayers set you on a positive course for the day. In the dawn is the remembrance of creation and re-creation; in beauty, the sacred promise of life.

The moment when night gives way to day, when the Dawn Walker moves upon the horizon, is the pause between cosmic breaths. The release of prayer into this pause is like the sending forth of a dove. Spoken or silent, this prayer moves like light into the heart of manifestation and is carried into the day.

It becomes the thought the Earth wakes to. The prayer is passed among the birds with their songs and travels with the morning breeze through the trees. It grows with the vivid colors of the day, riding the sun's path across the sky. It falls with the rain and soaks into the fertile ground. Let it be a good prayer. Let it be a song of joy.

PRAYER SMOKES

A prayer smoke is a ceremony of making visible the breath. When you put prayer into smoke, you act within the belief that the purifying fire and the traveling air will help actualize your spiritual intentions. The smoke is sent with the breath, the precious gift of life. It is carried in all directions.

The medicine pipe is an instrument of truth. In its use, only truth is invited. That truth is used to instate peace, to connect in prayer, or to heal. Its smoke permeates the realms.

The plants used for smoking add their medicines to the prayers. When you use plants this way, you must be sure you are in good relationship with those herbs. Marijuana is not a plant traditionally acceptable in conjunction with medicine pipes. Some of the plants in smoking mixtures include red sage, chamomile, meadowsweet, lavender, skullcap, passionflower, catnip, violet, dandelion, cinquefoil, coltsfoot, mullein, plantain, horehound, damiana, borage, muscadine, and mint. Native peoples often use red willow bark or uva ursi as well as native tobacco.

Using a personal medicine pipe is distinctly different from carrying a nation pipe or conducting a traditional pipe ceremony. Having a personal pipe, even if you share it in prayer with others, does not make you a "pipe carrier."

SMUDGES

Smudging—using the smoke from a burning plant to rid a person, place, or object of undesirable influences—is a simple and potent act. Smudging creates a cleared space into which spiritual presence may be invoked.

The plants most often used on this continent for smudging are sage, sweetgrass, copal, pine, and cedar. Each has a different characteristic medicine.

Pine (all varieties). Purifies, calms, and renews. The needles are used. East on the medicine wheel.

Cedar (*Thuja occidentalis* or *Libocedrus descurrens*). Clears and invokes, also brings visions. Use with care: many people are allergic to cedar. Burned in cut pieces or small branches. South or West on the medicine wheel.

Sage (the artemisias or *Salvia apiana*). The purifier, disperser of unwanted energies. Used bundled or loose. West on the medicine wheel.

Sweetgrass (*Hierochloe odorata*). The blessing herb, bringer of sweetness and grace. Used in braids (grandmother's hair). North on the medicine wheel.

Copal (*Bursera odorata*). The resin is burned to clear a space and to attract benevolent energies. Used widely in the Southwest (also by the Catholic church, along with frankincense).

Loose smudge herbs are usually burned on a stone or in a bowl; then the smoke is moved with a feather or directed by hand to the person or object to be smudged. Some people use an abalone shell for a smudge bowl, but this is considered by some to be disrespectful to the shell and to water.

The way the smudge does or does not burn gives indications of the energies present, so blowing on smudge herbs to encourage their ignition is not recommended.

Smudging is done in preparation for any ceremonial or medicine work. It is a good subtle-level housecleaning to incorporate into daily life. Medicine tools, altars, feathers, crystals, and other spiritually charged objects should be smudged regularly; or they can be kept bundled with sage or sweetgrass. Smudging daily can be an act of self-blessing and a remembrance of spiritual responsibility.

During This Week

Offer dawn or morning prayers—try at least a few times to do them at the moment of sunrise.

Address your relationship to smudge and smoking herbs. If you use tobacco as a habit, conduct some dialogues with the Tobacco Spirit and come to a more honest and clear understanding of your relationship with this being. Do the same with marijuana or opium if you use these plants as habitual smokes or in an abusive way, that is, with a confused or negative intention. Self-delusion—"spiritual" rationalization that obscures the truth—is very easy in these relationships.

Try to get a sense of how these plants affect your chakras, pacing of energy, and relationships with others. Observe yourself. Ask for perspective from others. Do without the plants and note the changes in yourself. If there is abuse in these plant alliances, it will touch any use you make of smoking herbs. It is worth delving into honestly but without prejudice toward yourself.

Your breath is your most intimate tool for directing how your energy moves and aligns. If you are using your breath wrongly in an unbalanced relationship with a plant, you are sabotaging your own well-being. Clarity of relationship is vital to good medicine work.

Without self-blame or demonizing of the plant, try to find ways to move into a place of freedom regarding the plant you seek relationship with. These plant spirits can be strong allies, once alliance is unclouded by illusion and addiction.

Let the teachings of addiction give you perspective, but don't use them to define yourself. Be free in body and thought.

BIRD MEDICINE (PART 1)

THE WINGED ONES, OUR BIRD ALLIES, BRING MANY GIFTS TO OUR LIVES through their songs, their jeweled colors, their grace of flight, their workings within the natural order.

To work effectively with bird medicine I believe it is helpful to have some understanding of feathers. It is thought that birds came from reptiles two hundred million years ago. What first distinguished birds from reptiles was their feathers.

The largest wing feathers of a bird are the primaries, from midwing to tip, and the secondaries, from midwing to body. The small overlapping feathers on the wings are called coverts. The medicine of wing feathers is in general that of motion, lift, flight, and power.

Long, narrow, pointed wings are suited for long-distance flying over the sea (albatrosses have these). Long, broad, and rounded wings such as the eagle's are good for long-distance flying or soaring over land. Short rounded wings, like some owls have, are suited for slow flying through forests and over fields, and rounded concave wings such as are found on grouse work well for quick take-offs and rapid escapes for short distances. Birds like the killdeer have pointed flat wings for quick wing action and swift flight.

Hard-edged flight feathers are for speed and maneuvering; soft feathers enable silent approach. The hawks don't worry about noise. By the time the prey hears a hawk, it is too late. Owls cruise more slowly and rely on their noiseless flight style.

The tail feathers are called rectrices (rectrix is the singular), and they also have little shingled feathers called coverts overlapping them. The rectrices are paired; they overlap each other except for one rectrix in the center pair. This feather is often prized as a medicine feather. Tail feathers in general are for balance, steering, guidance, and braking—for the bird and for the shaman.

Each feather is made up of a shaft with vanes on either side. There is a groove running the length of the back of the shaft. The parallel branches of the vanes are called barbs; each barb has many tiny barbules, which hook into the barb below it like little zippers, so that the vanes maintain a smooth surface. Birds keep these zippers in order by preening them with their beaks—you've probably observed this activity.

The vanes are not symmetrical. The inner vane is wider than the outer vane, and this difference increases in the direction away from the bird's body, so the innermost feathers have the most symmetrical vanes.

Bird feet with toes for perching, climbing, catching, carrying, and manipulating food are sharp and curved. Toes for running and scratching are sturdy, with large blunt nails, and toes for swimming are webbed. In medicine work talons are used for psychic defense, for grabbing energy in some kinds of healing work, and for housing the power of birds of prey on staffs, bundles, or other ceremonial objects. I have also used talons as acupuncture-like healing tools. The energy in talons is very intense and needs particular care in using and keeping.

Why is this information helpful in your work? First, many people using feathers and other totem body parts never truly look at what they are making use of; they don't bother to learn much about the being from whose body the object came. Each feather is a work of creative artistry, elegant beauty, and admirable function. Second, these physical details reveal a great deal of information relevant to the medicine the bird is sharing.

Besides the flight and tail feathers, there are many other kinds of feathers found on birds: down (prevalent on newborns of many kinds of birds and on waterbirds and hawks); semiplumes, plumes, filoplumes (sensory function); bristles (stiff hairs beside mouth, tactile function); powderdowns (down feathers whose bases disintegrate into talclike powder, found on herons and parrots). Other specialized feathers may be ornamental, sound-producing, iridescent, and so on.

The plumage of young birds often is different from that of adults. Differences are sometimes gender-related or seasonal. All birds periodically replace feathers by molting.

When you find a feather, you can sprinkle boric acid powder on it to get rid of feather mites, which will otherwise eventually destroy the feather. After two weeks, the powder can be shaken out and the feather used. Boric acid should be kept out of reach of children.

If you cut the whole wings from a bird you have found dead or skin the bird with feathers intact, you want to be sure to dry the skin properly. Wings and talons need to be tacked up in a spread-open position or they will not be openable when dry.

Feathers should be smudged when found and kept smudged regularly, especially if they are not kept wrapped. Otherwise, they will gather energy the way a feather duster gathers dust and will quickly become clogged and loaded. Always handle feathers with clean hands. Minimize the touching of a live bird's feathers: human and bird oils are not compatible when it comes to preening feathers.

It is currently illegal in North America to possess feathers or body parts of songbirds and birds of prey unless you have a permit to do so.

During This Week

Inventory any feathers you have. Make a list and note any patterns in the kinds of birds represented in your collection. Check feathers for mite damage. Smudge them all.

BIRD MEDICINE (PART 2)

IN THIS LESSON YOU WILL LEARN ABOUT BIRD MEDICINE AND FEATHER use. Begin by holding a feather.

Try to identify what kind of bird the feather is from. Practice, experience, and a good field guide are all useful. If you cannot identify the specific bird, try to discern whether it is a water bird, a bird of prey, a perching bird, or from some other general category. Often just sitting for a while in meditation with the feather will give you a feel for the kind of bird it is from.

Once you've identified the bird, try to tell where on the bird's body the feather is from—is it a flight feather, tail feather, specialized body feather? This will give you further clues about the nature of the bird's gift to you. Look at the qualities that stand out on the feather; examine the size of the shaft, the shape of the vanes, its colors and textures. Reflect on the circumstances under which the feather was given or found. Reflect on what you know about that kind of bird:

- Time of day or night that it is active
- What it feeds on, how it feeds
- Whether it is migratory
- Terrain it lives in, nesting habits
- Parenting habits
- Social patterns
- Spatial niche—ground bird, cliff bird, bush hopper, and so on
- Ecological niche, relationship to other species
- Kinds of songs or calls
- Style of flight or movement

All these physical details tell a story of the bird's medicine. Use your intuition to divine how that feather should be used and ask for guidance from the spirit of the bird. Be sure to leave an offering when you find a feather and to care for the discarded body of the bird in a respectful manner.

The following is an account of a ceremony done by a medicine sister named Starfire with a hawk feather. It is an example of an experience of asking a bird spirit for guidance on what medicine a feather is bringing:

Made a circle, called upon seven sacred Directions [the Six Directions and Spirit], asking for protection, strength, wisdom, and blessings.

Smudged self with sage—smudged feather, spoke to the totem, singing and calling seven sacred Directions, Divine names, around the totem.

Blessed with sweetgrass, making prayers to the totem, asking it to show its medicine to me, asking it to show me how to use its medicine in good ways. At the end, blessed with sweetgrass again, gave thanks, blessings, honoring to All.

What the Spirit spoke during the ceremony:

"I am the way of the medicine, I am balance as shown in the color on my feather. I am the way of Spirit—I hear and see the medicine, I hear and see the people.

"I sing and dance the medicine songs and make the prayers. I send them forth. I am one with the medicine. I am one with the Great Mystery.

"I am Spirit manifested, returned to Spirit, yet my feathers are still the manifested. I perceive and judge not. I hear the medicine songs and am drawn forth. I come. My medicine shows the way.

"All is done in honor, in recognition. I see the people and their need—I am the connection.

"Yes, I may be used for healing, for I bring forth the medicine. I am truly a shower of the medicine way—I see far and I honor the honoring.

"I have come to you from Spirit, for you have sung the honoring songs. I will show you the medicine way. I will bless you along the way. I am the one who carries the messages, the prayers.

"We may fly together and see and hear. You will learn. I honor you for the honoring. You are one who recognizes the sacred, and I bless you.

"I am the bridge between the worlds. I come as the medicine way. Starfire, it is good."

There are many ways to use feathers:

- On medicine bundles or totem bags

- On mandalas or shields

- On staffs or pipe stems

- As medicine fans or smudge feathers

- On prayer arrows or hung in trees or as flags

- As part of ceremonial regalia

- As guardians in a room

- In letters, as message carriers

- For healing work

The medicine of individual kinds of birds is suggested in the appendix. General categories of birds grouped according to their prevalent medicines would be as follows:

Birds of prey (eagles, hawks, owls, etc.): protection, power, hunting, vision

Carrion birds (vultures, ravens, etc.): retrieval, transformation, consequence, transition

Rainbow birds (parrots, macaws, hummingbirds, etc.): ecstasy, healing, renewal, blessing

Water birds (herons, ducks, egrets, swans, geese, gulls, etc.): guardianship, mediation, cyclic change, invocation

Earth birds (turkeys, quail, grouse, pheasants, etc.): secrets, prosperity, endurance, family nurturance

Working birds (woodpeckers, flickers, etc.): strength, removal of obstacles, purposefulness, drumming (thunder)

Peerless fliers (terns, swallows, swifts, falcons, etc.): evasion, freedom, achievement, agility

Heyoka birds (cuckoos, nuthatches, wrens, sparrowhawks, etc.): reversal, strangeness, paradox, spiritual responsibility

Message bringers (jays, doves, mockingbirds, crows, etc.): warning, tale telling, chants and songs, teachings, omens

Birds can also be grouped in other ways: by coloration, by medicine wheel orientation, or by whatever is meaningful to you. It is the personal relationship with the bird and the feather that is most important, not what a book or tradition tells you is the right view.

The birds listed in the appendix are birds I have some familiarity with through experience. The qualities I attribute to them may be different from the associations that develop for you. It is through experience that these things come.

Each bird, each feather has its own purpose. Because the big birds, like the large four-footeds, are the totems most frequently looked to, I discuss them briefly here as examples of the totemic qualities of the wingeds.

Eagle.   Despite the numbers of people using Eagle in their medicine names, there are relatively few two-leggeds who truly carry this medicine as totem. Eagle is aloof, flies high, and generally avoids human contact even at the cost of having its nest violated. Eagle sees the larger perspective and traffics in important messages and medicine, having great spiritual strength. Eagle is associated with the sun, with courage, pride, and aspiration.

Bald eagles hold different energies from goldens. Usually placed on the North of the medicine wheel, balds stay near water, eating fish (often carrion fish). The white tail feathers of mature bald eagles are prized for the spiritual light they transmit, the purification they emanate.

Golden eagles are awesome hunters, and their energy is of the wild canyons, prairies, and mountains of the west (though they represent East on most medicine wheels). Their feathers, spotted in young males and ghost-marked when older, are the traditional feathers signifying bravery, leadership, and connectedness to Spirit. They should be carefully kept off the ground. Female eagles are usually a third or more larger than males.

Hawk.   Unlike the lofty eagle, the hawk is quite willing to engage itself with human activity and is thus a frequent ally of shamanic practitioners. Hawk comes in many varieties but generally is a message bringer, protector, journeying totem, or helper of success in business or action. Most hawks are quick to defend their nest space. Their keen senses, speed of flight, fierceness, and independent confidence give much power to persons allied with this medicine. Hawk is a good bird to travel with between the realms, and its talons and feathers are versatile in healing use.

Owl.   Counterpart to the sun birds is the owl, the bird of the moon. Fearfully associated by many with sorcery and death, the owl is actually a totem of transformation. Moving from West to North to East—from power and dreams, to completion and the release of old patterns, to renewal and return—Owl carries wisdom, vision, prophecy, and transmutation in its silent flight and strange nocturnal calls. Totemically, owls and cats are closely linked, and a person having one as a totem often has the other also. Some owls, such as the snowy, barred, and marsh, are daytime hunters, and their particular medicines reflect that light; but most owls are night birds, guardians of that rich time of seeing with the inner senses, communing with stars, and confronting shadows.

Heron.   The great blue heron, stately monarch of the waterside, teaches patience, attention, accuracy, and grace. Heron's elegant feathers, subtle slate blue, calm the spirit. Heron's medicine is truth, judgment, intuitive knowledge. In flight, or walking in its deliberate way through lake shallows, Heron does not like to be hurried or distracted by inconsequential matters. When it comes time to grab its prey, Heron strikes like a rattlesnake, fast and sure, without compromise. Heron is discipline within beauty.

Vulture.   Vulture is patient also. It is one of the very few big birds that do not kill to eat. Rather it takes death and, by nourishing itself, turns it into life. To Vulture, a decaying body radiates heat and light; it sparkles. Vulture's amazing physiology can consume and thrive on microorganisms found in putrefying flesh that would sicken or kill other creatures. This is one reason their feathers are valued for doctoring.

The shaft of a vulture's flight feather is pale yellow, a ray of brightness through the dark vanes. Vulture is a protector and possesses the totem medicine of justice and karma. Master of spiraling soaring flight, Vulture rides the air for hours with scarcely a wing beat.

In approaching the realm of the winged ones we touch the intimacy between Earth and Sky, we learn to lift our eyes, minds, and hearts, and to honor the mystery of flight. Used to things dropping downward from the hand's release, it is a rare gift to the spirit to feel the body of a bird push from the palm and spring upward to the winds, the blue freedom of space and destiny.

During This Week

Be especially aware of the birds you encounter. Do some bird visualization work. See yourself as a particular bird and experience the world from that perspective. Make something with feathers. Start your own system of categorizing bird medicines.

PERCEPTION (PART 1)

LOOKING AT SOMETHING AND ACTUALLY SEEING IT ARE OFTEN NOT THE SAME experiences. To see, you first need to be attentive. Much of what you are looking at as you gaze at the world is the reflection of your beliefs and expectations.

In my experience of helping people with vision quests, I have found that it often takes several days and nights of sitting in one place to begin to see what is present. The modern mind often takes that long just to slow down and take a break from its internal preoccupations.

The East is the realm of vision. In this lesson you will focus on visual awareness; and in the lesson that follows, on perceiving the invisible worlds.

Perception is your individual "take" on reality. In meditation, you learned that there is no separation between subject and object—purely objective or subjective perception is an illusory concept (see part 1, week 2). Mind does not exist in separation, and no object exists outside pervasive consciousness. Subject and object are co-conditions of mind. The individual point of view is based on your perception of reality, so the way you see profoundly informs your beliefs, which in turn guide your experience of life.

In this lesson you are encouraged to integrate spiritual and physical perception so that they are not separate points of view, or views of separate worlds. From this integration comes a centering of vision and an expansion of reality.

Sit outdoors in the open, in view of the natural world. Begin, as always, with breath. Relax and be in the present moment with yourself, with the universe. Notice your state of physical and emotional being. Breathe—acknowledge that you are here.

Call on Mouse's help. Mouse attends to what is close to it. Mouse totem teaches you to observe detail and interpret its significance. Open, vulnerable, the vision seeker's model, Mouse shows you how to use your senses to pay attention.

Start with light. Tune your awareness to light; see the world around you in terms of light and color, brightness and shade, in all gradations and combinations. See like an artist.

Let your attunement to illumination then lead your attention to the world of form. Marvel at the diversity and beauty of the forms around you. Make a visual inventory of them, acknowledging and appreciating each one.

From form, become aware of movement, the dance of light and form in its interaction with other life. Observe the interrelationships of movements—see how they harmonize and interweave. Feel your part in these relationships. Breathe, see, name aloud and greet what is there.

Shift your attention to listening. Close your eyes. Listen to the separate sounds, naming and acknowledging each one. These are the voices of life on Earth. Notice the emotions evoked by the different sounds. Listen to the full orchestra of them—their relationships to one another, their conversations. Now open your eyes and see and hear at once, consciously, fully.

Touch the Earth around where you sit. Feel its textures and temperatures. Smell what moves on the air around you. Smell the Earth. Maybe taste it. Open your senses to these gifts. Be present with them. Thank Mouse for these teachings.

Call on Eagle's help. Eagle's vision is superlative. Eagle sees the big picture with clarity, with courage and purpose. Eagle's perspective is from the heights, detached from petty limitation, free from fear.

With an eagle's view, look upon your world. Breathe with the land and sky; merge with them. What comes to your consciousness now? What calls your attention? What flows from that attention? What is realized and understood? What are you feeling most connected to? What question is being asked?

See your world in wholeness, with your perception part of that wholeness, permeating it, yet unbounded by it. Feel your freedom within this vast web of relationship. Thank Eagle for these teachings.

During This Week

Practice paying attention to what you are looking at. Practice Mouse and Eagle seeing. Work with three other vision modes:

1. *Peripheral vision.* It is with your peripheral vision that presences from the more subtle planes are most easily perceived visually. Practice using and strengthening your peripheral vision. An old technique for this is to take a flat feather. Hold it about eight inches from your right eye. Cover your left eye with your hand. Focus your vision beyond the feather as you slowly rotate it until the feather is perpendicular to your face and almost invisible because of it flatness. Gaze past the feather or walk around maintaining the feather's position. The edge of the feather will occupy your central vision, forcing you to use your peripheral vision.

2. *Scanning.* Sit outdoors where you have a long-distance natural view. Relax into a meditative calm. Let your gaze become unfocused and then slowly scan the distances in front of you. Tune to movement or objects that catch your attention, but keep your gaze unfocused and your mind calm. Sense what is signified by those objects or movements rather than applying your analytical mind to them.

3. *Visual travel.* Sit outdoors where you have a long-distance natural view. Relax; breathe. Look into the distance until a tree or rock or place draws your interest. Ground and center yourself. Unfocus your gaze but keep it

fixed on the designated place of interest. Extend your attention like a bridge to that place; project your consciousness over that bridge so that you are now in that other place. See it in detail. Now return to your physical orientation. Steady yourself in your body—breathe, reground. Adjust your chakras if needed, particularly the third, sixth, and seventh. Focus your breath into the lower chakras and your eyes on something close by. Briskly rub your hands over your plexus, brow, crown, and back of your neck.

PERCEPTION (PART 2)

DEVELOPING PSYCHIC PERCEPTION IS MORE A MATTER OF PATIENCE, practice, and trust than a matter of technique. The biggest obstacle is conventional belief, not lack of ability. The second biggest obstacle is thinking that any one method of perception is more valid than any other. Each person interacts with the subtle planes in his or her own way, according to individual strengths and tendencies.

For instance, perceiving auras may mean visual colors to one person, sensations through the hands to another, inner messages to another, and "just a feeling" to still another. All are valid, if they are a result of a clear interaction with what is present.

Find your own portal of psychic sensitivity. Experiment—ask yourself questions about how you best receive input. Trust that what you need to perceive will make itself known to you, and open yourself to that interface.

Perhaps try different divination methods. They are often ways of finding your arena of sensitivity: I Ching (intellectual), scrying (visual), pendulum (body currents), and so on. See if you have an affinity for one of these and explore its applications.

Release obstructive beliefs about reality and about your abilities. Think in terms of "knowing" rather than "seeing."

Practice on yourself. Do observation meditation and become familiar with your chakras. Get to know your own energy in a friendly, nonobsessive way. Learn to be present with yourself.

Use the suggestions in the previous lesson to become more sensitive to your world, more aware. One world is overlaid on another; if you see more acutely in the physical world, you will also find the subtle planes more accessible. This is not a matter of keen eyesight but an attention to context. Know what is around you.

Realize that there is communication and interaction continuously going on, and that you can participate in this communication. It begins with being able to be quiet in mind and body so that you can hear and see what is around you.

Work on issues of ego and intention. Pray. Be honest. Ego and power are longtime dance partners. There is power in seeing, knowing, and working with the subtle realms. There is power in the admiration people give to psychic adepts. For power to be approached beneficially, there must be honesty, true service, equanimity, and appropriate relationship.

In developing your sensitivity, become familiar with natural forces and with the characteristic energies of presences that are usually found in your vicinity. Getting to know these enables you to perceive what may be present at any given time. Your peripheral vision will help pick up these clues to identification.

Verbal processing is an effective way of allowing more information to move into awareness. Just speaking of what you are perceiving, in an uncensored flow, acknowledging without judgment or analysis, draws more information into consciousness, like a siphon. It also aids your memory—a boon when you want later to retrieve and ponder your experience.

When and if you help others through your psychic perceptions, verbalization helps include them in what is going on. Other recommendations for beginning psychic practitioners include the following:

1. Give credence to your own observations, but don't be attached to them or to how others respond to them.

2. Deal in raw data rather than interpretation. (More on that later.)

3. Look for relationships, matrices, and patterns. These are where your most useful information is found.

4. Closing your eyes while you work may, paradoxically, enhance your ability to see. It will help you concentrate. Be *with* someone's energy, not looking *at* it. Relax! Take your time.

5. Don't ignore fast or easy information. Don't make it harder than it needs to be.

6. Sometimes strangers are easier subjects for practice than people you know.

7. Don't be afraid of mistakes. Be honest, patient, and unafraid. Be in the present moment without assumption.

8. Work in a spirit of service that is uninvolved with particular outcomes or performances. Be guided by what needs to happen, not by your neediness to be helpful or well regarded, or by the other person's expectations and neediness.

9. Discriminate between that which is presently useful to report and that which will rob a person of his or her own path of discovery and understanding. Timing is always a factor in how people are able to use knowledge. Resist any urges to be the savior, the revealer, the powerful one.

10. Practice.

The gathering of information can be divided here into four categories: the physical, the sensory, the intuitional, and the "knowing." (Information gathered in trance and dream will be discussed in later lessons.)

The first category, the physical, is the research level of books, teachers, conversations, and so on.

The second category is the sensory level. This is where input is received through both the physical and the psychic senses—clairaudience, clairvoyance, and so on. As you can see, this level overlaps the physical on the one hand and with the intuitional on the other. But it has greater dimension than the research level and is more controlled, deliberate, and conscious than the third way of accessing information, the intuitional.

Intuition is a function of mind that combines memory with subtle perception of present-moment clues to produce conclusions. It is often considered a magical process because clues are being noted and cross-referenced through memory in a quick and unconscious way, suddenly popping up into consciousness fully formed as information.

Intuition is an important tool to nourish, valuable in any aspect of life. But it is also tricky, in that the perceptive and interpretive processes happen almost simultaneously. Thus the information yielded by intuition is only as reliably useful as the belief patterns of the individual allow it to be.

I know very perceptive people who are often way off base in their interpretation of the data from their intuitive processes. It is not that their intuition is faulty; it is that their emotions and beliefs, which inform their intuition, are tied up with inappropriate projections and associations. Remember the suggestion about trying to present raw data instead of interpretation when you are working with subtle energies.

As you become more aware of how your mind functions within the intuitive process, then perception can become more distinct from projection. It takes close attention and knowledge of your own patterns because of the instantaneous overlay. The best practitioners are the most free of unconscious projection. Information and belief can of course never be really separate in consciousness, but an awareness of their interplay greatly improves your application of intuition.

For example, I may be listening to a woman talk about her rheumatic pain. I ask her some questions and pick up on subtle indications that I hear in her voice, see in her manner, feel in her energy. I don't focus on these things—I'm just listening and being receptive. These clues are being processed unconsciously.

Suddenly I know that her pain is the result of anger with her husband. I tell her. (She's asked me to do this.) I don't add any interpretation. I don't tie my memories of pain, anger, or husbands onto my perception of her situation.

We talk more, and she arrives at some insights. I give her feedback—observations. She goes home to reflect on those possibilities. I have not taken on her anger and pain or imposed mine on her.

Intuition is useful in counseling or in working with people through conversation where you are absorbing impressions and input. It can be a good basis for response and action.

The fourth method of accessing information is through "knowing": a direct interface with the cosmic realms of knowledge. I find this the most accurate and far-reaching method. The "knowing" is not dependent on clues or informational input, as is intuition. It is rather an opening of consciousness to receptivity beyond conventional time-space pathways. The best way I can describe it is as a state of not-thinking that is conscious of cooperative universal resource. I'm not sure how to teach it yet, but I know it is worth speaking about nonetheless because it gives important perspective to the other levels.

Knowing offers an experience free from ego involvement; it bypasses all mediators, interpreters, beliefs, preconceptions, and opinions. If you apply interpretation to what is perceived, it is done as a deliberate act and thus is not likely to be confused with the knowing itself. This level is accessed through a consciousness shift, so usually requires a time-out from conversation or interaction.

Nothing exists on only one level of expression. If you spend time sensitizing yourself to the subtle currents of your own energy and to those of the life that surrounds you, your sense of reality will expand. It takes quiet time—meditation and prayer. It means using your senses to their fullest potentials and releasing limiting concepts and habits. It may take some profound shifts in priority. It takes knowing how to be still, to listen, and to pay attention.

When love is applied to this process, the world begins to unfold its gifts, petal by petal, in the light of kinship. It lifts its own veil and lets you see within. Love is the path, and the treasure is found every step along the way. There are other paths to psychic development and other paths to esoteric knowledge, but the path of love is the teacher of liberation and peace.

I see the worlds and the life within them as interconnecting networks of light. Awareness can penetrate any of the layers of manifestation that cloak these living webs, through to the primal matrix itself. Seek your ways of accessing perception and then follow them through the layers. Try not to be distracted by stimulating phenomena or sensations. These are not your goal.

The lion's roar can teach you much about the lion and about yourself, and it can lead you to the lion. It can holographically carry the essence of lionness. But the hearing of it is not the whole knowledge of Lion, unless your consciousness is refined enough to thread the needle of emotional reaction and enter the space of truth, to use the personal to understand the cosmic. For most people, emotional reaction is simply constrictive.

Phenomena can be exciting—scary or fun—but not always reliable gauges of your nearness to the sacred. Any time someone comes to me wanting to be a shaman or thinking it is their destiny, I know almost certainly that that person is not suited for such a path. Desire for power and for the trappings of power is a gaping pit that can swallow other intentions. It is not an auspicious way to begin a path of spiritual service.

Instead of psychic phenomena, pay attention to stillness, to birdsong, to the gold of a frog's eye. Attune to the breathing of the seasons. Attend to the fears of a child or the loneliness of an elder. Feel the tremors of a birch trunk as the wind pulls its branches. See the way the mountains hold conference with the clouds.

From these will come a deepening of perception and alignment with the currents of healing. From these will come the secrets that all newborns know.

Learn how water flows, how flames dance, how winds travel, and how stones dream. Move with these patterns and let them be your medicine.

See the light in a leaf. You breathe that light. You bless another with it when you smile. In honoring the life in the leaf and the life in the light, you expand your spiritual resource. The leaf becomes your ally—as do the light, the tree, and the sacred Earth. They will speak to you. You will see.

During This Week

Practice seeing and perceiving subtle energies and presences. Make a medicine bundle for the East/Spring using simple items that speak to you of what is important to remember and express in this Direction. Use your intuition and your sense of connection to different forms and energies.

WIND CEREMONY

THE CLOSE OF EACH SEASON AND ITS SERIES OF LESSONS IS A TIME FOR ceremonial transition. It is for formally expressing gratitude to all the spirits that helped you in this aspect of your path's unfolding. At this time, you remember and gather to yourself the things you have learned and the gifts of the season.

In the East—the Spring—have come the powers of enlightenment and vision.

Bring your East medicine bundle to an open place that partakes of the breezes and the eastern light. Go there at dawn for your ceremony.

Smudge yourself and your place of ceremony. Smudge your bundle. Turn to each Direction and invoke the presences of these powers. Call to the Earth and Sky and to the Mystery. Invite the ancestors and the spirits of your place.

Face the East and make a prayer smoke. With each pinch of smoking mixture, make a prayer of thanks to the spirits of the East: the winds, the birds, the spirits that guide you.

Then send forth your smoke. Send it to the East. Then bless yourself by rubbing smoke over your body. Bless your bundle with the smoke.

Scatter the ashes to the winds. It is done.

Prepare for Summer Solstice.

> *Medicine Woman dreams*
> *she is the cat who*
> *walks alone.*
> *She is Kisewasewinkoko,*
> *whose moods create owls*
> *(I flew here to die).*
> *She comes to the place*
> *below the cliffs*
> *beside the water*
> *to listen*
> *to what rises there—*
> *stone spirits.*
> *She comes to the*
> *long sands walking,*
> *flute and knife.*

Her name is in the pipe
dreaming.
She-Who-Looks-Behind
is sighing.
Medicine Woman
gives everything
to the silence.

Part 2

SOUTH / SUMMER:
GUIDING THE WILL
Summer Solstice to Autumn Equinox

Powers of the South, the Summer, I come to you in prayer. In the midday light without shadow, I thank you for lessons of growth, passion, and relationship. I pray to be with the sacred fire of the South in a transformative way. I ask for courage in this place of action and change; I ask that my will be guided by right intention and that my medicine be good under the bright sun.

Let my idealism come not from self-righteousness or anger, not from arrogance. Powers of the South, I pray for the soul's awakening to love and for the vigor of youth to be within my sacred dance. May I express through every aspect of manifestation the joy and grace of life's vitality. May I fully live.

WE MOVE FROM THE REACHES OF THE MIND TO THE FOCUS OF WILL.
Summer is the season of outward movement, manifestation, and interaction. The
underground seeds have reached into the light and are now expressing their individual destinies. Eggs have hatched, babies have come forth from their mothers'
wombs. Life is on the move. Desire incandesces in heat, contact, and revelation. It
is a time of expansion and venture.

In this series of lessons, the focus is on right relationship, courage, and action—important attributes of spiritually directed will.

The will is powered by desire (that which reaches toward fulfillment) and
commitment (that which is unwavering in its intention), so will combines an impetus of doing with a determination of being. This can be a formidable power.

In order to keep the personal will in alignment with the good of all, right relationship becomes paramount. But relationship with what? With yourself of
course. Ah, but this is a tricky business: If right relationship with self is what is
needed to align personal will with the good of all, where is your place of perspective? The self advising the self is a hazardous mirror, prone to distortion and erro-
neous assumptions.

That is why you need the web of kinship to give you perspective. For this
sharing to function properly, you must be in right relationship with the web and
with the forces governing its harmonious purpose. So to be in good relationship
with yourself and thus in alignment with spiritually guided will, you must look to
your alliances. All your relations. It always comes back to this truth: the well-
being of one is intrinsically linked to the well-being of the whole and vice versa.

With courage—the facing of your shadows—you can untangle yourself from
ill will, yours and that of others. In courage is an expansion of possibilities, a
greater freedom of movement and experience. Strength of right will is not measured in success or failure to reach a preconceived goal. It is known through its
faithfulness to that which nurtures well-being. This is the uncompromising teaching of the South.

The solar plexus, the third chakra, is your center of personal power and ego
identity. It is the sun around which aspects of your personality orbit.

You'll notice that persons who are feeling insecure or defensive will often fold
their arms over the solar plexus, protecting that vulnerable sense of self. Women
have been conditioned to cinch in that part of themselves to be more attractive to
conventional males. Its correlation to personal power, which is seen as threaten-
ing in women, is no coincidence. Its overinsulation by fat, in those who feel a

need to buffer their sensitive egos from others, is another sign of how modern society has abused our balances.

A healthy third chakra is important to right relationship with will, so this week you will work with opening and being aware of the energy of your solar plexus.

Sit comfortably or lie on your back. Relax, breathe, relax, breathe. Let your thoughts float up and away from you like helium balloons. Let your body sink toward the steady Earth. Let your feelings drain away into the dark transforming ground. Breathe.

Focus your attention on your solar plexus. Breathe deeply into it, then push out all the air so that your next breath is even deeper. Explore this part of yourself—what do you find here? Ask your solar plexus some questions—what does it need, what patterns need changing? How can you come into better relationship with what abides there? How has it been hurt? How has your will hurt others? Ask, listen, and do not blame or judge. Do not criticize yourself.

Now breathe golden light into your solar plexus. Breathe it in like sunlight and with your exhalation let it radiate, clearer and clearer from your center. Breathe golden light and feel it relax and warm your center. Feel it melt fear and tension and pain. Feel it dispel the shadows held in that part of yourself. Feel golden sunshine lighting you from within, as you become radiant.

Breathe this way until you feel clear and centered. Now place your palms over your solar plexus. Feel the circulation of vitality through your solar plexus and hands, a circuit of goodwill, confident of the presence of right guidance. Connect the energy of your hands with that of the chakra. Then lift your hands away and relax them, palms up, at your sides.

Draw light from your crown chakra down through the sixth, fifth, and fourth chakras to the third chakra and collect the light there, intensifying the radiance of the third chakra. Feel the cosmic blessing and direction coming through and infusing your solar plexus, your center of will. Now open the gate below and allow the energy to flow through the second and first chakras, then into the Earth. This is a flow that keeps you in balance—your will poised between cosmic guidance and physical manifestation, engaged with both. Breathe, in this place of balance; renew it in times to come, as needed.

During This Week

Work with your solar plexus. Use visualization, observation, meditation, and physical nurturance. Wear comfortable clothes that don't constrict your center. Massage your solar plexus. Drink lemon balm tea to strengthen it. Belly dance. Walk with your shoulders back, not hunched. Remember to let your sun shine.

Basic to paths of nature-related spirituality are systems of totemic alliances. In this book, the term *totem* is used loosely to refer to both allies and medicine helpers, although there are differences in those categories as defined in the glossary.

Totems give aid; they bring information, perspective, assistance, and revelation. They summon certain qualities and knowledge from the seeker. Totems and allies are points of reference in consciousness—providers of perspective, something that is vital to right relationship with yourself and with all else. Each totem has its particular strength, its predominant medicine which if misunderstood or misused can be confusing.

I believe that one way the Mystery communicates with us is through all creation: stones, trees, animals, other humans, insects, lightning—everything is an opportunity. Each material form is an aspect of the cosmic spectrum of purposeful energy.

In relating to a stone with the intention of understanding and interacting with some expression of sacred wholeness, there is possible a resonance between stone and human; power moves in that resonant current. When consciousness is in harmony with the rhythms of the natural world, it finds resource there, including and beyond the material realm.

A stone speaks to you as part of the universal hologram, each part carrying the blueprint of the whole—different doorways into the same infinitely large room. The stone with its individual vibratory qualities of color, composition, shape, accumulated influences, and context of existence has a specific message or effect within your relationship with it. The foundation of that relationship is a common spiritual source. When you recognize this sharing, the resulting resonant interchange is the beginning of alliance.

The medicine or intrinsic truth of a totem is its beauty. "Walking in beauty" is living in awareness of these truths: seeing the medicine of the ocean wave, the rock outcropping, and the twisted juniper while knowing its relationship to the unified web. Beauty is what radiates from life when that life is expressing its essential harmonious nature; beauty is truth.

In coming close to this world of beauty, where clarity of identity and purpose guides action and form, you can learn about your own essential nature and how to touch that core of spirit within. When you sit in peace watching a pine tree, you can see beauty glowing in every cell of that tree. You see how it connects Earth and Sky, demonstrating balance. You feel the subtle dance it does with sun, water, air, and earth—its magic of giving oxygen, shade, food, and shelter. Its pineness is heard in the calming sigh of the breeze through the needles and felt in its evergreen watchfulness in all weathers and seasons. Its fragrance is a gift of clean renewal, as is the medicine of its bark and needles. In these ways and more, it radiates the beauty of giving and being. Survival and growth depend upon the harmony of this balance.

When you perceive and appreciate this beauty you may be able to find your own beingness within the web. In being respectful of these teachers in nature—elders on this planet who live the vision we so struggle for—you plant seeds that will grow into a world of peace.

When you open yourself to something seemingly outside, you make room for recognition of common ground and expand yourself to include more aspects of sacred expression; you increase your medicine. Everything is part of your wholeness, and the more you are conscious of, the more you have to call upon in need. You lose that deadly isolation that breeds violence and despair.

For one person, a shift in wind direction and the appearance of particularly shaped clouds either is not noticed or is not perceived as significant. To another person, these may be clear messages that a storm is approaching. In the same way, to a person attuned to movements in the subtle realms who understands their meanings, the messages presented by totems and guides are clear and significant. For this person, there is coherence and articulation in the seemingly random events that make up daily experience.

Coming across an object, having a dream, hearing a bird, seeing a rainbow, all can be part of the language in which the Mystery addresses you through your alliances. This is how the earthly plane becomes your grounding for spiritual realization; this is how you enact truth and make room for more knowledge to be accessed. This is how you participate and reconnect with the larger web.

Modern Western devotion to individuality is belied by its persecution of difference—be it race, religion, class, gender, sexual orientation, species, or bodily or mental condition. Modern society promotes severance from the mother, from the Earth, from other species, from Spirit, from awareness. The fear of losing one's self, one's personal identity, is a phobia arising from the cult of severance, not from the reality of integrity of relationship. Your individual uniqueness is not nourished by alienation, isolation, and insistence on otherness. It is cultivated in the garden of loving connectedness where the individual is supported, common ground is realized, and you find your reflection in the myriad mirrors of other beings.

We are all made of earth, of minerals, water, gases, and elements shared with plants, animals, stones. There is nothing about you that is so different, so "other," that you cannot resonate with all other beings on this Earth in one way or another. It is through your living surroundings that you discover what about yourself is special, what is shared, and how both these aspects are dependent upon respectful linkages.

In understanding the nature of the totem with whom you are allied, you better understand your own nature. You do not confuse the totem with yourself but realize that the power offered through alliance is accessible because of relatedness, the capacity to attune to connection.

The occupation of self-analysis should be secondary to just being in truth, in beauty. If your attention is centered in truth, then you act intuitively in ways that serve truth. If your attention is on figuring out who you are, then entire lifetimes can be spent in quest of identity. If trees did that we'd never have apples.

The process of totem understanding appears to me in four levels:

1. *Physical experience.* This is the interest you have in the form of the totem: the way it looks, moves, behaves, sounds, feels. It is your factual knowledge and physical plane encounters.

2. *Emotional engagement.* This is your response to the totem, be it of attraction, liking, sympathy, love, empathy, admiration, awe, or perhaps fear, discomfort, hostility, ambivalence. Your feelings about the totem can teach you much about your beliefs, your preconceptions, and your family and religious influences.

3. *Mental images.* This is a symbolic association: what the totem represents. These are metaphors, abstractions, translation into intellectual terms. This is where you ascribe certain powers or specific qualities to the totem, based on information and feelings.

4. *Spiritual connection.* This is the level where all the dimensions of the totem become clear, and the totem ceases to be objectified, romanticized, used as a substitute for self-esteem, or as a target for projected desires. This level is where the totem reveals its reality as a medicine and a sacred being. This is the level of power.

It is through exploring without prejudice all these levels and seeing how they inform each other that totem alliance becomes a medicine you can apply in daily life. This process is not linear; awareness percolates through all levels. You focus at different moments through the lens of feeling, thought, or sensation, but always with integrating perception. What you glean from the cumulative experience can yield clarity and open the way for the reality of the totem to emerge.

Using relationship of any kind as a source for self-understanding always carries the peril of narcissism and lack of sensitivity to the needs of your partner and the effects of the partnership on others. Alliance is meant to teach and reveal. It is also servant to the needs of the larger community of life. It is important to respond to this essential purpose that goes far beyond personal growth for its own sake.

The medicine wheel offers a helpful model when you are seeking ways to promote the well-being of your totems:

❧ *West.* Heartfelt prayer. Ask for guidance and express gratitude. Send a voice for protection, nourishment, freedom, and fulfillment for the animals, plants, and other beings. Do ceremonies, make medicine, focus your spiritual energies. Ask the totems what they need, what they suggest you do for them and for the whole.

❧ *North.* Wise action. Walk your talk. If your totem is Salmon, work to clean up the rivers or get dams removed. If your totem is Owl, take action to stop deforestation. Protect and restore natural habitats, curb pollution, change your consumptive and waste-producing habits, consider dietary changes. Do what you can or what is right for you, whether it is giving money to environmental activists, lobbying for legislation, civil disobedience, lifestyle changes, or getting out and sweating to guard and renew the integrity of the natural world.

❧ *East.* Communication and education. Talk to others, spread the word. Write books, articles, poems. Create art, music, dance. Much has been done to change people's attitudes through creativity. Think of Paul Winter, Barry Lopez, Annie Dillard, Bev Dolittle, Brooke Medicine Eagle, Farley Mowat, Jane Goodall. Teach children to respect and relate to nature. Talk your walk.

❧ *South.* Relating with love and courage. Express the truth of your path through your peaceful relationships and encounters in the natural world. Work to transform whatever fear and conditioning impedes your experience of love and kinship. Live good-heartedly amidst all your relations.

During This Week

Ask yourself some questions about your attitudes toward nature: What animals or other life forms do you fear? Which ones do you dislike? What did your family upbringing teach you about nature? What did your religious upbringing teach you? Did you have childhood allies? Intense encounters in nature? Dreams about certain animals? What attracts you in nature? What would you be if you were an animal? A tree? A fish? A bird? A mineral? An insect? Why?

MANY ALLIES AND HELPERS MAY PASS THROUGH YOUR LIFE IN DREAMS, trance, or physical encounters, but usually the relationship with a totem is more of an enduring marriage. How can you tell if something is your totem? Sometimes it is a slow process; sometimes you misjudge; sometimes you just know.

The bond with a true totem grows deeper and deeper, and its reality becomes undeniable. When I see a cat, any cat, something in me says, "I know you." It is a knowing on all levels—a knowing that is close to a shape-shifting—and it carries the potential for an intimacy of consciousness that distinguishes it from other kinds of alliance.

The totem is your counterpart from another realm—what you would be if you were four-footed, finned, leafy, or winged. The totem bridges the realms for you, and you for it. It is your entry, through right of kinship, into a world that enables you to examine the implications of your humanness and allows you to extend beyond them. It challenges you in ways that the human arena cannot, providing vital teachings and realizations.

Allies, on the other hand, are usually short-term though perhaps quite intense relationships. Allies may help you through specific stages of life, particularly times of change or reassessment. They provide important insights and offer their medicine to empower useful transitional work. The form an ally takes may surprise you at first, but if you engage deeply enough, you'll see what is being reflected.

Alliance is intimate but fluid, so it cannot be safely used as a way of defining or confining yourself, any more than can your relationship with a spouse or child, even if you share a name. The closer the sharing, the more attention must be given to each being's integrity and selfhood. The intimacy that allows profound insight is the closeness that also must respect freedom; interdependence is a balance.

In the complex web of life, all beings give and receive as part of the natural flow. Such reciprocity renews, strengthens, and maintains the hoop of life.

Deer depend on wolves to keep the essential truth of Deerness—quickness, grace, alertness—at the peak of expression. Without wolves and other natural predators, deer would lose that distinctive beauty of Deerness. The giveaway that the deer make to the wolves benefits both wolves and deer, and because both are intrinsic to the health of the hoop, they also benefit all else in their dance with each other. The agility of the deer demands that the wolves maintain keenness of sense, strength of body, and intelligence of action; the good of one species is inseparable from the good of another or from the whole.

In that way all life is linked. When in right relationship, nothing is lost; nothing is made lesser than another; nothing is at odds when the larger perspective is realized. The prey and the predator act not out of hatred, arrogance, or spiritual conflict but out of a natural pattern that governs their well-being. When you are in a true totem relationship, the medicine of the prey or food of your totem becomes significant; and the nature of the alliance with the prey or food is a facet of the relationship with the totem.

When asked why I am a vegetarian when most of my totems are predators, my answer is that I have so many animals living inside me that I do not need to eat meat.

That is not meant to be a glib rejoinder. I feel that real totem relationship is not demonstrated by physically imitating an animal but by engaging with the essence of a totem's medicine. This is an alchemical experience of spirit purpose. I don't need to pounce on deer to resonate with Panther. When I involve myself with the spirit nature of Panther and encounter the connection between the panther and the prey, it is through that connection that power flows and teachings are revealed, not in the eating of meat. The ratio of panthers to prey in the natural world is deliberate. We don't need a lot of humans invading that niche. Knowledge of and experience with the physical manifestation of your totem is important and too often neglected in our modern world, but how this is mirrored in your own physical life must be consonant with the highest good. Otherwise, totem alliance becomes a tool of the ego and a rationalization for perpetuating habitual behaviors. Pinning your morning grumpiness or overindulgence in sweets on your Bear totem is not fulfilling the responsibilities of right relationship. Awareness is often the signal for change, not for complacency. Knowledge becomes responsibility.

During This Week

Begin to get a sense of the presences of totems or allies in your life. Do some work in the medicine wheel directions to see what appears there. Be aware of what you are encountering during the day and in your dreams. Talk to what is around you. Attention and communication are two of the best ways to discover alliances. Often, in searching, you overlook what is already there.

Develop a sense of the different roles of totems and allies and of the potentials of these relationships.

Keeping in mind the differences between totems, allies, and medicine helpers, here are some ways that these find you and are found by you:

1. Vision questing (more about this in a later lesson)

2. Receiving totem objects: repeatedly finding or being given such things as fur, feathers, claws, and so on, relating to a certain totem or ally

3. Significant interactions: meaningful encounters with a totem or ally on the physical plane

4. Affinity or likeness that extends well past casual interest

5. Dreaming: repeatedly dreaming about or having visions of a totem or ally

Learning to live in harmony with the physical representatives of totems teaches you much about how best to conduct inner relationships with them. The first step is studying the totem. It is all well and good to say that Bear is your totem, but if that stems from a romantic notion about bears and you don't know much about real ones, then your totem concept is bankrupt. To know Bearness you must learn about bears. To do this:

1. Become factually knowledgeable; read, make drawings, write things down. Don't go to zoos. They are prisons, and the creatures there do not look natural or behave naturally.

2. Use any encounters to learn and communicate. If you live with an animal, ponder the differences between a pet and a totem (not that an animal living with you cannot be your totem—often it is).

3. Invite the totem into your dreams. Be patient and persistent. Sleep with a totem object nearby. Keep a record of your dreams.

4. Learn to dance your totem and use its voice. This is a powerful technique for aligning your energy with the totem's and for both learning about and applying totem medicine.

5. Meditate at the medicine wheel direction that corresponds to your totem. Make an offering there and invite its teachings and presence.

6. Spend a night outdoors in a wild place after a day of fasting. Set out an of-

fering and wait in quiet meditation and prayer. If you sleep, invite the totem to come into your dreams.

7. Make visualization journeys with your totem, and do shape-shifting visualizations (see the lessons on visualization skills in part 1, weeks 3–5).

8. Use a totem object—a physical part or representation of your totem—as a connector for receiving information about the totem's medicine in a ceremonial way (see Starfire's ceremony in part 1, week 9).

9. Talk with knowledgeable people about their perspectives and experiences regarding your totem.

10. Communicate directly with your totem.

What is the medicine being offered by the totem contact? How do you know what its powers are?

The physical manifestation of the totem gives you many indications. In thinking about the spiritual attributes of a totem, ask yourself some questions about its physicality:

∾ Is it an urban or wilderness creature? What is its habitat?

∾ Is it solitary? A herd member? Sociable?

∾ Is it nocturnal? Daytime medicine? Does it hibernate?

∾ What is its ecological niche, its relationship with other species?

∾ What are its courting, mating, and parenting styles?

∾ How is food obtained? What does it eat?

∾ Is it migratory? Territorial? A roamer?

∾ What is its mode of locomotion? How does it pace its energy?

∾ Where does it sleep? What are its patterns of activity?

∾ What color(s) is it? What textures?

∾ How does it deal with aggression toward it?

∾ Is it adaptable to change and pressure?

∾ What are its predominant physical characteristics?

All these clues give a wealth of significant information. The totem's powers are clothed in its form and way of living. By looking at those things in terms of medicine, it is simple to begin to understand what gifts the totem brings to you.

After applying the intellect to this process, you can seek counsel from your intuition:

☙ Where in your aura do you feel this totem?

☙ What images are associated with it?

☙ What does contact with the totem awaken in you?

☙ What does it mirror?

☙ How does it make you feel?

☙ What is the pattern of your dance together?

These sorts of questions allow information from the other realms to emerge. Don't forget that the most important way of understanding is through communication.

Once you have gained some knowledge of the totem, you will want to seek more inner contact. One way to begin this is to go to a space where you will have quiet and security, perhaps a place that would also be natural for your totem's comfort.

Smudge the space and set out an offering. Settle yourself, perhaps holding a totem contact object. Make a prayer for insight to flow from the alliance. Make a prayer for right relationship.

Ground, center, and relax into trance. Use drumming if needed to access a deep state of trance consciousness. Take plenty of time.

See the totem. This will come easily if you have done the preparatory work and made your intentions clear and if the totem is interested in alliance with you. This seeing is not a visualization in the sense of imagining—it is a seeing of presence.

Focus on the essence of the totem. At this time you can either work with the totem from the vantage of your own perspective or shift into the totem's perspective. To shift, allow your full being to immerse itself in the totem—your responses, ways of perceiving, physiological functions, all become those of the totem. Sometimes this takes practice; sometimes, particularly with people experienced in shamanic work, it is spontaneous.

At the end of this contact you must be sure to shift entirely back to the human. With spontaneous experiences the return is usually automatic, but with deliberate immersion it often takes conscious shifting.

As your experience grows, your contacts will be made almost instantaneously because of your familiarity and attunement. In your counseling with the totem, you may want to ask for a name or song that will carry the totem's essence. It is important that you approach the totem realms with definite purpose. They are not for spacing around in—psychic sightseeing—but for specific work.

The totem relationship can be aided by use of objects that serve as connectors, focal points, and reminders of the totem's medicine. You may have pouches containing bones, fur, feathers, claws, stones, plants, and other representatives of your totem. You may also collect things that relate to your totem's medicine.

Totem objects must be cared for properly—their care is a reflection of the quality of your relationship with the totem. Maintenance of medicine objects will be discussed in the lesson on rattles.

Totem carvings or fetishes carry the energy of the substance from which they are carved, the energy of whoever made them, and the energy of the totem. If you work with carvings, you need to be congenial with all those facets of their medicine.

These objects focus your attention and invoke your feelings and past experiences with the totem. People will sometimes use a circle of them as a form of totem council for seeking advice and receiving information. Like all totem contact, remember that each totem has its special areas of expertise and is not infallible. One of the most crucial parts of medicine work is keeping things in right perspective, which is why prayer is such a vital aspect. It returns you to the center, the source.

People are drawn to what our culture perceives as the more glamorous totems. Beware of preconceptions! Take an honest look at your own responses to various plants, insects, animals, and so on. In respecting all expressions of life you enlarge your capacities and nurture harmony.

Contrary to popular belief, there are no bad, useless, or expendable parts of the web of creation. All forms of life have the same right to be here. We are dependent for survival on the balance we maintain together. Let there be an end to our species' arrogance and the obsession with managing nature; let us abide together in dignity and peace.

The primary purposes of totem relationship are:

1. Strengthening certain qualities and aspects of being

2. Teaching new strengths; bringing balance

3. Teaching and reflecting behavioral patterns and responses to situations

4. Helping when in need—finding things, protecting, getting information, withstanding severe conditions, healing, dreaming, receiving whatever is that totem's forte

5. Bringing messages from the other realms

6. Teaching respect, gratitude, connectedness, expansion

7. Being a companion and partner in medicine

8. Releasing belief patterns about self-identity/definition

During This Week

Focus on conscious relationship with the totems and allies in your life.

DANCE AND MOVEMENT

IN THE EAST OF THE WHEEL YOU THINK, YOU CONCEIVE AND PERCEIVE, you speak, you sing. In the South you will, you relate, you move, you dance.

Sacred dance is the medicine of motion and gesture. Dance is an alchemy of intention and form in action that is expressive of beauty. Patterns of movement, like arrangements of sound, bring change. They have an effect on the planes of manifestation.

Ritual movement directs currents of power. If you stir the soup with your spoon, it swirls, carrying along anything that floats in it. If you stir the ethers of power, they too will respond, if your "spoon"—your focus of energy and intention—is strong enough.

Ritual gesture is an act of will. It is a rearrangement of the universe, whether slight or widely encompassing. As such, it needs to be guided by understanding and love in order to be within right universal relationship.

The power of ritual gesture is used by all religions and spiritual paths. Sound brings energy into the world of physical manifestation; ritual gesture sends manifestation into the subtle dimensions of causation.

Sacred dance is a series of gestures and movements that are both expressive and nourishing of vital energies. Sacred dance is a bridge between realms across which power moves in configurations shaped by choreography and by the will of the dancer.

Traditional healers often use dance to focus themselves in a trance that opens them to the particular medicine they are intending to bring to their healing work. Totem dancing is used this way. Body and will are the implements that stir the energies, creating openings and flow between the worlds. Dance connects the realms.

Ceremonial movement is traditionally used by groups to direct and harmonize intention in a consensus of wills. This unifies the group and brings a cumulative power to its purpose. Will is described and channeled through the eloquent patterns of the dance. Repetition increases the field of energy and exhausts peripheral thought and emotion. All this peripheral energy, freed from self-identification, is drawn into the pattern of the dance, where it adds more and more power to the dance's purpose. Once completed, dance of this sort will have not only bridged the realms but also cleared the individual group members of locked-up emotions and thoughts.

Dance can be used in a similar way by individuals to exhaust mental and emotional patterns and to circulate freed-up energy through the whole body and aura.

This unlocked energy can be redirected through the individual or sent elsewhere in the universe in accordance with clear intention.

Acts of great power are demonstrations of alignment with cosmic forces. The greatest personal power of all is that which is personal only in the sense of a living being's unity of consciousness and will with something far beyond the ego's concept of selfhood. In this state there is no illusion of power as something to be owned or as an aspect of individual personality.

Movement articulates relationship. How you move in the world—each gesture, touch, and interaction—is indicative of relationship. In remembrance of this is much opportunity for change.

I've often thought of myself as clumsy and out of step with my body. As I grow older, I become less concerned with outward appearances and more absorbed in a connectedness to the beauty that moves in all life. In recent years, when people have remarked about a sense of grace they see in my movements on the land or water, I have been surprised and blessed in the affirmation that we can be truly brought into that natural dance on all levels.

The way you move upon this Earth, the way you walk your talk and embody the sacred dream, can reveal much about the level of reality at which that dream is awakened in you. The act of walking is a gift that many of us—for reasons of injury, illness, or condition of birth—do not have; for these people life moves in a different way. But for those of us who do move about on our feet, we must ask ourselves: How aware am I of the spiritual implications and possibilities of how I tread this Earth?

The angry stomp, the arrogant stride, the intoxicated stagger, the depressed shuffle, the stab of high heels, the pounding run of fear—all vibrate through the realms just as surely as does the ritualized step into the consecrated circle. In following a spiritual path or enacting a sacred journey, you must pay attention to how you move. With every step, you imprint the ground, visibly or not, with the resonances of your state of being. It is not on arrival that you become your true self, it is on the way.

Listen to the sound of your walk and to your heart and breath. Feel your feet and knees. Be mindful of where you are stepping and what you are stepping on. You talk with your feet—to the Earth, to others. Your walking is a cadence, a drumming, a code tapped out on sidewalks, floors, and this ground you call home. What tracks are you leaving, and what do they say to those who follow?

Let each step be a prayer, an honoring, a love of the Earth. Walk in beauty.

During This Week

Practice walking with awareness:

- ❧ Feel the surface under your feet; attune to it.

- ❧ Feel below the surface, deep into the core; speak to the Earth.

∾ Be aware of the mechanics of your walk—the sequence of how each foot makes contact and the related movements of the rest of your body.

∾ Be aware of the sound your walking makes, of the vibratory impact on the ground and your body and aura.

∾ Pay attention to the pace of your walking and the length of your strides.

∾ Feel your poise between Earth and Sky.

∾ Sing or chant while you walk, sometimes, or use the eight-count breathing or counting of breaths.

Other suggestions:

∾ Wear comfortable shoes.

∾ Learn t'ai chi or some other movement form that strengthens your centeredness in action.

∾ Go barefoot when sensible.

∾ Wear garments that do not hinder free movement.

∾ Massage your feet often—treat yourself to foot baths of herbs or salts.

∾ Think about the different ways you use your style of walking to express moods.

SEXUAL FIRE

THE SEXUAL FIRE IS A POWER OF CREATIVITY AND UNION, THE JOINING OF doing and being. It is an energy of life's core. To connect spiritually with the life force is to experience the sacred fire that manifests within natural desire, reaching to fulfillment of purpose and transformation—an eternally evolving cycle of realization.

Sexual fire free from confusion is a primal, sacred medicine. In human interactions, this power is so shadowed that rarely is it used with clarity. More often, it is the arena for abuse—the misuse of will and power—or it is a landscape that engulfs the wisdom of the explorer.

Mainstream religions vilify or seek to domesticate it; the counterculture tries to liberate it without first liberating the dysfunctional patterns of belief that make the sexual fire a dangerous torch.

Fear-guided beliefs about sexuality, love, union, desire, intimacy, gender, and relationship must be transformed if the ills of this age are to be healed. Separation from truth about these things has brought catastrophic violence into the world. In the search for a security of understanding, the separation of the sexes has continued in New Age preoccupation with "men's mysteries," "women's spirituality," and other similar definitions of identity-through-otherness.

For the sexual fire to be experienced as a medicine of the sacred, we must release the beliefs of separation. Like the illusion of a subject-object universe, the divisive categorizations of male and female that prevent wholeness need to be seen as impositions of fear.

The act of sexual union is only one aspect of the sacred fire's dance, though indeed this aspect can be far-reaching and volatile. The sexual fire is present also in the making of medicine and in any creative use of the life force. It moves within all pure desire. It is the essence of the South, the energy of Spirit-aligned will.

To use the sexual fire rightly, you must see yourself as whole. If you see yourself as one part of a duality, you are in a fragmented consciousness of identity that will inhibit your experience of the sacred.

In wholeness, you encompass the yin and yang, the in-breath and out-breath, the creative and receptive, the doing and being. You see these as inseparable, not opposites but interwoven aspects of one thing.

In wholeness, the sexual fire is not a servant of neediness or ego. Instead, it can embody love, celebrate life, and lead you into the dimension of life's core desire.

Fear constricts possibility. Its shadows distract you from the source of light. Love expands your potentials and keeps your priorities tuned to wisdom. In the sacred fire is refinement of will and purification of intention. With this can come the gift of courage—participation in transformation.

During This Week

Examine how you involve yourself with the sexual fire. Look again at your attitudes about sexuality and gender. Look at your fears. Be aware of how you define yourself in terms of male and female and in what ways these definitions box you in.

Reassess your patterns of sexual relationship and see if your beliefs are constricting the possibilities of a fuller experience of joy and love in relationship. Seek clarity in your embodiment and interaction with the sacred fire. Awaken to its medicine.

TRANSFORMATION AND HEYOKA

LIKE THE ASTROLOGICAL SIGN OF AQUARIUS—RULED BY TWO SEEMINGLY opposite energies, Saturn and Uranus—those born under the sign of Heyoka are governed by cosmic paradox. Heyoka preserves through change and is guardian over the ways of the people. It is like putting a coyote in charge of the henhouse, and if humans are as reluctant to change under pressure as chickens, then we're in trouble.

Heyoka is the visionary, one step ahead. Heyoka is the rememberer, looking back over the shoulder. All this makes Heyoka energy unsettling within the present moment. Heyoka energy is not of the same world as the mainstream, yet its response to the world is informed by an extended knowledge that allows instinct to reflect truth. It is playing with more cards than are in the standard deck: reference and resource beyond ordinary vision.

Heyoka actions rattle the cages of complacency. Wake up, wake up, howls Coyote in the middle of the night; Coyote then hides, embarrassed by the attention. Transformation is not always a welcome message, even wrapped in silly gift paper or sent anonymously.

No one can follow in the tracks of another Heyoka. It is a singular path, yet found in every society and tribe, in every time in history, in some form. It is not a sought-after path, not aspired to. Different societies have in varying degrees accepted, honored, feared, dreaded, and misunderstood Heyoka.

Most modern people who think they are Heyoka are not, or they are but not in the ways they think they are. Most of these people like to make fun of what other people are doing or to disrupt groups. They like to make scenes, get attention, and justify anger, irresponsibility, resentment, and insecurity by calling themselves Heyoka. These people cannot bear to be poked at themselves. This is not Heyoka, it is neediness. Many of these people carry the seeds of true Heyoka, expressed inadvertently and unconsciously, but the banner of trickster they proudly or ruefully wave is a guise that does injustice to true Heyoka.

This is fine, however, because it is the nature of Heyoka medicine to be misjudged. Such hostility keeps Heyoka's power of elusiveness in top form; and elusiveness, as Coyote knows, is a valuable ace in the hole. Heyoka will not be fenced in by fear, trapped by definitions, or boxed by pretensions.

Wanting to be Heyoka is like wanting to be a shaman. It is a desire usually born of ignorance of the reality of what such a path entails. Those whom such a path chooses often feel ambivalence, resistance, or resignation to the process, though some souls accept such life agendas gracefully, grateful for the opportunity to grow and committed to transformation.

Heyokas are self-taught. They may have advisors, guides, and allies from both the human and nonhuman communities, from the physical and spirit realms, but essentially they must come to terms with their medicine within the solitude of their own naked souls. That is why, in some Native tribes, it is said of Heyokas, "They know something about themselves."

Heyoka is a mirror, neither distorted nor dirty, not clouded by limiting beliefs, attitudes, and habits. It is a clear mirror without secondary intention or abuse. In this clarity abides innocence and the space for transformation, healing, release. The mirror is service, not need, so what is reflected is freed from personality; there is no put-down. Being a mirror is different from disguising intimidation and manipulation under a coyote mask.

Heyoka has license because Heyoka is accountable to Spirit, has surrendered the illusions and privileges of conformity, the insulation of the group, and the security of the mainstream. It is painful/it is powerful, it is demanding/it is liberating, it is scary/it is hilarious. (Coyote gets tired of all this analysis, trots off. Coyote has all those abilities and no station in life.) Tremendous power is associated with Heyoka, which is why so much humiliation is also involved.

Turning things backward or upside down reveals hidden truths and dislodges assumptions. Secrets get chased into the sunlight. Realizations are stirred up from the depths; tension is made conscious and used to create crisis and change. Heyoka does not orchestrate these activities but is their instrument. Heyoka is wild card, fool, X factor, the uncompromised. Heyoka is direct, allied with lightning; Heyoka makes no sense. Those with this medicine cannot forget the sacred dream—it is their law. They are committed.

In tribal cultures, Heyokas, Coshares, False Faces, Contraries, and other eccentric roles were accepted as intrinsic to the healthy functioning of the society. In modern cultures, it is often an unsupported path. People are afraid. There is no explicit community, no consensus of what our roles are in relation to one another.

On the ranges, coyotes are despised, shot, trapped, poisoned, and bad-mouthed; yet Coyote endures, adapts, eludes, and continues to sing its medicine song across the sacred Earth, as full of conspiring vitality as ever. May you live long and well, Coyote, may you never get caught.

Axis, a true shamanic Heyoka magician, gave permission for this song to be used in this book. It was given to him from Coyote.

> *I am Mirror show-er*
> *and glass breaker,*
> *I am between the worlds.*
> *I am shadow show-er*
> *backward dancer,*
> *I am on a healing path.*

I am sweet law-breaker
that laws of the people
may live.
I am Heyoka,
Coyote sings in me.
I am my own enemy/friend,
light in darkness,
darkness when it's bright.
I am Heyoka.
I am death in life,
and life in death,
I am Anpu-Anubis,
I am Heyoka.
In silence do I speak
and sing,
in words I hide,
moving I rest,
at rest I move.
I am between the worlds,
I am Heyoka.
My path is twisted
and direct.
I am crazy dog,
I am Heyoka.

Some years ago, I participated in a large pipe ceremony—a marriage of pipes, based on a traditional Seven Nations peace ceremony. There were a hundred or so people in the circle under a hot afternoon sun. Two pipes were used, one lit from the other.

I stood and filled the pipe, praying aloud, and the people were quiet and attentive, respectful of the sacred occasion. As a shy person, I have to focus entirely on the medicine during public ceremony or I can't function.

The pipe was lit and the blessing of prayer flowed forth on the smoke. I felt the presence of Spirit. I reached down for the pipe tamp that had been set out on the blanket with other articles from my pipe bag. As scores of sincere people watched closely, I tamped the burning tobacco.

The mysterious smell of melting plastic mingled with the fragrance of tobacco smoke. I realized with a shock that I had somehow picked up my rainbow-striped pen instead of the tamp! I heard Coyote snickering in the astral distance.

With great and foolish dignity I finished tamping the tobacco with my pen, and the pipe was passed to each person in the circle, for smoking. One woman had a baby in her lap who tugged two of the three feathers off the pipe. After the ceremony, I gave them to two people I met at the gathering.

The person I gave the owl feather to brought teachings to me years later in the form of intense suffering. The one I gave the macaw feather to brought teaching to me years later in the form of healing and love.

Everyone liked the ceremony.

During This Week

Do something different.

USING THE RATTLE

MEDICINE RATTLES ARE OF MANY KINDS AND MATERIALS. SOME SOUND like rattlesnakes, some like rain, some like hail, some like a mother shushing her child.

Rattles are used to wake and call the spirits. Sometimes they're used with drums, or other percussion, or with songs and chants. The rattle speaks with authority, or it whispers and cajoles. The rattle knows secrets and sometimes tells them. The rattle moves to make medicine. Whether its voice is a liquid swish or a dry rustle, it is a medicine of the South, a dancer, a shaker.

Rattle sounds can break up stagnant patterns and scatter the shadows of ill will. The rattle can disperse, shatter, and guide as well as invoke. It is a tool of change.

Rattles are part of healing work and can affect the chakras. Rattles are part of ceremonial dance when spirits are being invited. Rattles are totem callers, made of deer toes, turtles shells, and buffalo horns. Rattles are Yuwipi medicine. They participate in many ceremonies.

Inside the rattle may be stones, crystals, seeds, teeth, or beads. The dance of the rattle's womb with its hidden contents is part of the particular medicine of that rattle.

Some rattles are plain, some decorated—painted, feathered, beaded, anointed. Each rattle is a being whose life is motion, sound, and form. Sparks fly from some rattles, others are more introspective. All rattles like to dance.

If you have a rattle, pick it up. Look at its shape and what it is made from. Is it decorated? What does the rattle mean to you? What part does it play in your life?

Feel the weight and balance of your rattle, the way it fits in your hand. Smudge your rattle. Smudge yourself. Address a prayer to the rattle's spirit and to the powers of the South.

Sit with your eyes closed, holding the rattle. Breathe, be aware of your heartbeat, center and ground yourself. Slowly tip the rattle until it speaks. What does it remind you of? Begin to shake the rattle gently. Tune to its voice. Find a rhythm that suits the moment and continue to rattle until you are immersed in the medicine of it.

Sing if that is what rises in you to do. Feel what happens when this rattle moves. Feel what is summoned and what is sent. Feel what presences are attracted by the rattle and your use of it.

Now let the rattle become quieter and slower. Breathe and relax. Let it become still.

What has happened? What has shifted? Is all well with your space? If anything is there that should not stay, smudge, speak a dismissal, or use whatever mode you are familiar with to make your space clear.

Thank the spirits that blessed you with their presences. Thank the spirit of the rattle. Put it away on an altar or in a wrapped bundle until you are ready to work with it again.

All your medicine objects should be cared for conscientiously. Proper maintenance is one safeguard against accumulating objects that you are not really using or more things than you can give proper attention to. The allure of beautiful things, or objects that make you feel important through association with them, can lead you astray from appropriate relationship. Power is not in an object or in being seen with it, but in the quality of your relationship with the medicine.

With the proliferation of New Age shops and catalogs, and the popularization of shamanic thises and thats, all kinds of wonderful-looking stuff is available, ready-made. Just as money can't buy you love, money can't buy you spiritual power, though it can certainly make you look dazzling.

Medicine objects are not for decoration or image enhancement. If you are sincerely looking for spiritual alignment, you must look honestly at what role your "stuff" plays in your work. Here are some suggestions:

1. Inventory what you have, including stones, crystals, feathers, drums, rattles, shells, fur, bones, antlers, claws, talons, skins, carvings, pipes, esoteric tools, shields, ceremonial regalia—everything along those lines. For each item, ask yourself and the spirit of the object some questions:

   ᚙ When was this acquired? Under what circumstances?

   ᚙ How long since I've interacted with it?

   ᚙ What is my relationship with this object?

   ᚙ What are my intentions toward this object?

   ᚙ What action needs to be taken in relation to this object?

   The results of this inquiry should give you insight on whether you need to change how you work with something, maintain it differently, pass it on, put it away to reassess later, return it to some element of the Earth, or take some other course of action.

2. Smudge, wash, or otherwise clear your medicine objects regularly. Some objects need it more often than others, particularly ones used in healing work, ones exposed to random energies, or those that are very energy sensitive or energy productive. The same goes for those objects you carry or wear frequently. New moon is a good time to take care of this.

3. Recharge objects that you use to emanate certain kinds of energy or to maintain particular vibratory conditions. It may be helpful to rotate these

objects with others in order to give them periodic rests. Clear, rest, and renew any objects that seem to need it. Waxing to full moon is a good time to recharge.

4. Keep medicine objects wrapped, in containers, or on a maintained altar when not in use. Sage, sweetgrass, or other herbs can be put in those bundles and containers to help keep the objects clear and protected.

5. Be aware of how your objects affect others, especially animals and children, who are vulnerable to random energy. Be responsible.

6. Realize that your relationship with your medicine is an evolving process, so what was a fine way to work with something in the past might not be true for the present. Inquire into these relationships regularly.

7. Feeling love and appreciation for an object doesn't necessarily mean that you should keep it. The movement of medicine objects through the world is part of how power finds its path of healing and how people respond to Spirit guidance. When there is sharing and freedom of movement, there is increase of medicine.

8. When you pass an object on to someone or give it to the elements, clear it first, very thoroughly. Give it only to someone who can be responsible for its proper care and use. Let it go completely. If something is given you, know that you don't have to accept it. If you do, move slowly in bringing it into your intimate psychic space. Clear it. Don't immediately wear it, use it, or put it on your altar. Meditate on what its right place and use is. Communicate with the spirits associated with it. Get to know it. Smudge it often.

9. Treat your medicine objects with respect and attention to relationships. This treatment reflects your attitude toward yourself, your spiritual path, and your allies. If your respect is only a formality or show, your objects will be empty of true use. If your treatment of them is haphazard, your use of them will produce erratic effects. If your interactions with your medicine objects are Spirit-guided, your work will be blessed by their use.

10. If you have objects that have a history of traditional application—either the objects themselves or ones of their nature—be particularly mindful in your use and keeping of them. Be clear about the appropriateness of your involvement with them, and try to become knowledgeable about the protocols surrounding their use in the past. These objects have certain associations for people of the cultures from which they came. These associations and traditional patterns are part of an object's matrix, and thus are part of your relationship with an object.

If you can't make medicine without objects, can't be safe without your protective crystal, can't clear your energy without sage, can't shift into trance without a drum, then you are losing touch with your primary alignment, which has no reliance on objects. When you lose your roots, you become top-heavy and fall. The grounding in Spirit will allow you to find a balance of form and formlessness in the embodiment of your medicine path.

During This Week

Implement whatever suggestions from this lesson seem like good ideas to you.

FOCUSING AND PROJECTING POWER

POWER. WHAT IMAGES AND FEELINGS THAT WORD INVITES! IT IS A WORD that pushes buttons. There is much talk these days of personal power, empowerment, sharing power, giving away power, coming into your own power, and so on.

What is power? Something invisible that exerts deliberate effect—movement under will. That definition includes a lot of territory without reference to value. Let's be specific: What is the role of power in a spiritual life?

Power is intrinsic to Spirit and thus touches all aspects of the path. My Native teacher once told me, "I won't talk to you about power," and indeed he rarely even mentioned the word. In alignment with the sacred, power is not taught, not pursued, not considered an object or an objective.

You do not teach children to grasp at consciousness or to possess curiosity. You guide their maturation so that their use of mind will be, as a matter of course, ethical, inquiring, and effective. So it is with power. If you are in harmony with the sacred, power will naturally be present. If you are not trying to attach that power to yourself—an act as unwise as holding your breath—it will flow, becoming part of the current of medicine manifest on this Earth.

Your focus needs to stay with alignment, not with desire for power. Alignment informs will, and will, action. Alignment guides intention and present reality. Alignment is where you're at and where you're headed. Power is the current that carries intention like a river's flow carries a boat. Will is the paddle with which you steer. Alignment guides your use of the paddle.

You can't hold on to the current; you can't own it. You can engage with it, move with it, use it with purpose, deal with it skillfully, or you can be swept away by it, spun willy-nilly into rocks, drowned, or confused in its eddies. You can even dam it up and build your own hydro plant to harness the current for personal profit. But this will take you nowhere.

Power cannot be given or stolen, shared or owned. It can only be interacted with, or not. This interaction can be receptive or projective.

Receptive engagement with power is a trademark of many healing techniques, such as laying on of hands and Reiki. It is a channeling of particular universal energies for the purpose of balancing and healing. This mode is attractive because it tends to bypass many ego-related pitfalls and complications. It is an invoking of power, though, and requires skill in its calling and in its application. Persons using it must provide an unobstructed passage for power to flow through, and they must be able to maintain their own balances during this transmission.

Conduction of power does not leave you unaffected. For some it can be a vitalizing experience; for others, draining. Many factors within the situation contribute to these effects.

It is an oversimplification to say that you are doing a good job—letting the source of sacred power do the work—if you feel vitalized by acting as its channel, and that you are doing a poor job if you feel weary afterward. Each healer participates in this process in her own way, with her own purposes and realizations within it, her own personal responses.

More useful, if you work in this receptive mode, is to be aware of how you are being affected and what understandings can be gleaned. This will help you evolve in your relationship with power and with healing.

Learning to work with power as a receptive channel is applicable to more than healing. It is an exercise in spiritual alignment, a connection to the sacred, and a path on which subtle energies can be brought into the levels of material manifestation.

Formal training for this is often an initiatory experience—an opening. Some people just have the knack for it, either from birth or because of some transformative event. Here are some ways to encourage this ability in yourself:

1. Clear, balance, and align your chakras, and try to maintain that healthy state. (See the next lessons, on chakra work.)

2. Maintain a resourceful level of physical vitality.

3. Examine your intentions and relationship to power. Be clear about what role your ego plays. Work on aspects that need changing in these areas.

4. Strengthen your meditation practices—learn to be still.

5. Learn to pace your energies effectively and consciously. (More about this in later lessons.)

6. Strengthen and expand your alliances.

7. Develop a sense of compassion and service (shouldn't take more than a few days!).

8. Focus on opening and being available to Spirit. Clear away obstructive patterns, fears, and beliefs.

These are long-term projects that are worthwhile in themselves, whether or not you ever become a hands-on spiritual healer.

The touch that conveys love is a healer. Stroke a cat, comfort a baby, brush your friend's hair, hug someone who's lonely. These kinds of contact channel power too—love power, the strongest embodied energy of all.

Smudge yourself. Sit, breathe, be peaceful. Breathe clarity and balance along the path of the chakras. Open yourself to universal power and invite its presence. Pray in the Mystery for sacred alignment. Breathe it in. Center yourself in it.

Breathe and become calm. Feel the gathering of love within you—nourish it with your trust and acceptance. Feel it move in you. Feel your hands begin to pulse with energy. Let it fill you, healing, clearing, transforming. Let it overflow, radiate, stream from your hands. Let it expand into the universe, carrying blessing. Ground yourself. Make a prayer of gratitude.

This practice can be used, as given or with modifications, as a basis for work with channeling loving and healing touch. It is similar to what I did as a midwife before touching a laboring woman or newborn baby, and to what I did as a mother preparatory to soothing a stressed or sick child. It can be used in general, for healing work or in personal interactions. Once centered in it, with power flowing, you can sense where to put your hands—what kind of touch is needed— and love will move rightly.

The active, projective mode of interaction with power can be used in healing also, but it requires greater discipline and clarity and strength of will than the channeled mode. This means it also has more opportunity for abuse or random effect. The power used in this mode can be tapped from the universal source or generated within the personal energy network.

Personally generated energy can be readily available but is quickly depleted. If the personal matrix is well aligned and integrated with the larger web of alliances or with the primal matrix, however, energy will not diminish until concentration and will slacken.

Impressive acts of power usually require either a high level of alignment and alliance, an extraordinary control of the personal matrix, or a combination of these. Magical adepts, yogis, and the best of the shamans are examples of that level of ability.

During This Week

Work with charging such things as stones or crystals in an appropriate way. This is a form of projective interaction with power. Elemental charges can be given through such means as

1. Intentional exposure to a specific context such as fire, wind, water, or earth for a period of time

2. Singing or chanting with a focus of infusing something with the energy pattern of the song or chant, such as using a mantra to charge a crystal

3. Immersion for an extended period in colored water or colored light, to impart the attributes of that color

4. Visualizing a beam of light energizing something as you hold it

5. Exposure to lightning, moonlight, or other natural charge

New moon to full moon is a time conducive to charging things. What you charge will radiate or house the charge until the energy naturally dissipates or is deliberately cleared; the charge needs to be periodically renewed. The more often the charge is renewed, the stronger the pattern of energy will become and the more easily the recharge will be accepted. Thorough and possibly repeated clearings will be needed to remove such a charge and to completely dismantle its pattern.

When you are charging something, the first consideration is the appropriateness of doing so. Permission should be sought from the spirit associated with what you want to charge, and your intentions clarified and assessed.

If all is well and you proceed, set yourself in alignment with your purpose and the energies involved. Smudge yourself and what you are charging. Make a sacred space. Hold the object of your attention in your hands and attune to it. Breathe and move your consciousness into nonordinary awareness. Make a prayer for right relationship and right action.

Connect with the universal web. Breathe in its power. Speak aloud your intentions and invoke the medicine from the spirits and allies related to the particular charge you are wanting. Be specific.

Let the current of energy flow into what you hold. Feel the pulse of power in your hands being absorbed by the object. Feel the blessings and gifts of the forces you have called settling into the object's underlying energy pattern. This can be done in a ceremonial way or, if your focus is skilled and strong enough, by simply holding or touching what you want to charge.

Continue until the charge is complete, then disconnect your attention. Make a prayer of gratitude. Store, use, and care for the object in a spiritually responsible way. Renew or clear the charge as appropriate.

CHAKRA WORK (PART 1)

THE WORD *CHAKRA* HAS POPPED UP IN ALMOST EVERY LESSON. THE following two lessons turn your attention completely to the chakras. Why are they so important?

The body is your classroom for this life on Earth—home base for your consciousness. The physical senses are portals of learning and communication. The chakras are vortices where your personal system of energy intersects with the larger grid.

Energy moves to and from the chakras and is circulated through your body and aura, affecting your perceptions and state of being. The health of the chakras, then, has a great effect on your physical, mental, emotional, and psychic well-being, and on what you experience.

Whole books have been written about the chakras. The brief exploration these lessons present will touch on a few practical techniques for maintaining and working with your chakras, and on the interrelationship of chakras with totems and allies.

The chakras are easily worked with. Don't be put off by all the esoteric language and mystique surrounding traditional knowledge of them. Have you ever felt butterflies in your stomach? Ever experienced your throat closing with inhibition? Ever curled up in a fetal position to comfort yourself? These are responses linked to the chakras, which in turn prompt physical reaction.

The chakras regulate the movement of energy through your system. Each chakra is associated with particular physical regions and systems, and with corresponding types of energy. The chakras can be pictured as flowers—they can be tightly closed, fully opened, or anything between. Their degrees of openness govern the traffic through them.

For instance, when you are physically threatened, the first chakra, which is concerned with survival, opens wide. Energy is drawn to that fight-or-flight instinct; your physical reserves gather so that you can run extra fast or struggle extra hard. But if you were to walk around in your everyday activities with that wide-open first chakra, your resulting actions would be quite unbalanced. The state of the chakra needs to be appropriate to the circumstances. To a large degree, this is automatic, but unless you are well balanced to begin with, the chakras need some conscious adjustment in order to reflect optimum functioning.

You can adjust your chakras as needed; gradually, as your awareness deepens, this can be done on the go without having to take time out for frequent assessment and balancing. Your power to choose your state of being—through meditation, pacing of your energy, and awareness of the chakras—can profoundly change your life.

When you go out into bright sunlight, you can squint, close your eyes, or put on sunglasses. What if you didn't use those options but just suffered the circumstances? That is what most people do in terms of their chakras. They have lost connectedness with healthy states of being and relationships, and thus cannot respond wisely to life's varying circumstances.

Balance does not necessarily mean that all the chakras are at the same degree of openness or activity. It means that they are in beneficial relationship to each other and are functioning in intelligent ways within any given situation.

The basic chakra correspondences are

1. Base of the spine	Red	Earth	Survival and grounding
2. Lower abdomen	Orange	Water	Emotions and sexuality
3. Solar plexus	Yellow	Fire	Personal energy and identity
4. Heart	Green	Air	Love and compassion
5. Throat	Blue	Sound	Creativity and communication
6. Brow	Indigo	Light	Imagination and intuition
7. Crown	Purple	Thought	Knowledge and understanding

(Remember the chakras are not in the body itself; they are in the aura.) Within the chakra spectrum of energy, no greater or lesser value is placed on particular chakras. The lower chakras are just as important as the upper—all need tender care. There are chakras in the hands and feet also.

Adjustment possibilities for the chakras include

1. *Size.* You can increase or decrease the radiant extension and density of energy.

2. *Color.* The clarity of color will reflect clarity of energy.

3. *Openness.* The degree of openness will affect volume and velocity of flow.

4. *Position.* Sometimes chakras will tilt, droop, or be in unusual relationship to the body and aura.

5. *Directional spin.* Chakras have a clockwise or counterclockwise vortex.

6. *Flow between chakras.* Movement of energy through the system can be obstructed or free, and the flow can move in various patterns throughout the entire system.

7. *Introverted or extroverted.* Consider whether the chakra is primarily drawing or projecting energy.

Doing general chakra maintenance can increase your awareness and control. The seven areas of adjustment all have significant bearing on your well-being and experience on all levels. As you experiment with various adjustments and become sensitive to your system of energy, you will see what changes are needed in other areas of your life. Much healing can be accomplished through your care of the chakras, and such skill is of vast benefit in your spiritual work. The healthy use of power depends on healthy chakras, and dysfunction in the chakras inhibits your range of relationship with the larger web of life.

The following is an exercise for clearing your chakras. You should decide what pattern of circulation best suits your needs any time you adjust chakras. Some possibilities for this: a pattern of movement from the Earth up and out the crown; from the crown down and into the Earth; from Earth up and back down, into Earth; from crown down and back up, and out; down from the crown and up from Earth simultaneously, meeting and circulating in the center, and then continuing up and out the crown and down into the Earth, respectively. In this exercise you'll use the first of these.

Sit or lie on your back. Relax, breathe, center. Feel your place between Earth and Sky.

Let your attention sink to your first chakra. Feel its connection to the Earth. Observe it, see what is there, get a sense of how it is doing. Then breathe energy up from the strong Earth and into the chakra: red light from the core of the Earth. Fill the chakra with this rich light until it is brightly suffused, warm, and steady. Feel the security of the ground in the chakra, and its power to warn and protect you at need. Be glad of your presence on the Earth, in this life. Feel your sacredness as a created being, part of the luminous web of relationship alive on the Earth. Feel your commitment to being.

Breathe your attention up through the first chakra to the second. See what is there, feel what is there. Breathe orange light into this chakra—clear, courageous light. See the chakra as a bright flower. Fill the chakra with this glow; breathe it. Feel fear unwind and dissipate; feel the sensitivity of this chakra, its awareness of the feelings of others. Let the light be strong in it to guide right relationship and to guide right use of the sacred sexual fire. Bless yourself in the light of this orange flame.

Move your attention to your solar plexus. See the chakra; feel what is there, its state of being and movement. Breathe golden light and let the chakra expand with shining light. Fill the chakra with light, dispelling shadows and constriction. Feel what the right balance of this chakra is, how far your will needs to project and how it must also respect the space of others. Feel a strength of character that is not aggressive or wrongfully imposing, that balances self-knowledge with attention and service to Spirit. Feel the clarity of this balance.

Draw energy up through the lower chakras and into the fourth chakra, the heart. Observe what is present and what you are feeling there. Breathe love, bright green like the green fire of spring leaves. Breathe clear compassion and love.

Expand the chakra with light and breath. Feel your limitless connection to love—your access to receiving and passing it to others. Feel surrounded by the power of love; feel it radiant in your heart. See the presence in your heart of those you are close to. Bathe their images in the beauty of love. Fill the chakra with luminosity.

Move your attention to the throat, the fifth chakra. Observe its state of being; feel the breath in your throat. See it become the color of clear blue sky. Feel it ease any tightness in your throat. Relax as you breathe; relax your jaw and shoulders. Breathe calming, soothing blue light, cool and glowing, peaceful. Feel your ability to speak and breathe beauty, truth, from your intimate connection with the sacred source. Feel the gift of expressive life. Feel the flow of light within you, in communion with grace, with spiritual resource. Let the light extend along your outer arms and flow from your hands.

Breathe your awareness into the sixth chakra, your brow, place of deep indigo mystery. See what is there; be with this chakra. Relax your face, your eyes. Breathe indigo light into this center of psychic vision. Travel into the light, deep places beyond your ordinary perceptions. Relax and flow into the light. Travel, as through a velvet indigo sky, unbounded, vast. Release yourself from the inhibitions of belief. Open this chakra with light, breath, and the desire to see. Let your awareness move in freedom, carried on the energies flowing through the chakra from your connection with the strong Earth. Be peaceful in this place; let the vision unfold its dream.

Now the energy moves upward to the crown chakra. Feel this place at the top of your body. Feel its closeness to the Sky and the universal cosmos. Breathe purple light. Open this chakra and send the light cascading from your crown, to rain down through your aura with diamond-bright purple and silver light. Breathe in energy and send it up through all the chakras and out the crown. Feel it wash over you, clearing your aura, energizing your body. Be an open channel for the light, its power infusing and flowing unencumbered. Breathe and relax. Be connected to Earth and Sky; be at home in yourself. Move your chakras' states of being into right balance. You will feel when they are as they should be. Give thanks for this energy. Sit up when you are ready. Move slowly until you feel reoriented in your energy pattern.

During This Week

Work with your chakras. Do some long sessions and some brief tune-ups. Clear chakras as you are going to sleep, to give your dreams more clarity and your body better rest. Some questions to ask when you are assessing the states of your chakras:

- ❧ What is the relationship of this chakra with the world?

- ❧ What relationship do I want, in terms of this energy, right now?

- How is this energy affecting my experience?

- What changes would benefit my interactions with the world?

- What are my habitual patterns of energy?

- Which chakras get the most attention from me?

- Which chakras do I relate least with?

- Which colors do I like? Dislike?

- Which chakras are most affected by others, without my being responsive to my own choices?

- Which chakras need the least conscious adjustment in order to function well?

- How are my chakras affected by what I wear? How I walk? My usual position for sleep? The way I make love? What I eat and drink?

- What kind of energy do I attract? What kind of people?

- What part of my body seems most vulnerable to illness or discomfort? What chakras are related?

These kinds of questions will get the ball rolling and help you see where chakra work will bring balance and healing to different aspects of your life. Chakras can lead you not only to insight and understanding but also to specific ways of asserting your commitment to awareness and change.

CHAKRA WORK (PART 2)

IN WORKING WITH THE CHAKRAS, TOTEMS, AND ALLIES, YOU MAY FIND that certain allies are associated with specific chakras. Seeing these connections can give you some leaps of realization about what role the ally has in your current interaction with it. If you are already working with totems and allies, you might want to ask if they are involved with specific chakra functions or if your association with them would be more effective through correlations with the chakras.

These correlations may be short- or long-term and thus should be reexamined periodically as your alliance unfolds. These correlations also conjoin revealingly with other orientations such as the medicine wheel directions, opening deeper dimensions to explore.

For example, Eagle is my East (Air) totem but is currently involved with the energy of my third (Fire) chakra. Knowing this gives me much more to work with than if I just have a general sense of Eagle as my totem. When I communicate with Eagle I often feel its energy in the solar plexus, and I can call upon its help in situations where the energy of the third chakra can benefit from Eagleness. It also teaches me to use the Eagle aspect of my ego and will in responsible ways.

The effectiveness of this work is dependent on my knowledge of the chakras and my clarity of relationship with the totems and allies. It should be remembered that totems and allies can mirror apparent weaknesses as well as potential strengths—they reveal as well as reinforce your tendencies. With each of the chakras, the totem can give insight into how you are functioning in that aspect of life and can lead you to positive ways of growth and alignment.

An ally for the first chakra could help with issues of physical orientation and success. If you had Eagle, for example, involved with this chakra, you would give thought to this airy being's relationship to groundedness. Perhaps you would need to pursue a course of bringing your high aspirations into physical manifestation.

If associated with the second chakra, Eagle would be addressing matters of emotion and sexuality. Eagle's style of mating in midair would give food for thought, as would its pattern of lifelong partnership. Eagle is aloof and picky about friends; Eagle keeps its cool.

Finding Eagle in the third chakra, the place of personal power, could make you reflect, as I did, on being Eagle-egoed—distancing yourself from mundane affairs and not wanting your will to be challenged. Eagle likes to maintain position in the heights. It has the courage to be itself, however, so does not get drawn into petty bickering. It just does what seems right.

In the fourth chakra, a totem would give teachings about giving and receiving, about relationship with the larger community and the maturation of emotion. Eagle here might indicate a tendency toward universal love that is also loyal to specific individuals.

Eagle's correlation to the fifth chakra might indicate a drive to bring high aspiration into right livelihood through self-expression. It might also warn that you are not much of a team worker in terms of communication.

If Eagle was nesting in the sixth chakra, it would bring tremendous keenness and accuracy of insight to this chakra of intuition. It would be a guide through the subtle realms, but a different one from, say, Owl with its nightly powers.

Finding Eagle in association with the seventh chakra would greatly reinforce the airy quality of that chakra and perhaps indicate a need to make sure your grounding is secure. Eagle's involvement in the crown chakra would reinforce a strong connection to the cosmic powers that give a larger and more inclusive perspective than that afforded by daily personal concerns.

Working through the chakra functions, a totem or ally can promote healing and redirection of natural qualities. Taking what you know of the totem and of the chakra and maintaining an active communication with the totem, you can make choices, be more aware, and move your energy in productive ways.

Your intimacy with the totem or ally allows you to look at yourself without fear and to choose what to nurture and what to release. It brings you closer to the totem and to the web of relationship that is your family of resource. This mode of partnership gives a path of cooperative appreciation and makes the relationship more real and particular. It forms a basis for daily interaction—aspects to focus on and directions to investigate.

The chakra-ally correlation is not meant to inhibit the range of the totem's medicine. The chakra approach to relationship is only one perspective—perhaps a starting point, perhaps an adjunct to other views and accesses. Alliance is a living truth, so it is always in movement, flow, and transformative unfolding.

Finding a totem or ally associated with a chakra can come through contact with the ally or through your work with the chakra. Either way, there is a gift.

During This Week

The following exercises can be used for seeking knowledge of your chakra-ally correlations or for communicating with totems and allies through focus on the chakras. The first exercise is applicable if you already know your allies; the second, if you are seeking to know.

Smudge yourself and your working space. Ground and center. If your totems and allies are mostly nocturnal, perhaps do this exercise at night.

Gather before you images of your various allies (photos, drawings, carvings, and so on) or objects representative of your allies (talons, fur, feathers, stones, and so on).

Make a large rainbow from cloth or paper using the seven chakra colors. Sit for a while, gazing at this vibrant rainbow. Clear your chakras. Perhaps do some drumming or singing. If you have songs for your allies, sing them as you gaze at the rainbow. Make a prayer or invocation appropriate to your path.

When you feel ready, sit in stillness and focus on the red color in the rainbow. Ask if there is an ally associated with your first chakra, and if so, if it will reveal itself to you now. You may want to close your eyes and direct your attention to the chakra, or you may place your finger on the red arc of the rainbow and attune to the chakra with your eyes open.

You may see or hear or feel something to indicate what ally, if any, is associated with that chakra. Take the image or object that corresponds with that ally and place it on the red arc of the rainbow. Express gratitude for this information, and move to the second chakra and color. Repeat the process for each chakra. It may be that some chakras do not at this time have any allies associated with them. This may be similar to an astrological chart with some of the houses empty, or it may be something that changes with time. It may be that one ally is involved with several chakras.

When you are finished with this exercise, give thanks again, perhaps putting tobacco, corn pollen, or sage on the rainbow arcs beside the objects or images. If your concentration is still strong, this may be a good opportunity to meditate on the possibilities inherent in the chakra-ally correlations that have been revealed. You may want to commune awhile with your allies.

This rainbow arrangement can be kept on an altar for later reference and meditation and for strengthening this aspect of your alliances, or it can be respectfully dismantled.

A variation of this exercise is to hold each ally's image or object and ask for its chakra correspondence to be shown. The image or object can then be placed on the appropriate rainbow arc. With this approach, you are focusing on the ally instead of the chakra.

Another variation is to lay relaxed on your back and hold an ally's image or object in your hands. Ask to be shown its corresponding chakra. Begin slowly moving the image or object over the chakras from root to crown.

Tune your awareness to any tug between the image or object and one of the chakras. You may need to retrace your movements slowly a few times, or you may know without moving at all where the ally belongs.

Once you feel a pull to a chakra, set the image or object on the corresponding part of your body and feel if the correlation is comfortable. Then move on to the next.

If you are not familiar with your totems and allies and the time seems right—that is, if you have done some preparatory work—then the following exercise may help open the way to knowledge in the realm of alliance.

Smudge yourself and your working space. Invoke your guardians; make your space safe and sacred. Speak of your intentions to the spirits—pray. Access a trance state through drumming or other means.

Direct your attention to your first chakra. Energize it with your breath. Clear it and fill it with light. Ask if there is an ally for you relating to this chakra at this time. If one makes itself known to you, greet it and ask what issues or aspect of your life it is there to help you with. Then ask how you can best honor this relationship. Give thanks, sending loving energy to the chakra, the ally, and the universe.

Move to the next chakra and repeat this process, continuing up through all the chakras. It may be that you will not find allies relating to all the chakras, or per-haps you will find one ally associated with several chakras. Work with what comes.

When you are finished, breathe through all the chakras, distributing a balance of well-being throughout your aura. Bring yourself back into ordinary conscious-ness. Open your circle, releasing whatever energies you have invoked or attached to your work.

This week, make a bundle for the South Fire.

FIRE CEREMONY

SUMMER HAS ENDED, AND BEFORE MOVING INTO YOUR WORK OF AUTUMN, it is time to make a ceremony to honor what has come to you in this season of transformation.

Take your bundle, at noon, to a place of sunlight. Smudge yourself, your bundle, and your place of ceremony.

Lay a small fire. Then call to the Directions to be witness to your prayers. Call the Earth and sky, the spirits of place, and the Mystery. Invite the spirits and allies who have helped you in your work of Summer.

Light the fire from its South side. Sit awhile and watch its flames. Reflect on what you have learned and experienced through Summer.

Bring out your rattle and let its voice speak to the spirits that are present. Sing your medicine songs. Then stand and face the South. Hold tobacco in your hands and make a prayer of gratitude and alliance. Focus your energies into the tobacco as you speak, and when the prayer is complete, toss the tobacco into the flames of your fire. Sit and watch the fire die down. When there are only ashes left, stand and open the circle.

Prepare for Autumn Equinox.

The sacred dream,
matrix of remembrance,
stained-glass leaf where I pray
and something flows like
mother's milk
into the core of desire.
The shadow and the light say
one thing—love's brightness—
it is only a turning
that makes the worlds seem
divided. Like the seasons,
you must travel the round
to know them, and their
wholeness, held like an apple
in your hand.

Part 3

WEST / AUTUMN:
USING THE INTUITION
Autumn Equinox to Winter Solstice

Great Mystery, powers of Autumn, of Water, I send a voice in prayer. I am asking for entrance through the gates of inner knowledge. I am seeking to cross the realms. Spirits of the waters, help me be fluid in consciousness, to move easily in this work.

I turn to the setting sun, in the place between day and night, asking guidance for intuition. I pray for the right doors to open, for the ability to look within and make good medicine from what I find there. I pray that I can grow within this work and be of service to others.

Powers of twilight, I walk in your mystery and open to your gifts.

OPENING THE CENTER OF FEELING

THE TURNING OF THE WHEEL BRINGS YOU NOW TO AUTUMN, THE harvesting of the fruits of consciousness and will. The outward flow of manifestation has reached its tidal peak and now returns inward to the work of the heart.

In these weeks, the lessons will focus on taking awareness to deeper levels. In the deepening of consciousness comes emotional maturation. Perception and will are expanded beyond youthful ego centeredness to become more encompassing. In the West is acceptance of self, where there is freedom for giving and receiving. This acceptance also makes possible movement into realms where fear, doubt, and shadows of self-image would otherwise impede the way.

To use your intuition you must first trust yourself. Without self-acceptance and trust, clarity of perception is distorted by emotional turbulence. The steps to self-acceptance are awareness, understanding, compassion, and love, the East-West road on the medicine wheel.

Autumn is for exploring the depths, carrying with you the enlightenment of spring and the courage and alliance gained in summer. Autumn is the time of going within. You release what is finished, like a tree setting free its leaves, and store what will nourish the work to come, as the squirrels do in gathering food for winter.

Intuition, a perceptive-interpretive power of mind, is dependent on attention and acknowledgment in order to be useful to you. The more it is used, the stronger it becomes. It can take you into the heart of things. It can enlarge your arena of spiritual practice, giving more levels of information and resource, and more complete views on which to base choices.

Acting on intuition brings it out of the speculative distance and onto the bedrock of reality. Experience gives confidence; confidence gives impetus for further exploration.

The second chakra, the waterlike center of emotional sensitivity, is often a vulnerable place. Its association with sexuality makes it particularly prone to buffeting and imbalance. Overstimulation of this chakra yields an empathy that is extreme to the point of being self-abusive. In this state, one's own feelings cannot be separated from those of others. This kind of empathy serves no constructive purpose; it can be moderated by a healthy solar plexus and by steady grounding from the first chakra.

Keeping the second chakra in balance will help you be discriminating about what you take on of other people's emotions and about your sexual interactions. A healthy second chakra will reflect a growing emotional responsibility.

To clear and open this chakra, sit or lie on your back. Center in your breathing, relaxing, relaxing, relaxing. Breathe so that your lower abdomen rises with your in-breaths and falls with your out-breaths. Loosen your waistband if necessary.

Bring your breath through the chakras, starting at the crown. Feel yourself relax. Breathe into the second chakra. See it like a peaceful pool of water, gently stirred by the life within it. See it reflecting an orange sunset, its waters shining with color. Breathe orange, a blessing of light.

Focus on the waters of the pool. See the gentle light making the waters clearer and clearer—a pool you can drink from, waters you can see into, pure and calm. Breathe this clarity and feel your emotions become untroubled. Feel the sacredness of this pool and of yourself in the truth of being. Feel the sacredness of your sexuality, and be within the integrity of this sacredness. Be in your wholeness.

Allow light to become brighter and the energy to flow down through all the chakras to the first chakra and into the holy Earth. Breathe through all the chakras, Sky to Earth. When you feel ready, sit up and go about your day in remembrance of right emotional balance.

During This Week

Nurture your second chakra. Try to keep tension and emotional debris cleared out of it. Remove any unwanted sexual presences or connections from it. Fill it often with beautiful light. Love yourself—do things that bring you pleasure.

Pay attention to how you interact emotionally with others. What do you take in? What do you project? Stop yourself when you are about to engage in unproductive emotional reactions. Disrupt those patterns. Just stop—take a few moments to reconsider whether you really want to respond in that way. Breathe. Relax your second chakra and breathe into it.

Don't stuff down the reflexive emotion or deny its presence. Breathe and observe. Understand what you are engaging in when you link yourself with a particular emotion. Is there good in it? Is there transformation of an unhappy situation? Do you like how it makes you feel? Is this a pattern you want reinforced?

The more you remember to stop and reconsider, using your breath in a meditative way to restore calm and clear perception, the quicker you can disengage from harmful patterns. The more you free yourself from outdated emotional patterns, the better you feel and the more willing you are to look within without judgment or fear.

Be careful of limiting your emotional options. Stop, look compassionately at what is happening, then make choices that honor your wholeness and your birthright of love. Nothing is unchangeable. You have perception and will and are moving into a maturity of feelings. Be present in the truth of this.

Sometimes ingrained emotional patterns can be dismantled through extensive verbalization, either alone in prayer or in the listening presence of another person. The person listening must understand that you are not asking for counsel, comfort, or solutions, but only for another's hearing of you.

A fully emotional and exhaustive verbalization may empty the pattern of its energy, making it easier for you to reorganize the freed-up energy into more useful patterns or to transform the emotions into healing, understanding, and compassion. You must be sure not to leave a vacuum into which the old pattern will tend to re-form itself. These changes need to be reinforced affirmatively. Identify your core intention—happiness? spiritual growth? peace of mind?—and the practices, responses, and behaviors that will fulfill that intention. Make these your priority in situations that invoke old, harmful patterns. Consciously keep shifting energy from the harmful to the helpful response patterns. Gradually the balance will tip and the positive patterns will be where vitality moves.

PURIFICATION,
TWILIGHT PRAYERS, MOON MAGIC

TWILIGHT, PLACE BETWEEN, PORTAL OF MYSTERY—IN TWILIGHT THINGS appear different than in the day. Shapes shift; shadow and substance dissolve, one into the other, or exchange places. The seen and unseen slide from realm to realm. Power moves toward night—rather than form, feeling is revealed.

Like the transition of dawn, twilight is a pause for prayer, as day comes to rest and nocturnal beings take their turn. Twilight prayer is gratitude for work finished, for being alive another day, for entrance into dreams.

The evening prayer asks guidance and protection through the night and through the dimensions of disembodied mystery. It remembers the gifts of friendship, family, and allies. It thanks the body for its work. Evening prayer murmurs through the soft dusk, in awe of life's beauty, in words that echo the heart's longing for intimacy with the powers that guide the panther's leap and the rose's unfolding.

At twilight the heart's fullness flows into speech of gratitude and desire. The setting sun—you watch and cannot follow; dark wraps its cloak around the shoulders of the land. There are places only dreams can find, and so you stand, sacred embodied being, and watch the light fade. It is a magic time, a haunted time; and prayer within it keeps the heart strong on its journey through night. It is a time to remember what has been given and to give something back—love of the universe in all its power and vulnerability.

The moon, with its mysterious silky light, pulls us with the tides and influences of its cycles. The moon's influence is something you can work with consciously or be an unwilling party to. Tuning to the moon cycles increases the effectiveness of your endeavors.

The moon has a fairly short cycle, making it easy to use as a transformative vehicle and easy to keep track of with its visible nightly changes. A moon cycle, or lunation, takes about twenty-nine days. It begins (if a circle can be said to begin) with the new moon. At this time the moon rises and sets with the sun, so it isn't seen at night. The new moon represents beginnings. It is a biological high tide, when the moon's gravitation is strong; it is a good time for planting or starting things, including inner seeds that you want to see flourish during the coming cycle. There is potential at this phase for sending healing energies. It is a space for clearing, and solitude is helpful with this. Avoid impulse and emotional outbursts or brooding.

Each night after the new moon, the moon rises and sets an hour later. As the moon waxes, or grows, the horns of the moon face left. This crescent phase is a time of realignment. The first quarter moon, which looks like a half circle, is a good opportunity for revitalizing your personal energies. You begin to nurture the seeds of the new moon and make sure the momentum culminates in positive forms.

The gibbous moon, shortly before full, brings forth the fruit of what has been sown. It is when the inner realms become illuminated and creativity is expressed.

The full moon rises and sets opposite the sun and thus is fully present in the night sky. The seeds of the new moon come into completion. It is a perfect time for making medicine, for dreaming, for magical sexuality—a phase of fulfillment and completion. If you are stressed, the full moon will amplify this; if you are centered, the moon will boost this also—it is a matter of resonance.

After full moon comes the waning part of the cycle. At its onset, you can release and disperse energies of the past. The third quarter is a time for change and making decisions.

Balsamic moon, with its horns pointing right, is when you can attend to unwanted patterns and prepare for renewal, the fresh start offered by the new moon.

The moon cycle, like all natural influences, does not control or victimize. It presents a framework for harmonious growth and alignment, constant in its circle, in its opportunity.

The word *purification* usually evokes the image of making clean something that is dirty. Another way to view this, one less judgmental, is to experience spiritual purification as a process that reveals inherent truth—a refinement of perception. It is a realizing rather than a becoming and an acting upon realization. In transformation of consciousness, objective manifestation follows suit. Likewise, physical action can remind consciousness of its spiritual purpose.

Smudging, ceremonial washing, reorganization of emotional patterns, chakra clearing, are all ways you can purify and realize your alignment with sacred being. They are acts that affirm your capacity to participate, make choices, and experience wholeness.

In the refinement of perception, will, and intuition through sacred intention and alignment, the heart is opened to the freedom and abiding strength of love. Insecurity and neediness release their holds and love then flows as it should, and with it, power. Inward and outward acts of purification offer that state of grace that is your opportunity to move transformatively on your path.

During This Week

1. Offer twilight prayers.

2. Pay attention to your responses to moon energies. Write down your expe-

riences with each phase of the moon for several consecutive cycles and see
what insights emerge.

3. Integrate the moon phases with your mundane or magical work. Respectfully greet the moon each night that you see it.

4. Consider the connotations, for you, of the word *purification*. How do they
reflect your attitude toward yourself? Toward spirituality? Toward transformation?

PLANT ALLIES

PLANT AND TREE TOTEMS, THE GREEN FOLK AND STANDING PEOPLE, ARE GREAT healers. They constantly give their blessings to the planet. They are the medicines, the shade, the shelter, the air, the wood for heat, the building material, the soil stabilizers, the food. The Earth cannot live without them.

Trees connect Sky and Earth, bringing equanimity. Plants teach you about rootedness and reaching upward, about grounding and growth, and about cycles and seasons. Each part of the plant—seeds, roots, stems, leaves, and flowers—has lessons for the spiritual student as well as for the botanist or herbalist.

When working with plant totems, study their physical representatives as you did with animal totems. Plants are more easily studied because they don't run away when approached, but as with animals, always stop a distance away first to greet the plant or tree before going close.

Practice the art of intuitive plant study as well as reading texts. Intuitive plant work involves using all your senses to find out what a particular plant is about.

At first sight—look at the plant and ask yourself such questions as: Does it grow alone or in a group? What sort of soil is it in? Does it grow near human habitation? Is it in sun or shade? What does the plant look like—tall, short, woody stem, toothed leaves, bushy, prickly? What of the flowers—what color, number of petals, and so on? Take a long look and make notes.

Then focus on scent—of the leaves, the flowers, the ground around the plant. What associations begin to form in your subconscious? Let the information link with past knowledge, and let your imagination roam.

Now touch the plant gently, feeling the textures of the various parts. Close your eyes and send your attention into your fingers. What do the textures remind you of? What purposes would they serve?

Next comes taste. Take a small bit of leaf and hold it in your mouth a moment, if you feel comfortable doing this (some plants have poisonous leaves!), then chew but do not swallow. Don't do this with mushrooms or berries, please. What is the immediate taste? The aftertaste? Spit the plant out; what taste lingers? How do these tastes relate to memory and knowledge?

Last, use your hearing—your psychic ears—to communicate with the plant spirit and ask what special qualities the plant offers. Be patient with this. If you are working with a tree, lean your back against it awhile or take a nap beside it and invite it to speak to you in dream. (I learned this mode of study from Susun Weed.) Leave an offering when you are finished, or perhaps, if it is a tree, tie a medicine bundle or prayer feather in its branches.

Spend some time visiting trees and plants. Feel the different qualities of forests and plant groups. Each is unique—some seem to welcome and embrace you, while others may feel foreboding or uninviting. Experience the difference between the day and night plant energies. Meditate on green.

If you live in the city, work with houseplants, small gardens, hardy sidewalk weeds, and street or park trees. There is always a plant somewhere in your habitat. One caution—don't taste or consume plants that have been exposed to car exhaust, chemical sprays and fertilizers, or other pollution.

When you form a close tie with a plant totem you will be able to work with it in ways beyond the normal ranges of its use. The plant spirit will guide and inform you.

The forces of life are vibrant within plants—expressed in the luminous green of leaves and grasses, in the vivid hues of flowers and berries, in the richness of nutrients and medicines the plants share with us. Life moves most gracefully in the gestures of trees—resilient, responsive, unafraid. It dances and sparkles in the caress of sunlight and wind on twinkling leaves.

Come into the peace of a cedar grove or a cathedral of giant firs. Listen to the Earth's secrets whispered beneath pine boughs. Seek the elegant company of birches, and commune with your muse on the smooth branches of a beech. How blessed is the company of trees.

Water is essential to the well-being of plants and animals alike. The medicine of water is its fluidity and power to refresh, cleanse, and bring movement. It is part of all our bodily fluids—blood, tears, urine, sweat—so it is intrinsic to circulation and balance.

In spiritual practices, water is used for purification, for divination, and as a carrier for certain energies and charges. It conducts power, dissolves boundaries, and is a multileveled realm of surfaces and depths—reflective interfaces and hidden reaches. It has currents, tides, waves, eddies, whirlpools, and ripples, and it has crystal calm, responsive to the most subtle touch.

The spirits that abide in water are elusive, changeable, sometimes capricious or perilous, but also hauntingly beautiful or teasingly inviting. There is age-old allure in the mystery of the waters.

Moving or still, water can be hypnotic in its mirror quality, beneath which dwell the refractive, otherworldly depths. Its moving sounds and patterns can also entrance. In all its contexts, water evokes emotional response, touching and beckoning you. From tiny stream to vast ocean, it is a restless power linked with feelings. Think of a roaring waterfall, the sound of rain on your roof, a looming tidal wave, or a murky swamp. Feel the strong emotions associated with water, characterized within different contexts.

Like emotion, water can quickly shift or relentlessly persist. Like emotion, it will tend to flow in riverbeds that become deeper and more pronounced with time. It can be sweet or bitter, clear or muddied, wild or placid. In your work in the West, emotions are the element of self that is accentuated, and water is the metaphor and power that can help your understanding and healing.

During This Week

Look into yourself as though into a pool of water. First observe what is growing along the verges of your pool. Observe the weather, the time of day, and the season. Be relaxed and in a light trance as you do this.

Observe the surface of the pool—what is happening there and what is reflected? Then gaze into the depths. Can you see the bottom? How deep is it? What do you see below the surface? What lives in this pool?

Touch the water—what is its temperature? Is there sediment stirred up in it? What feeds this pool? Taste the water. Do you like this pool? How do you feel being here?

Slide into the water—float around. Sink or dive to the bottom. Swim underwater. What are you experiencing? Climb out of the pool. Sit and gaze at it as the water calms. When the surface is still, look into it and see what is mirrored. Say "I love you," to whatever appears there, then come back to ordinary reality.

Most of the time when people look within, they tend to dump a lot of judgmental opinions in the water, so what is seen is stirred up and distorted. To see clearly, be centered in your perception, not in your beliefs about yourself. Be willing to see and accept and love. That will give you the emotional room for useful response to what is perceived.

Also work with plants this week. Explore the possibilities of alliances with different plants and trees. Nurture the green beings in your habitat. Learn their names.

Get a sense of medicine wheel orientations for the plants you work with. Realize all the different ways you interact with plants: food, shelter, wooden objects, fibers, incense, smudge, tea, coffee, smoking herbs, oils and perfumes, medicinal remedies, and so forth. Come into a more conscious relationship with all these interactions. Honor the life and spirits of plants.

TRANCE (PART 1)

IN THE EAST ARE THE SKILLS OF MEDITATION AND VISUALIZATION. IN THE South are action and relationship. In the North you will find wisdom and giving counsel, and in the West are dreaming and trance.

Trance is a consciousness of nonordinary reality. Some people are born with or naturally acquire the ability to access trance states, probably because of both organic and spiritual circumstances.

Others experience trance through hypnosis, use of mind-altering plants and drugs, or through shifting into trance inadvertently during some extraordinary occasion. Such experiences can be profoundly life changing in their revelations of the potentials of reality and consciousness. They can also be disorienting and frightening for the same reason.

Still other people may gradually and intentionally develop a skill for entering into trance. For these people, the learning process needs to include conscious control of emotional patterns and training of the mind and will, otherwise it will founder on the rocks of limiting beliefs or an ego-centered self-identity.

What many people label trance is actually more along the lines of relaxed visualization—a trancelike state. As said in earlier lessons, there is no gradation in value between trance and visualization—each has distinct purpose.

In the East of the medicine wheel is nurturance and concern with self—personal point of view and perception and experience. Visualization is a tool of these. In the South is involvement with the extended family of alliance; and in the West, perception and alliance are applied in the unseen realms that influence the forces of manifestation.

Comfortable rules and parameters of reality dissolve in the West. For some it may be a place of madness, illusion, and confusion of alignment. It is important when working with the nonordinary to be ready for spiritual adulthood or to have access to counsel from those wise in the powers of the West. In terms of experience and karma, it is worthwhile to do the preparatory work. If fear and belief keep you from the deeper potentials of consciousness, or if need for stimulation and desire for power propel you into trouble, you'll probably need to backtrack anyway, so shortcuts are of little value.

Once your involvement with Spirit takes you into a relationship of service and commitment to the medicine, trance will be more meaningfully attuned to universal resource. Trance can be employed as a condition of resource where information, insight, and aid can be obtained.

Trance states enable you to sense priorities and see the forces at work in a situation. It is a perspective from which you can summon spiritual helpers and do work that goes beyond the abilities of the physical form.

Diagnosis and healing can occur in trance. Travel to other places on Earth and communication with distant people are possible, as are travel and communication with other worlds. Totems and guides can be consulted and their medicines transmitted in trance.

The dismemberment of ego and its beliefs is often preliminary to or experienced within trance. Altered reality has a disconcerting effect on ego, which depends on known boundaries and definitions in order to function efficiently.

For ego to maintain itself in deep trance states, it needs to be either powerfully developed, as is true for many ceremonial magicians, or well integrated with the cosmic web so that it is not discombobulated by nonordinary reality. Traditional shamans tend to be in this latter group, with their calling and training for service, their intimate engagement with allies, and their reliance on Spirit.

In my experience with trance, there are several levels and realms. These include:

Levels	Trance that encompasses a simultaneous awareness and ability to function within both ordinary and nonordinary reality
	Trance in which the physical body is ""left behind"
	Trance that is a direct interface with the mind of the Mystery—cosmic consciousness
Realms	Visual perception of nonordinary worlds or terrains (sometimes there is auditory perception also)
	Molecular awareness
	Formlessness, chaos, void
	Multidimensional realms
	Realms of totems, allies, guides, entities
	Elemental realms
	Parallel and past life realms
	Astral "garbage" realms
	Realm of pure knowing

There are others, but this gives you some idea of the scope of reality afforded by trance consciousness. There is a state I sometimes find myself in unintentionally, usually at night, waking from sleep. I think of it as a free space. In it I don't know who, what, where, or when I am, though I am awake. Nothing has a name or orientation to ordinary time and space. Things pulsate, and the scene around me seems to be a series of translucent overlays that shift in predominant substantiality.

This state used to make me panic and mentally grope for identity—a name, place in time, body, context. I remember once looking at my clock, and its hands were spinning backward as the clock pulsated back and forth on the shelf, which was supported by a wall through which I could see.

Gradually things would sort out and settle down. A few years ago I decided not to be fearful of this state anymore. I know that ordinary (for me) consciousness reasserts itself on its own, so I don't need to search for it.

This state, which seems to be extremely right brained or possibly in between, can be used to reroute energy from unproductive belief patterns. Because the space is free of opinions, self-image, and other conventional dimensions, I am not confined, when in it, by assumptions that limit my range of belief. If I am not fearful or agitated, I can work in this context in radically transformative ways.

I recall waking in this state and sitting up to gaze around calmly. The cat came and sat on my lap. I could not name the cat or its species or even its identity as animal, but I felt clearly its pleasured purr, its life force, and its consciousness touching mine. It was very peaceful just being with that. I lay down and went back to sleep still having no name for anything, but knowing it all, in love, as part of me.

During This Week

Examine your beliefs about reality:

- What are your criteria for "real"?

- Where and who did these criteria come from?

- What are your beliefs and experiences regarding nonordinary reality?

- How do you see yourself in relation to it?

- How do your beliefs compare with those held by your family and childhood religion?

- How comfortable are you when discussing nonordinary reality with those who believe differently than you?

- What are your fears regarding consciousness-altering practices?

- What are your desires?

- What category of trance induction methods do you feel most drawn to? Least? Why?

- Do you divide your mundane life from your spiritual life?

❧ How much integration of realities is present in your life?

❧ What do you consider to be the real world?

❧ Do you think reality is relative?

Take some time to delve thoroughly into these questions.

TRANCE (PART 2)

IN THE LAST LESSON, SEVERAL VEHICLES FOR ENTERING TRANCE WERE mentioned. There are many more, including possession or channeling, but most of them fall into three categories:

- ❧ *Exhaustive:* fasting, dancing, marathon prayer, sleeplessness, and other physical and emotional techniques that empty energy from the mundane aspects of the personal matrix that preoccupy perception, thereby releasing the mind from ordinary reality

- ❧ *Alterative:* psychotropic plants and drugs; those that change perception by directly intervening in mental and emotional functions

- ❧ *Resonant:* soundmakers, such as drums, rattles, Tibetan bowls, chant singing, didjeridoos, and drones that entrain the brain patterns to trance levels

Sometimes techniques from several categories are used at once, such as drumming, peyote ingestion, and marathon prayer. There is some overlap in these categories—they are presented as a perspective on some of the approaches commonly used to access trance. You may find some methods more effective for you than others or some more in keeping with your personal sense of what is right for your path.

Each method of access has its pitfalls when relied on in abusive or needy ways. Sometimes it is helpful to have the doors of consciousness opened by an ally or a technique in order to see where those doors are in yourself and what is beyond them. But once that is known and you have included the reality of that experience in your belief patterns, you need to either reach these doors through your own will and powers of perception or develop an honest and healthy alliance with the vehicles used for trance. Reliance placed outside yourself can distance you from the discovery of your sacred gifts and also may take you too quickly in certain directions.

Walk your road when your spiritual legs are strong enough to carry you. Helpers and companions are a blessing, but if they do all the work, you'll never experience the freedom and joy of your own wholeness.

Drums are popularly used these days by people interested in alternative spirituality. Their appeal is somewhat due to their shamanic associations, wide and legal availability, ease of integration into urban lifestyle, and gratifying simplicity of use.

Trance journeying has been presented extensively through Michael Harner's workshops, and drum journeying tapes are used by many psychologists and trance practitioners.

The drum's sound is loud and compelling—persistent—so it is capable of getting the attention of even the most "shamanically impaired." It is an ancient spiritual tool that is applicable to modern times.

My main concern with its present-day use is that it has been separated from an important context of belief, understanding, and relationship to larger experience. In addition, its use is often accompanied by illusory or half-baked assumptions of the elements of belief, understanding, and cultural relationship.

The use of the drum needs to come out of the shadow zone of imitation without honoring. People feel the good medicine of the drum. In bringing greater clarity to its use, that goodness can only grow.

If you have a drum, pick it up and sit with it in a special place. Smudge yourself and the drum. Look closely at your drum and at what it is made from. What animals or plants are part of it? What do those animals or plants mean in your life? Honor them as you hold your drum. Thank them by name and put an offering on the ground for them.

What is the shape of your drum? How many striking surfaces does it have? Is anything depicted on these surfaces? What meaning do these things have to you?

Smooth your hand over the drum head in a circular motion. Feel the resting spirit of the drum. Pick up your beater and look at it. What is it made from? How does your beater relate to your drum; to you? Feel the balance of it in your hand.

Feel the relationship of the drum in one hand to the beater in the other and how this affects the movement of energy in your body and your aura. Feel the balance of the circular drum and the linear beater.

Breathe and center yourself. Make a prayer of right alignment and understanding. Begin to strike the drum gently. Hear the drum awaken. Let the drum choose a rhythm and pace that is harmonious with your spirit.

Listen to the drum—let your consciousness dance to its beat. Let all other preoccupations cease. Feel the drum sounds in your body and aura; they are the speech of your heart and will.

Listen to the drum—what do you hear? What do you see? Be the drum's dancer; ride the drum's beat. Where is it taking you? Let the drum speak loudly. Breathe and integrate the drum's resonance so that you are one with it. Feel its vitality, its assertion, its endurance of movement.

Let the drum walk slowly now, like a horse after an exhilarating run. Let it tiptoe, taking you to quiet places. Then let it come to rest.

Breathe—feel your chakras and your balances. Ground yourself if necessary. Again, caress your drum's surface in gratitude, affection, respect. Thank the drum's spirit and any spirits whose presences were felt during your drumming. Put the drum and beater in a good place.

During This Week

If you have a drum, work extensively with it this week, doing a variety of things: singing or chanting as you drum, dancing as you drum, drumming as trance induction, drumming in conjunction with prayer at different times of day, trying various rhythms and feeling how they shape energy, working with chakras and drumming.

Develop a friendly relationship with your drum that is based on your own beliefs and experiences, whether or not it includes teachings from other peoples and cultures.

If you feel it is right within your own path, trying working with trance and altered states of consciousness. Try finding these doors without outside induction. Altered states are readily accessible to my own nature, so it is difficult to instruct others in how to enter those realms, but some general suggestions may be of use.

Trance challenges ordinary beliefs far more than does meditation or visualization and is more of a shift away from standard modes of consciousness and perception.

Even using traditional or contemporary methods of induction such as those categorized earlier in this lesson, deep trance will not necessarily be achieved or effectively employed. Belief, intention, and understanding are key elements in accessing and working with altered states. As with meditation and visualization, the more often you move your consciousness into these modes, the easier it becomes and the further your intentions can carry you. Preparation and practice can make a difference.

If your consciousness is predominantly fixed in mundane preoccupations, it may be harder to awaken the areas of brain function and awareness needed for altered states. The questions asked in last week's lesson address some issues that pertain to this: your beliefs about reality and your integration of various states of awareness within daily life.

When approaching nonordinary reality, you need to let go of all anchors except those that maintain basic physical survival—and those can be put on automatic pilot. You want to be sure your body is in a safe situation and won't be disturbed by noise, touch, or other intrusion.

In light trance you can monitor this and continue to be active in the ordinary realm. In deep trance your body is more vulnerable and your consciousness may distance itself from the physical. Too big a distance or too profound a disturbance may cause spirit and body to lose connection with each other or with ordinary reality. Work with light trance for some months until you become adept at shifting your state of consciousness and at maintaining physical well-being during these shifts.

In letting go of your anchors, your intentions will guide your journey, so be wise in your intentions. If they are not clear or your will is not strong and spirit-aligned, your experience will be influenced by whatever asserts itself. That may be guidance from another person, random emotions, or the energies present in the context of your trance.

Concentration within trance is not like that of other modes. Your thoughts are not conventionally directed or observed—neither are your emotional or bodily sensations, except peripherally. You are in a more expanded cosmic awareness.

In the beginning, trance may be a passive experience. As your inclusion of it in your spiritual work grows more particular, it will combine a depth of letting go with a strength of purpose, and your work within that state will take on clearer direction.

PAST LIFE AWARENESS

ONCE WHEN MY SON WAS AN ADOLESCENT, HE EXPRESSED THE WISH THAT he could remember his past lives.

"What if you knew that the man who is now your father had hacked you into tiny bits with an ax in a former incarnation?" I asked. "Would that enhance your ability to relate positively to him in this life?"

Most people are born, or reborn, with a haziness or loss of memory of other lives. Even the Dalai Lama, who reputedly reincarnates into the same destined role over and over, says he doesn't have specific remembrance of his former lives.

Some people seem to achieve recall through hypnosis, trance, or other extraordinary circumstances. Many of us have moments of déjà vu in which we witness or do something uncannily familiar, or have encounters with strangers who feel like old friends.

Whether or not all these can be attributed to a reality of reincarnation is a matter of personal belief. In this lesson you will not be learning particular techniques for accessing past life memory. My sense is that if these memories are important to your spiritual path, they'll be made known to you in the course of your journey.

At best, such recall can give valuable insight into emotional patterns, relationships, and karma. At worst, they can lock you into limiting beliefs about yourself and others and obstruct transformation of patterns, relationships, and karma. It is challenging enough for most people just to deal with memories from their immediate incarnation.

Would you consider the memory of a life as a fishwife as important as the memory of being queen? Would you be as eager to share your remembrances of the life in which you molested sheep as you would the incarnation when you were a master magus of Atlantis? Often, the appeal of past life awareness is in the desire for glamorous roots. Modern reality can sometimes seem rather pedestrian.

Past lives are often conceptualized as a linear progression—a time line. Try, instead, visualizing time as an ocean. You are where you are in it, but if you desire it and your consciousness is a good enough swimmer, you can go anywhere (or any time) in this ocean. It all exists simultaneously, so all there is, in truth, is the present moment. Awareness in the present moment can be awareness of past and future and of all alternate realities.

Pondering the past is useful only in its relationship to awareness and choice in the present moment. It is never too late for situations to change or heal. The gift of life is in the present moment. Within the power of that gift is the opportunity, moment by moment, for renewal.

If you change your patterns by abiding in love and compassion, by forgiving or asking forgiveness, or by seeking right relationship, you are healing the past within the reality of the present moment. Each moment offers the potential for transformation. The past cannot condemn you.

Past life awareness is serviceable only if you are grounded in present mindfulness, otherwise it tends to be a fantasyland or a replacement for responsibility within present circumstances. Is it harder or easier to deal with your phobia about dogs if you know your cherished baby was torn apart by one a hundred years ago? That depends on whether you are wanting justification for fear or understanding of its roots in order to heal your phobia. Sometimes knowledge is a tool, sometimes a barrier. Knowledge from the past can crystalize or amplify a fear, providing a basis for what before seemed irrational. If so, the knowledge is not serving healthy change. However, if this understanding is used as a pathway to freedom and reconciliation of relationship, it can bring healing.

If you have a particular fear or phobia that has power in your life, bring it into consciousness now.

Sit. Relax and breathe, breathe and relax. Center yourself in the present moment. Take time for this. Breathe, go deeper and deeper into your breath, into the present moment.

Meditate on the phobia. Look at it in the present moment, without denial or distraction. Look at it without judgment or opinion. Go deeply into the heart of this shadow, remaining all the while centered in breath, in well-being. Be kind with this fear. Be calm.

Where in your body or your aura do you feel this fear? What images are connected to it? Look into these feelings and images. Breathe understanding into them. Ask questions of them. Follow the path these questions open—the path of present reality.

If you are able and it seems good to do so, shift from meditation to trance. Shift with the intention to see anything at the roots of this phobia that would be of use in healing. Breathe and allow your consciousness to travel the hidden realms. Perhaps you will see or realize something that answers this intention.

When this process seems complete in some form, return to the meditative mind. Breathe, relax, balance your energy. Be a still lake, peaceful and reflective. If this fear seems related to a particular chakra, attend to the balance and clearing of that chakra and to the overall circulation of vitality in your aura.

Then take three deep cleansing breaths. Say aloud, "I release myself and anyone I have bound from the pattern of this fear (name the specific phobia). I take this pattern out of the law of manifestation. I forgive and ask forgiveness of any who have harmed me or been harmed through this fear (name it again), including myself. I celebrate my freedom now, in the truth of the present moment. I send the energy of this pattern of fear into the universal source to be transformed."

Breathe deeply three more times, allowing the mental formation of fear to leave you. Smudge yourself and breathe in light and joy. Fill and balance yourself with light. Repeat this clearing process if needed until you are no longer troubled by this phobia.

During This Week

Work with past-within-present, whether past life or memories from this incarnation. Do some understanding, clearing, and healing. Besides the exercise described in the lesson, work with the following:

Consider a relationship that you have regrets about in terms of your conduct toward another person. (If you can't think of one, I salute either your obliviousness or your impeccability.)

Sit in relaxed meditation, focused within the present moment, within the power of the breath. Call to consciousness images of your relationship. See again the regretful episode(s) without miring in the emotions associated with it (them). See those feelings with kindness in your understanding of them. See whatever needs to be seen. Unlock memory and emotion compassionately.

Ask for any additional information that will help your understanding of this relationship. Shift into trance for this if appropriate. Then return to meditative consciousness.

Breathe. Let your breathing clear away or transform the unwanted emotions connected to that relationship. Then visualize a still lake, very beautiful, very calm, under a peaceful night sky. Look into the surface of this dark mirror and see the image of the person with whom you felt at odds. Say to that person "I am sorry for the troubled feelings between us, and for my part in their creation. I love you."

Let that image ripple and vanish. The lake becomes very still again. Look upon the surface and see yourself reflected. Say to that reflection "I forgive and love you." Know that the present moment is truth and that you have summoned the healing of love into present reality. Present and past are one, so you have healed the past also, whether the person is now living or dead.

Smudge yourself and reaffirm this truth whenever old patterns try to assert themselves. If relationship is ongoing, remember to stop and reconsider your habitual responses. Make healthy relationship with yourself a priority over habit.

DREAMING (PART 1)

I HAVE A THEORY ABOUT DREAMING: PEOPLE WITH A FREUDIAN WORLDVIEW have Freudian dreams, people with Jungian beliefs have Jungian dreams, and people with a shamanic sense of reality have shamanic dreams. This theory arose from many years of listening to people's accounts of their dreams.

Contemporary interest in dreams as mirrors of the subconscious has provoked the publication of numerous books on the subject. In the two short lessons presented here, the discussion will be about dreaming from the shamanic perspective—an outlook (or inlook) that has been, for the most part, co-opted and significantly altered by Jungian approaches. It is important, I feel, to retrieve and differentiate shamanic dream work from Jungian analysis.

Dreams, from a shamanic viewpoint, are not any less (or more) real than waking experiences. They are not merely symbolic images of thoughts and emotions released by the subconscious mind during sleep. They are a level of enactment.

Dreams, trance, vision, meditation, and waking life are all states of consciousness, awarenesses of various realms and aspects of reality. They do not represent things about life—they *are* part of living in an expanded, integrated spectrum of perception. To be prejudiced in favor of certain levels—ignoring, trivializing, or walling off some states of consciousness and fixating on others—is to handicap yourself.

Dreams and waking life both are experiences in which you engage with many layers of manifestation. In waking life you tend to be more occupied with the physical and dense layers of manifestation; in dreams you are more involved with the more subtle and unattended-to forms. These all inhabit a spectrum of consciousness. In seeing and using a continuity of perception, you can apply your dreams to waking life and be more intentional in your dreamwork. Traffic between these states of consciousness will enhance both.

To a psychologist, totems, dream images, and trance visions are all symbolic and only symbolic. To a shaman, they are multidimensional actualities—they are alive. They are Spirit-in-form.

What Coyote does is not myth; it is what Coyote does. Coyote is not an archetypal projection of group mind; Coyote is a Sacred Being. Medicine is not a concept; it is a living, embodied power. That is why shamanism is not to be toyed with. Its experience of reality walks through many levels.

Dreams can bring added clarity, insight, and expansion to waking life. When your waking and dreaming bodies work together lucidly, you can accomplish much more in this flow than you can from a fragmented perspective. The more you treat your dreams as the equal of waking experiences, instead of interpreting and setting them off on a separate shelf, the more resourceful your work with dreams will become.

The power is in your participation—as with all events in life. You can do things in dream. Change can be enacted. Information is accessible. Communication is possible. Work can be accomplished, healing realized, memory tapped. All can be done lucidly, intentionally, actively, experientially, consentingly.

As indicated at the beginning of this lesson, your dreams tend to reflect your beliefs about dreams, reality, and yourself. Dreams are mind looking at mind, following mind's directives, blocked by mind's closed doors, governed by mind's sense of possibilities, operating in the grooved pathways of mind's experience.

You can open new pathways and doors, extend your possibilities, and offer innovative directives that bring to life more of the mind's potentials of consciousness. You can be active in consciousness.

In sleep your body rests. You don't need to be mentally engaged with it. This allows more freedom for activity elsewhere. If you practice giving yourself specific directives before sleep or consciously clear and prepare yourself as you do for other altered states, your dreamtime will begin to change. Instead of just passive (though revealing) rehashing of thoughts, emotions, and events, your dreams will become more purposeful, responsive to intention, vivid, and productive.

You will be aware in your dreams that you are dreaming and will have more control over what happens in the dreams. The more you work in this way, the easier it is to do, and the more fluid your beliefs about reality become.

In dreams you can explore options and their outcomes; you can find insight to apply to problem solving; you can retrieve information, consult with guides and totems, enter other realms, receive medicine gifts, work with relationships, and do many other things that may be difficult to accomplish in ordinary states of consciousness.

Dreaming, unlike trance, is something everyone does. It is only a matter of bringing deeper awareness and participation into this nightly opportunity, so that it can become an arena for spiritual unfolding: awakening within dream.

During This Week

If you haven't started a dream journal, consider doing so now. If you have been keeping one, read it over. Consider these questions and what they say about you:

- ∾ How would you categorize your dreams?

- ∾ What patterns are you finding?

- ∾ What images, elements, or participants recur?

- ∾ What are your beliefs about dreaming?

- ✤ Are you aware you are dreaming?

- ✤ Can you voluntarily wake yourself from dreams?

- ✤ Do you have nightmares?

- ✤ Do you have recurring dreams?

- ✤ Are you always your same sex, age, and appearance in dreams?

- ✤ Do you usually dream about people you know? About family? About animals?

- ✤ Do you dream in color?

- ✤ Do you dream about your totems and allies?

- ✤ How many dreams per night do you remember?

- ✤ How does your dreaming change in different sleeping positions? In different seasons? Different locales? Different company?

- ✤ Do you tell your dreams to anyone?

- ✤ Do you interpret them? How do you use them?

- ✤ What part do they play in your spiritual practice?

- ✤ Do you remember significant childhood dreams?

DREAMING (PART 2)

BEAR IS THE TOTEM OF DREAMERS. BEAR IS CLOSELY RELATED TO HUMANS and is a hibernator, so dreamtime is given a special place in the medicine of Bear.

If you have difficulty remembering dreams or want to become a stronger dream worker, call on Bear's help. Ask Bear to bring your dreams to you in the morning when you wake. Meditate on Bear consciousness. Keep Bear medicine near your bed. Talk to Bear as you go to sleep at night. Make offerings to Bear in the West of your medicine wheel or altar.

In thinking about your dreams, avoid classifying them as good and bad. Conventional images and experiences of good and bad may not be useful to apply if you are seeking a more shamanic dream practice. Being devoured by a tiger can be a great dream from the shamanic point of view. So, instead of seeing this as a nightmare in which you were consumed by your primitive appetites, try pondering the experience of merging with Tiger medicine, and see the dream as an offering of sacred, intimate alliance.

Dreams have their codes just as waking life has, but if you are using psychological decoding instead of shamanic decoding, you will continue to dream only in a psychological realm.

If you are truly plagued by dreams that feel evil, do some clearing work. Smudge yourself and your sleeping space—maybe your whole house needs it. Meditate and clear your chakras before going to bed. Make prayers for a peaceful, protected sleep. Ask your totems, allies, and guardians to watch over your dreamspace. Sleep with a protective medicine bundle nearby. Visualize a circle of light or guardians at the corners of your room.

Most important, clear yourself of fear. Use your breath to reclaim a balance of calm in your body. Encourage yourself with affirmations of centeredness and integrity of well-being. Identify and dismantle beliefs of weakness, helplessness, or unworthiness. Reconnect yourself to spiritual truth through prayer.

Meditate on the dream(s) that have troubled you. Understand their energy and face what you fear in them. As you fall asleep, tell yourself that you will transform any negativity that appears in your dreams. Your mind is your mind. You don't have to be victimized within consciousness.

Learn to wake yourself if need be. Learn to interrupt and resume dreams at will, to change what transpires in dreams, to remember dreams, and to invoke certain kinds of dreams through presleep directives and communication with guides and totems. All these take practice—sometimes sustained practice—but they are not difficult to do. Be patient. Enjoy dreaming; explore its potentials. Try to get a sense of how dreamtime connects to waking life and what purpose these bridges serve. Be creative in your work with dreams.

I see dreams as falling into nine main categories:

1. Emotional and mental maintenance dreams usually incorporate events, issues, or people from waking life that have unresolved energies associated with them. These are ordinary or psychological dreams—though they are often very creative, funny, or revealing—and serve an important function.

2. Other-dimensional dreams involve the past, alternate or parallel presents, the future, communication with the dead, prophesy, or warnings. The warnings can be of personal events or of larger events such as earthquakes, wars, or societal changes.

3. Spiritual working dreams include presleep directives and may be responses to someone else's invocation; consultations or meetings with teachers, totems, or medicine people; or dreams of conducting ceremony, sweats, healings, teachings, or other spiritual work, whether spontaneously or due to presleep directive. Often you need extra sleeping time to rest from these dreams.

4. Occupational dreams concern your usual worldly work as the activity through which you deal with situations and energy. (Years after my last delivery as a midwife, I still have frequent dreams about birth.)

5. Medicine dreams are the most cherished dreams—they take place in the realms of magic. They renew, nourish, and expand your knowledge and medicine.

6. Empathic or telepathic dreams are those in which you merge with someone else's consciousness—human or otherwise—and dream their dream or experience their thoughts, feelings, or perceptions; they may also be dreams that are a result of someone else's thoughts.

7. Problem-solving dreams give answers. On waking from this kind of sleep, you find you have solutions, answers, understandings, realizations, or directions that were not present in your awareness the night before.

8. Encounter dreams involve form-embodied forces—not necessarily benevolent—who challenge, provoke, or seem to threaten you. These dreams often come at turning points in your path, like guarded gateways to another level of relationship with yourself and your spiritual work. If not effectively faced, these forces can become the core element of recurring dreams or nightmares.

9. Relationship work dreams are those in which you interact and communicate with people in ways that attend to or change relationships. They differ

from ordinary dreams in that they are actual interactions with the astral forms of people, not just mental and emotional mirrorings about relationship.

Each of these categories has a certain characteristic energy to it. Besides these, pay attention to recurring dreams or themes, to odd dreams such as narrated dreams, to ones in which you encounter your double, to ones that rewind and run through again, or to dreams that seem like intrusions into your space by outside agents.

One night I was lying awake, thinking about something. I slipped into sleep and dreaming. Realizing I was asleep, I began to pursue the thought process while I also continued the unrelated dreaming. This went fine until I became aware that I was in a double consciousness (at this point triple?) and I woke up.

The mind is capable of all manner of activities within multiple layers of function and perception. Modern Western peoples are conditioned to severely limit their range of consciousness. To begin transcending these restrictions, work fearlessly, intentionally, and without prejudice with dream states.

During This Week

Peruse the list of dream categories. How does it compare with your own list from the last lesson? In which category are most of your dreams? What kinds of dreams do you have least frequently? What categories don't apply at all to your experience? What does your own list reflect about your approach to dreaming?

Try bringing more depth into the dreams you have within each category. Dream states, like meditation, respond encouragingly to regular practice. Writing dreams down, following up on them appropriately, and using presleep preparation are steps that will lead you toward more awareness within dreaming.

For example, I had a relationship dream some years ago in which I saw my mother curled up asleep on the bottom of the ocean, wrapped in red and closely flanked by dolphins. I wrote to my mother about this dream and she told me she'd been wearing an old red sweater while she slept. In my dreams, I had traveled across the ocean of time and space and consciousness and seen her in the red of her sweater, watched over by dolphin allies.

The dream bridged the realms of physical and astral truth. To me, the nonphysical dolphin guardians are as real as the red sweater, and the physical red sweater is as symbolic as the presence of the dolphins. It is all a continuity—multilevels of actuality.

In another relationship dream, I visited some friends at their farm. As I approached the house, a white horse trotted back and forth in the yard (these people have no horses), blocking my way. I had to interact fearlessly with the horse in order to pass.

After I shared this dream with my friends, they wrote to say that a neighboring farm horse, a white Appaloosa, had got loose that week and come into their yard. Again, physical and metaphoric occurrence combined within dream as it does also within waking life. This overlap of worlds—which gives you the possibility of free movement of consciousness—shows you how much choice and volition there is in daily existence. You do not need to be separate from any stage of life's unfolding. In full participation (not manipulation) you see that you are a part of everything and everything is a part of you, in constant, transformative flow.

Dreams can be your psychological closet or they can be a world that helps connect you to all your relations.

CONDUCTING CEREMONY (PART 1)

IN THIS BOOK I TRY TO PRESENT KNOWLEDGE AND PERSPECTIVE DIFFERENT from that widely found in other writings. I try to present a path both old and new, a path of the present moment. It is not in opposition to other paths—how can it be when it has no dogma, no separate boundaries? Instead it suggests an awareness of and alignment with what you understand to be sacred.

Ceremonies within this path are formal acts expressing and strengthening that alignment. They are your respectful intersection with living truth. Their form must arise from your center of understanding and relationship.

Effective ceremony is within the present moment. Nowhere else is that fullness of transformative power to be found, only and always now. So to conduct ceremony, you need mindful presence.

Ceremony is where you recognize and align with that which will best serve life's harmony. You choose what reality to participate in and facilitate its physical expression. Mindfulness is vital in this—words and actions should demonstrate your highest understanding of right. In ceremony, use language and movement whose meaning you understand. Do not imitate the ways of others unless you truly perceive what it is they are doing and are in accord with it.

On the other hand, do not willfully alter the ceremony of others unless you are centered in understanding and guided by Spirit. You are on surest ground when you evolve your own way of ceremony from the fresh basis of your own skill, worldview, and connection to the sacred Mystery.

Traditional teachings can offer precious perspective to this evolution, but you must exercise a great deal of wisdom and vision if you conduct a ceremony that is your own version of traditional forms. These forms have their fields of energy and associated spirits. Experimentation with them is not a precinct for the aspiring freewheeling ceremonialist. As one Native elder expressed it, "All worlds meet in the sweat lodge." Unless you have the training, understanding, and wisdom to move competently at such an intersection, it is better not to play in the traffic.

Does this book offer too many cautions? Too narrow a road? I hope not, for fear is an oppressive companion. But there is a responsibility inherent in the role of teacher, even the teacher who walks beside and not in front of you. There is accountability to the medicine, to the spirits, and to Spirit. There is karma and consequence and concern with harmony.

Medicine work is similar to childbirth. You deal with natural forces and processes, and this can (and some feel should) be done without mediation from "experts." But natural processes also include death, disintegration, and chaos. To accept and work amid the range of possibilities within transformative states is not something most modern people have practice in doing. Spiritual physics—the knowledge of how things operate in the subtle realms—is still an esoteric specialty.

An intuitive sense of how to move in this arena is as valid as formalized training, but a basis of intuition alone, particularly if you are in a leadership role, is sometimes not enough. Challenging situations arise, or unexpected manifestations, or emotional and mental states that interfere with intuitive clarity. No one is exempt from occasions of uncenteredness or difficulty. If intuition is your primary guide and you lose track of that guide, what do you then use as a compass? I've seen even experienced, skilled medicine people struggle for alignment and clarity when doing their work.

Transitional and transformational shifts are times of vulnerability. Womb to world, ordinary to nonordinary, life to death, virgin to lover, personal to cosmic—all are movements that open to myriad possibilities. Whether opening to randomness or purposefully making choices for yourself, your actions are not without consequences for all else. Deliberately including others in your work means taking on a certain responsibility.

My warnings aren't meant to hinder your exploration and pleasure. They are only descriptions of possible terrain in these realms that your path may pass through. My swamp may turn out to be your delightful wetland, or you may fly where I trudged, and that is well and good.

As a parent I caution my child in ways I know he will sometimes ignore, preferring to be informed by experience. Experience may be more convincing than words, but there is a balance between the value of following your own instincts and desires—gaining wisdom through trial and error—and heeding the loving guidance of others. This book tries to urge both modes, aiming toward freedom within counsel that serves survival and growth. It is your journey, and no one can walk it for you.

Ceremony should be performed for a definite purpose. For energies to reverberate in ways that serve harmony, the intentions of ceremony must make spiritual sense and the elements of ceremony must be congruent with intention.

Ceremony sets things in motion—a pattern enacted in the subtle realms that echoes into physical manifestation. You want to be sure that there is reason for setting these energies in motion and that their fulfillment in life will be as desired.

If you request ceremony from a medicine person, or even just prayer, you are asking her or him to precipitate change, to invoke the attention of the spirits. Your are asking the person to stick an oar in the current of power, changing the flow and altering the boat's course. This has consequences in the subtle universe for the person who is the object of ceremony or prayer and for the medicine person as well. Do not forget this in your own work or in your requests of others.

The closer your alignment with the sacred, the easier it is to ascertain the correct ceremonial form or prayer to offer in any given situation. Alignment reduces risk of error. Alignment, not performance, is the focus in ceremony. Being attuned to Spirit allows ceremonial work to answer the true needs of the moment.

There is a beautiful sense of peace within power when you release anxiety and self-consciousness and let your energy become one with the Mystery. Instead of generating ceremony, you are then conducting it—letting your natural gifts honor their source.

To know what is needed *in* ceremony, first be clear about what is being asked *of* ceremony. What you do to ensure well-being is different from what rectifies imbalances. What you do to divine something is not the same as what you do to create something. Look inquiringly at your intentions—write them down, rewording them until what is written says precisely what you desire to have happen.

Then investigate the implications of your purpose. What short- and long-range changes will be set off? What energies feed these intentions? How will their fulfillment echo in people's lives?

Look at your purpose within meditation. Explore its layers and pray for guidance. If you are using traditional forms, look deeply to see if the chosen form and ceremonial purpose are well-partnered. Pray to the spirits linked with that form and seek their blessings and perspectives.

If you are conceiving your own ceremonial form, after clarifying and pondering your intentions, shift into meditation or trance and align that purpose with Spirit. In this process, the elements of ceremony will occur to you. You will know what form and sequence of actions need to be enacted. This knowing may come as a whole or a bit at a time. Return to meditation or trance periodically to gain a complete sense of what should be included in your ceremony.

Don't unmindfully manufacture ceremony from a book or other things you've seen or done. Conceive it in sacred alignment. In this way it will be right and strong.

During This Week

Bring to memory the ceremonies you have attended or conducted and consider these questions about them:

- ∾ Which ones did you feel best about?

- ∾ Which ones distressed, drained, or bored you?

- ∾ What were the elements that contributed to these feelings?

- ∾ Which ones were traditional or traditionally based?

- ∾ How do you feel about group-led ceremonies?

- ∾ How is your experience changed by leading, participating in, or just observing a ceremony?

    ∾ What ceremonial purposes are most appealing to you?

    ∾ What ceremonial forms interest you?

    ∾ Are you drawn to ritual as a spiritual practice?

    ∾ What is the role of paraphernalia in ceremony?

    ∾ Do you prefer solitary ceremony to group work?

Autumn/West is the time for introspection—looking within—so this group of lessons offers many questions to aid that process.

CONDUCTING CEREMONY (PART 2)

THIS LESSON WILL DISCUSS TWO OF THE MANY ELEMENTS OF CEREMONY: altars and offerings. The altar is often central to what is present in ceremony; offerings are often the agents of what is done.

An altar is spiritual terrain. Its lit candles enliven and illumine this landscape; they serve as beacons to energies and entities aligned with what abides there. Fire is power that is constantly creating and releasing—generative of light, heat, and change. The altar candles are sparks of the sacred fire and mystical enlightenment.

The arrangement of spiritually charged objects on an altar is like a map of mountains, rivers, and plains: it guides the flow of power as mountains direct light and wind, as rivers carry earth and moisture, as the plains allow space for expansion and movement. These objects are more than representation, they are function and manifestation; they are engaged in relationship with one another, with the Spirit, and with the person who works with them.

The altar invokes remembrance and focus. It is a consecrated space, present in many simultaneous interactive realms. It is a portal, a continuity, a stage, a meeting place, a telephone booth, an aspect of one's true face. Sometimes an altar is the illusion of privacy or the greater illusion of one-to-oneness. You may think of the altar as your space or your zone of communion with the One, but it is the center of the universe, accessible to all. Like the infinity of reflective jewels in the net of Indra, it is a mirror. It is how you recognize your kin.

No collection or arrangement of objects can ever fully describe transformative truth. The altar is more than you know but less than you need, or sometimes less than you know and more than you need. It changes. It shifts in candlelight, it does things in the darkness while you dream. It is portable yet molded to the Earth's core.

An altar is a configuration of gratitude, honoring, and connectedness. It is a mandala leading to the interface between intention and truth. It is the process of understanding and the acceptance of mystery. It unites your aspirations with the present moment. It celebrates, motivates, comforts, challenges, reflects, and inspires. It helps keep you safe and invites risk.

An altar can hide you from the emptiness of your spiritual practices or it can focus, direct, and amplify the real power of them. It can be a vanity, a pretension, or a decoration, even a mockery, or it can be a tangible commitment to beauty, to healing.

Making an offering is saying please and thank you all in one. The importance of this, and of doing it right, should not be underestimated.

Asking for something makes room for its reception. It is a realization of desire and a willingness to be part of the larger web. It is trust in that web, because the offering is gratitude as well as desire. Asking puts you in a position of relationship; it relieves your isolation and makes you cognizant of your own responsibilities within relationship. All this in an offering.

In asking, you must make desire specific, gratitude specific, and the act of relationship specific. Through this, power can flow, need can be addressed.

In making an offering, you are mindful of the present moment and its ripples of past and future. You touch your connectedness. An offering is your spokesperson, so you want to inform it with your asking and your gratitude. You want to be sure it is representative of your best. You infuse it with love. It is your emissary in the realms, your message to the Mystery, the impression you leave on the universe.

All that? Yes. Your salutation and signature, your heart's truth. Breathe a moment longer the next time you make an offering.

Offerings keep you honest on the path. Offerings invoke and reflect mindfulness. Offerings are the simplicity of power, the responsibility of maintaining the cycles of balance, and the verity of interdependence. What if the trees did not shed their leaves in autumn? What if the grain did not give its life to the harvest? Offerings teach you about giving and receiving in all their grace and practicality. They teach you to honor.

Anything can be an offering, though in truth you have nothing to give that is really yours, not even your life or your love. The gratitude implicit in asking reminds you that there is nothing you don't already have that is sacred, that can be given.

The offering that is right is the one that balances the universe. It is the one that makes your heart smile or gives you a feeling of well-being reflected like a crescent moon in a peaceful pond. Remember this when you stand in the ceremonial circle, tobacco in hand.

During This Week

Review earlier lessons that pertain to ceremony: part 1, weeks 6, 7, and 12; part 2, weeks 5 and 12. Also review the seasonal ceremony at the end of each part.

Do you work with an altar? If so, contemplate its meaning to your spiritual path. Sit and observe it, with all its elements and arrangements. How deliberate are those arrangements? What use do you make of your altar?

Look at the objects on your altar—are they happy there? Do you need to change anything? Meditate on the nature of your altar. Clean and renew it. Honor its spirit, and your own.

VISION SEEKING

AT THE HEART OF SEEKING OR CRYING FOR A VISION STIRS THE LONGING to know the sacred dream, the jewel within life's purpose. It is the pull to touch the ineffable and through that to know you are more than a messy toiling creature beset by worry, boredom, and stressful demands.

In years of helping people enact vision quests, I have heard the same voice speaking from their intentions—to know, to go beyond, to find themselves at the shining core of something that matters, that is real. They want to find that which is worth dedication and to realize some dignity.

People labor over the formulation of their quest intentions as if they were the three wishes to be granted by a bottled genie. Yet they know that they carry the vision with them into the questing wilderness—it is not conjured there. The fasting, prayer, and solitude in nature reveal rather than engender vision. The quester is the bottle from which the genie materializes.

Still, the articulation of intention is an important process that dispels vagueness, dismisses what falls short of core desire, and puts into motion the energies of quest and response. It is commitment's first step.

If you are planning to embark on a vision quest or want to better understand the process, I recommend books such as those by Meredith Little and Steven Foster. You might also read the accounts of vision seeking by well-known medicine people like Frank Fools Crow, John Fire Lame Deer, Black Elk, Brooke Medicine Eagle, and others. These writings give traditional and contemporary views of the purposes, procedures, and experiences associated with this ancient ceremony.

Unhappily, preparation is neglected in many modern people's vision quests—not only the important physical readiness to fast and be exposed to natural elements, but also mental and emotional preparedness.

What for many modern people is the peak of their questing experience was in older times a starting point. Why? Modern people are not spiritually inferior, but modern life encourages a different focus of consciousness. Consciousness conducive to spiritual vision is not a way of life for most modern people; consequently, their days and nights alone in the wilderness are mainly spent in these ways:

1. Struggling with the unfamiliar psychological and physical rigors of weather, hunger, fatigue, and wildlife

2. Struggling with fear of the dark, the weirdness of being alone, and the sense that they're doing something society considers off-the-wall

3. Struggling with the absence of their customary mental occupations—TV, radio, books, magazines, conversation, moving scenery, computer screens, journal and pen, crossword puzzles, embroidery—all the things that busily keep the mind insulated from silence, stillness, and the terrible fear that the center of the self is an empty room

These struggles were not big factors for tribal people. They lived with wilderness, so its elements were familiar, if not always benevolent. Their lifestyle required perceptiveness, patience, and resonance with natural rhythms, and their society honored vision seeking as intrinsic to its well-being.

The tribal worldview emanated from a spiritual center, so people did not learn the sorts of doubt and confusion about their nature that modern people have.

Another difference in experience is the vision itself. Tribal people had a rich cultural and environmental context for their visions. If a badger, a storm cloud, or a supernatural being appeared in vision, the quester—with the aid of the medicine person—could confidently interpret the import of those presences and identify the medicine of that vision. The beliefs of society and individual were aligned, the manifested forms of spirit recognized, and the quester's consciousness receptive.

Modern seekers go to the mountain carrying such societal images as Ninja Turtles, Rambo, the dog in the beer commercial, or at best, perhaps the Virgin Mary. Theirs is a lonely consciousness, wanting kinship with beauty, wanting healing of self, wanting something more expansive than religious doctrine, more alive than New Age commercialism, and more lasting than the pot illusion of hippie camaraderie.

It takes courage to make this quest, unnourished by society, knowing that the vision may have no welcome in the modern world. Preparation helps. If you work in the months beforehand to become aware of, to understand, and to clear fears and other issues that might loom up to obscure your vision while questing, you will make better use of your rare opportunity on the mountain.

Practice meditation—fostering calmness and perception. Practice being in the present moment with your breathing. Much of what happens during a vision quest is a process for becoming centered and receptive, and seeing what is present.

If you are looking at your memories and apprehensions, fidgeting at sitting in one place for four days, you will not know what is revealed right before you. So practice being still and in full awareness of the present moment.

Perhaps you need this quest as a time to face fears of darkness, solitude, cold, hunger, or bears. If so, that is a brave and worthwhile intention and should not be diminished by unreasonable expectations. Without restricting yourself, give that intention respectful place in your work.

One of the most enduring worries of questers through ancient and modern times is that, spiritually speaking, nothing will happen during the quest. Greet this concern kindly if you see it in yourself. It speaks of age-old human yearnings and vulnerabilities. This fear tells of needs and lost paths, of pride and private doubts, of the child's hope that there are answers—its hopes that life is watched over by something wise, that all within it are deserving of gifts, that something loving will hear its cries. It is the need not to be wordlessly dismissed from the presence of Mystery.

Know that your quest will give you what is right for you in the present moment. Your part is to be with that moment. When you are in the ceremony of vision seeking—for ceremony it is—in a sacred way, with purpose and prayer, what is needed will appear. It is for you to perceive and accept.

Do not overlook the small, the simple, or the quiet. You have appealed to spirit presence; now acknowledge it, remember it, and make your offerings. Remember that you do not quest only for yourself. In your solitude you seek the prosperity of the people. You take your turn to speak for the humans and carry the sacred dream back among them.

During This Week

Whether you are considering seeking a vision or not, these questions (*quest*-ions) provide avenues for introspection. If you plan to quest, these may be things to discuss with the medicine person helping you in this ceremony.

- What is the purpose of your vision seeking?
- What has led you to where you are now on your spiritual path?
- Who have been your teachers?
- What are your fears about doing this quest?
- What has your society, family, religion taught you about vision?
- What do you pray to—who is (are) your deity(ies)?
- Where do you stand on the medicine wheel?
- Who are your allies?
- Who is your community of support?
- What is the hardest part of doing this quest?
- Is your spiritual reality integrated with your daily life?
- What do you want to let go of before this quest?

∾ What are you expectations?

∾ What are you asking or expecting of your helpers?

∾ How will the planet benefit from your vision questing?

∾ How will you keep the vision alive after the quest?

This week, also prepare a medicine bundle for the West/Autumn.

WATER CEREMONY

BRING YOUR BUNDLE TO A PLACE OF BEAUTY AT SUNDOWN—A PLACE touched by the western light.

Smudge yourself, your bundle, and your ceremonial space. In the West, set a shell or chalice of water—smudge this also.

Sound your drum, or a bell, and call to each Direction, praying for presence, protection, blessings. Pray to the Earth and Sky, to spirits of place, to the Great Mystery.

Sit or stand looking West, holding the vessel of water. Center yourself in the magic of evening. Steep your heart's essence in this power. Remember the teachings of Autumn—center yourself in their beauty. Fill yourself with the mystery of Autumn, its light and color, and let it move through you, permeating your breath.

Draw upon love, look down at the vessel in your hands, and lightly blow your charged breath upon its waters—a prayer breath, a blessing.

Pour some of the water onto the Earth. Give thanks for the teachings and gifts of the West. Touch your fingers to the water and sprinkle it onto your bundle. Touch your fingers to the water and bless yourself with it on brow and heart. Then drink what remains.

With gratitude, open your circle and greet the night.

Prepare for Winter Solstice.

> *Wane of the year,*
> *solstice tale,*
> *clear moonlight*
> *on the past.*
> *Dream upon dream*
> *in evening's blue,*
> *they settle like birds.*
> *I remember*
> *relentless snow, and*
> *pines, wakeful—*
> *the story of the owl*
> *and ermine—*
> *the giveaway time.*

Longest night,
the laboring woman
brings the dawn to us.
I remember
the salmon's journey,
pattern of return;
the Earth is
not as it was
but some things still
teach continuity,
the dance of freedom
and love.

Part 4

North / Winter:
DEVELOPING WISDOM
Winter Solstice to Spring Equinox

North, great white giant, please hear this prayer. I greet the coming of Wnter, the coming of night. I give thanks for rest and peace and renewal.

Spirits of stone, of crystal, of bone, spirits of mountain, I pray for alignment with your ancient wisdom and endurance. Please share your teachings with me—tell me your memories.

North totems, keepers of lodge and ground, medicine of the manifested vision, bless me with your purposefulness, prosperity, steadiness, and balance.

I send gratitude to the ancestors and elders for your guidance and example. Into the night you walk, leaving me, leading me, singing your songs. I pray in the womb of rebirth for purification—power of the inipi—and for all passages to be blessed as we come again into the sweet dawn, the hoop unbroken. All my relations.

GROUNDING

NORTH, THE DARK TURNING, THE SPIRALING UNIVERSE, SLOW GUIDANCE of starlight. Where are you in this universe? Touch the Earth—you are here, embodied in the sensitive hand, in the Earth you touch. Breathe—you are here, in sacred life, in the intimacy of your breath, in its confluence with the breath of trees, of seasons, of galaxies. You are here.

Sacred fire, the core of stars, the center of Earth, the light within the matrix, soul fire—warmth of your smile—you are here.

Mysterious ocean, fluid fertility, your heart's realm of dreams, where consciousness casts its nets and learns the currents and tides of power. Here also you find yourself.

Touch the winter Earth, set your feet to the mountain's path. In this season, you will seek the high ground, learning to pace your energy, keep your balance, patiently commit yourself to the long haul, and at last stand free of the shadows with wisdom.

In the North you must embody truth, live spirit, teach by what you are. How can you do this, imperfect human? Winter tells you: it is not enough to be enlightened, to be in alliance, and to know the hidden realms; you must also put on your hat and mittens, shovel the driveway, and keep a weather eye on the wind's shift.

"Oh, no," you may exclaim in dismay, "I haven't journeyed all this way through the worlds of metaphysics just to be told that wisdom is a wool hat!"

Tut, tut. Didn't your grandmother teach you anything? Didn't she give advice with her cookies? Ah, well. My grandmother was fierce.

"What are the names of your friends?" she sternly inquired. "Are they good children?"

"Show me those dance steps," she would command. It bewildered me—her questions seemed like a form of divination. She knew about ferns and frogs and how to approach dogs. She conjured food. She wrote me letters on the backs of wallpaper samples. She was abrupt and bird-quick, and she called my mother "Sis." She kept me on my toes.

If you didn't have a grandmother to teach you the medicine of the North, you can apprentice in other ways. Spend some time with the mother of small children. Observe her shamanic capacity to do many things at once without resentment. Observe how she can also travel at a snail's pace in the company of a toddler, being completely in the present moment, admiring pine cones, adventuring in puddles.

Observe her strength of nurturing and protecting. Feel the love she makes available to her children. Realize that she gives her body, her time, all her personal resources, and the fruits of her alliances to the medicine of motherhood; instead of being diminished, she is more complete—a magic of the North. Winter is cronehood, but its wisdom is the fruit of motherhood.

Apprentice with a mountain. Observe how the busy clouds must heed the mountain's directives: "Go here" or "Don't go there" or "Rain on this side," the mountain says, and the clouds assent. In its solidity and strength of identity, the mountain is a convincing authority.

Observe how the mountain wears its weathers. It looks good in all of them: mist, snow, seasonal flowers, fall colors—all suit the mountain equally well. Its beauty finds inherent harmony with all aspects of what is natural, what is part of itself.

Feel the meditation of the mountain: its quality of vast and ageless perspective, its ability to sit a long time.

When you walk the mountain, it will tell you, "Pay attention to where you put your feet; be mindful of your breathing. Know your path—watch for rockfall and rattler. Keep your balance, carry water, wear sensible shoes. Did you bring an apple? Oops, that was bear scat you just stepped in."

At other times the mountain will seem to have nothing to say, for years perhaps, as it waits for you to mature in receptivity—as it waits for your medicine to grow. North is good at waiting, at proper timing, and at seeming to ignore you.

Snow, another wisdom teacher, is North medicine. Learning how to move in it—how fast, how hard, how to gain its alliance, how to let it lead the dance—you learn something about patience, humility, and perseverance. You understand something about survival.

There are all kinds of wisdom found in the North: herbal healing, midwifery, stone dreaming, business managing, and the correct making of things. There is much medicine to be found in the study of these arts, but the study that leads to and honors wisdom is the kind that learns through the old way, by paying attention to your elders in these medicines.

I once watched a Native grandmother doing quillwork. Having some experience of the ways of fierce grandmothers, every time I thought of a question to ask I clamped my mouth shut and watched instead of asking. At the end of an hour and a half, every unvoiced question had been addressed in the silence of this woman's skillful work.

During This Week

Work with your grounding. It is your orientation of balance, your channel of manifestation. When you are grounded, you have basis for movement. You are, once again, with the present moment, where action and being have reality.

Grounding gives direction and purpose to energy. It is more than a remedy for scattered emotions, short-circuited chakras, or power overload. It is a reference point for wisdom and a credibility factor in your capacity to engage in medicine work.

Sit or lie on the Earth. If it is snowy, pick a mild day and dress warmly.

Relax, breathe, feel the Earth, sacred being, nurturant home. Greet the Earth—feel its embrace. Feel your relatedness to this Earth. Remember the food, water, air, and minerals that are part of your body—gifts of the Earth—and the circulated gases, fluids, and solids that you return to the Earth through your physical processes. You are at every moment in a dance with the Earth. Honor this intimacy.

Breathe up from your connectedness to Earth into your first chakra. Breathe in red, the color of life, remembering the red pipestone, the red core of the planet, the red vitality of your blood.

Feel a steadiness in your partnership with Earth. Fill the first chakra with light that is strong like the heart of a mountain. Relax into that steady strength, breathing deeply. Feel the capacity of that strength to be impervious to anything seeking to disrupt your alliance with the Earth.

Send gratitude to that chakra for all the work it does to support your survival and grounding. Breathe energy up from the Earth through the chakras, giving each a balance with the Earth. Send the energy out through the crown in a cascade that gently rains down through your aura to the ground. Refresh yourself in that light until it is time to resume ordinary activities. Maintain and renew your grounding as you move through daily life.

NOURISHING THE BODY

VISUALIZE A BEAR—PERHAPS HIS NAME IS WILBUR. HE WAKES UP AND feels a bit slow and thick-headed, so he makes himself a cup of coffee. He recalls his amorous exertions of the previous night—that fine fat bear he met, breath like honey—and how they flattened some grasses together, bent some saplings in their passion.

Wilbur drinks his coffee (with a generous dollop of honey) and eats a few donuts. Now he feels more lively, but it takes another coffee and a cigarette to trigger his need to go off to the woods with his latrine shovel.

Wilbur comes back and looks in the mirror. Hmmm, a little ragged around the edges. He thinks fondly, if not regretfully, of all the dandelion wine he consumed in last night's romp, and he pops a pawful of spirulina tablets and vitamin C's into his mouth to restore himself, then rolls another smoke.

Wilbur's tumble in the grass with the she-bear improved his mood, but suddenly he's feeling all the more lonely, so he turns on the TV and sits down with some ice cream. . . .

Wilbur has lost the capacity for naturally pacing his energy. Animals rarely do this, except in captivity, but humans often find themselves in this kind of self-perpetuating cycle. The issues of what people do with their body are more volatile even than those of religion or politics. Avoiding touchy specifics, I will offer here some general thoughts pertaining to body wisdom.

To be responsible to Spirit and to your path of Spirit, you need to be able to respond intelligently to all situations. You need an intelligence of body, mind, and heart. All these are naturally intelligent if they are functioning from a basis of health—not from a social concept of health but from an individual well-being within the moment.

Observe the buffalo. It grazes and walks, walks and grazes. It moves steadily, maintaining its energy, and if need be it can run for miles.

Consider the cat. It lies around a lot, relaxed but often awake, alert. At mealtimes the cat patiently stalks, abruptly attacks in a fast short run or pounce, eats heavily, then lies around again.

The buffalo and the cat don't have similar pacing, yet each behaves intelligently within healthful rhythms, within the balance of its medicine.

What is the natural human lifestyle? That is for the individual's path of unfolding to reveal. To understand, you must first become aware of what you are using to pace your energy, and why. Food, drink, alcohol, tobacco, drugs, sex, sleep, mental and emotional stimulation (violence, fear, thrills), and other, more subtle, methods are the tactics used for externally adjusting your energy. They can be subtly or (as with Wilbur) obviously applied in daily life, but we all use at least some of them to pace ourselves, in conscious or oblivious ways.

Healthy balances are not necessarily fixed, even for the individual. In winter you may sleep more, in summer you may eat more fruit, if pregnant you may need a different sexual pattern. The key in all these adjustments is the attunement to natural rhythms—your own, connected with that of the Earth's. From the Earth you learn and develop or remember wisdom.

As you become aware (without being nasty toward yourself) of what you use to slow down, speed up, control fear, catalyze appetite and excretion, fend off boredom, be at ease in company, sexually perform or abstain, assuage loneliness, and accomplish tasks, you will discern some things about yourself. Meditate on these things.

Patterns of imbalance usually begin innocuously enough, or they may be the fruit of desperate circumstances. Either way, they are a remedy that becomes an illness itself as it spirals you away from consciousness, will, and well-being.

In honest awareness, you can see how these tactics are substitutions for respectful response to underlying needs. These are not small matters—deprivations and indulgences are emblematic of deep discontent with self, even if they only manifest in small acts of betrayal to well-being. Habit that does not nourish is at best neglect, at worst destruction.

This does not rule out short-term imbalances that are chosen because of a greater need than bodily nurturance. Staying up all night for ceremonial purposes or for a suicidal friend or for childbirth is different from not sleeping because you drink too much coffee or because you think you don't deserve sleep so work instead.

Moderation is not the answer, nor is eating only health foods and avoiding vice, nor is fearing any variance in your correct lifestyle, nor is being absorbed in only your own needs. These are not true nourishments or true alignments with balances. They are the flip side of the same coin whose face is abuse of self.

Freedom from addictions and from unhealthy modes of pacing your energy is more than a change in behavior, though that is powerful and important. The change must be partnered with awareness, compassion, and real understanding so that what follows is, indeed, tuned to wisdom, not to regimented belief or avoidance.

As your awareness leads to efforts of change, try to be simple for a while. Eat when hungry, sleep when tired, read all day if you want. How do these things make you feel? You've become aware of the imposed and compensatory patterns, now look beneath them. Where is your energy really located? How did it come to be this way? What has been suppressed or made aberrant?

As these needs manifest themselves, see them as interim behaviors that are speaking to you of what has not been heard, what has not been nourished. Let the insights and relief gained from them move you into clearer attunement to balances. It is not the cravings that instruct your choices, because those are apt to reflect suppressions, not accurate needs, but the insights that emerge from acknowledging those cravings.

From that animal simplicity develop body wisdom. Hear your body and recognize what it is reflecting to you. Let its advice be given place in your council of consciousness—the voices of self you hear—when you are making choices. Evolve a pattern of nourishment based on the freedom of the present moment. If your context of life or employment prohibits these healthy balances, ponder your priorities and be courageous in making changes that support well-being.

During This Week

Work toward a natural pacing of your energies. Some suggestions:

1. Become aware of and assess your patterns and their roots.

2. Meditate—know what you are doing; know the purposes and consequences of what you choose to put in your body.

3. Listen to your body, respect its needs, understand its language.

4. Begin aligning yourself with natural rhythms and learning what balances best serve your strength in the present moment.

5. Don't punish your body for the perceived shortcomings of self. Don't use the giving or withholding of physical treats such as food, sex, or pleasurable activities as a way of governing behavior.

6. Be judicious in your use of energy modifiers. Don't use them habitually or inappropriately.

7. Don't make categories of good and bad behaviors or substances. Be spiritual rather than religious in your way of life.

8. There is nothing wrong with pleasure.

9. Pleasure is not the only criterion.

10. Nourishment is not fulfilled through occasional pampering of the body. It needs to become an instinctive aspect of wisdom.

STONE SPIRITS AND EARTH RHYTHMS

THE MINERAL WORLD, LIKE THE PLANT AND ANIMAL WORLDS, IS ALIVE. Its life is expressed in subtle ways that are often unperceived by us—the minerals' quality of life is not characterized by rapid movement, growth, or sound, though stones indeed move, change, and speak.

Stones radiate, store, and transfer a variety of powers that can be interacted with for scrying, grounding, communication, and other purposes. Each stone is unique, though they are often grouped by kind, and their individuality should be recognized and addressed.

If you pick up a rock from the ground, first ask permission to do so. Many stones need to remain where they are. The maintenance of the planet is balanced to a great extent by the arrangement of minerals around the world. The mining and moving of many minerals is a threat to both the physical and the spiritual health of the planet. It may not seem a big deal to carry off one rock, but each such action represents a thoughtless egotism that, in the long run, is damaging to all.

In your enthusiasm to participate in the magic of crystals and stones, you must not overlook the implications of the means by which they are acquired and what impact these have on the Earth. Dynamiting mountains and pillaging the Earth's innards have never been acts of respect or healing. The pattern of creation is not a random game.

There is a deep and old wisdom to stones. If you reach out with your awareness, most times you will be rewarded with a response. The simplest way to listen to a stone's story is to hold or touch it, still your thoughts, and allow your consciousness to slow down and seek resonance with the mineral vibration. Images may appear in your mind's eye, or a sense of stone history and associations may become clear to you.

Sitting or lying on rocks is a good grounding experience in times of confusion, stress, grief, or spaciness. Mountains, cliffs, and boulders often give inspiration, peace, and endurance. They speak of life in terms of centuries and eons, tempering your perspective of daily changes.

Crystals have been used as allies by shamans of different cultures since ancient times. Crystals have unique vibratory qualities that make them ideal for focusing, transmitting, and transforming energy. Crystals can amplify awareness of other realities and dimensions.

Crystals come in all sizes—bigger is not always better. Small crystals are useful for children, medicine bags, jewelry, and certain healing techniques. Larger ones are used on rods, staffs, wands, and for work that requires more "juice." Crystals can aid lucid dreaming or can appear in your dreams, sometimes speaking or altering what is going on in the dream. Pay special attention to these dreams.

Clarity and intactness of points are two characteristics considered important in crystals. Energy moves from the base out the points, except in double-terminated crystals, in which the flow goes both ways. Crystals often change with use.

If you obtain a crystal, clear and charge it. When it is not in use, keep it on an altar or in a medicine bag. Meditate with your crystal and see what particular application it has in your life.

The mineral totems, like the plant and animals totems, require active relationship. It is up to you to communicate and work consciously with your allies. Merely carrying a stone around will not accomplish much. Intention, capacity, focus, and perseverance are the keys to effective relationship with all the totems, including the minerals. The properties listed in the appendix are not claims made for the consumer. They are experiences, traditional and current, that have come from serious practitioners of totem medicine. It is up to each person to find his or her path with these sacred beings.

If your totem is a mountain or cliff, remember that physical proximity is not necessary for medicine work—inner connection is sufficient if your alignment is solid. It is said that the herbalist has the eyes of a healer and a stone dreamer has the gaze of a prophet.

Stone spirits can be very enigmatic, being Northerners. They can be very close-mouthed. Stones teach the value of patience and enduring attention. Stone spirits have long memories. They are strong, but gracefully receive the changes brought by wind, water, fire, and the movements of the Earth. Their cycles are slow but ungrudging. They are the bass note in life's symphony. To be with them, you have to learn to think like a mountain.

The Earth's rhythm has rock as its deepest beat. The rock music of the Earth is not quite mirrored in the rock music of humans, but both have a steady pulse that can move the body. Breath and heartbeat can attune to the Earth's rhythms—the eight-count breathing technique given in part 1, week 1 is one example of this.

Aboriginal people on all continents have found resonance with Earth rhythms through their ceremonial dances and percussion and in their daily responses to the seasons and natural cycles. The simplest power of all is the alignment with natural rhythms. It is the framework of this book and all its teachings. It is an entry point into sacred wisdom.

Rhythm, vibrational pattern, spiritual codes within transformative cycles— they speak to consciousness through the body so that spirit can be manifested, so that spirit can be experienced.

In winter silence on the mountain, everything can be heard, and in the long nights you can feel the Earth breathing, dreaming, healing itself, cradling its seeds—the hibernation of light ensuring its renewal. The power of the North is the materialization of life's rhythms.

During This Week

Deepen your relationship with the stone realms, including representatives big or small. Consider the origins of any stones in your keeping—how they were taken from their natural contexts and how they arrived in your care. Perhaps you need to do something in response to these considerations. Reread part 2, week 8, the lesson on caring for rattles and other medicine objects. Are you properly maintaining the well-being of your stones and crystals?

Deepen your awareness of natural rhythms, not only during this week but throughout the year. Tune yourself to the seasons and cycles of the Earth. Try to decrease your reliance on electrical light. Try not to insulate yourself so thoroughly from weather—walk in the rain, play in the snow, run with the wind. Be aware of what phase the moon is in and how the arc of the sun's path changes with the seasons. Watch the stars turn in their dance of constellations.

Pay attention to the migration of birds and the hibernation of snakes. Learn the succession of wildflowers that bloom in your area. Keep track of first and last frosts and the cycles of insects. Do not live in a world separate from the rest of life.

Paying attention to and aligning your rhythms with the patterns of nature will in itself yield a wisdom that grows richer over time. Do not underestimate its power.

ANCESTORS

ANCESTORS CAN BE ABOUT NOW—JUST AS PAST LIVES CAN BE ABOUT now—OR they can be about something long ago that holds you like a leash from moving freely through life.

Here in North America, people come from many ancestries—we are a mixed bag as a people and as individuals. If you toss reincarnation into the bag, the mix gets even more genealogically boggling. I lay in bed once trying to decide whether ancestors are behind or in front of me. They are of the past in their having lived prior to my life, but they are of the future in their genetic influence affecting how my life unfolds. Before can mean either behind or in front of, and my ancestors are before me. It all, of course, resolves itself in the present moment, where the connection abides and time ceases to be a linear concept.

You can look in the mirror and see ancestry—a continuity, an inheritance—but how accountable are you to that destiny encoded in your cells? Some people are proud of their ancestry, some ashamed, some are ignorant or indifferent. Are you any more or less what you are as a result of attitude?

When I was in my thirties, I went to each of my parents and asked them to tell me about their families. Both my mother's and father's ancestors came to North America before the Revolutionary War—my mother's people supported the revolution; my father's were Tories. My blood is mainly Scots-English with a little Dutch and a dab of German—a basic northern European background.

As I listened to my parents talk and wrote down their stories, patterns emerged that I could see repeated in my own temperament. Nature or nurture—I won't argue the roots of family patterns—but when ancestry is brought into the spiritual path, its significance changes.

I believe that people on the "other side" can be teachers, allies, and guides. I don't approach them through seance but through the resonance within myself—if I can find them in my cells, I can find them in my consciousness. Even those ancestors not of my bloodline can be found in consciousness; there are no boundaries.

Regardless of imperfections in personality, there is in each person some aspect of the sacred dream, and it is this that you seek to reach when calling upon the help of ancestors. These aspects are yours to embody by right of kinship. The gifts may seem small, or for a time impenetrable, but they are there. Part of the path of compassion and acceptance is coming to peace with family and ancestry so that you are neither severed from history nor hiding behind its supposed glory.

Ancestry informs but does not define. Such things as appearance, family customs, religious background, cultural prejudices, physical constitution, and class status are not influences to be blindly reinforced in yourself or futilely ignored. They can be sorted through like objects in a house you've grown up in and recognized for their impact on the form of your life and beliefs.

Some of the furniture in that house may no longer be comfortable or may be despised for the memories it evokes. Some of the objects may be the sort needing to be put in temporary storage until you know what use to make of them. Some things may well suit your house of the present moment. Maybe you'll want to just burn the whole thing down; but the memory will remain, and at some point along the path you will have to address these ghosts.

Anywhere you enact ceremony or live, there are ancestors of place to consider. In some places these spirits are formidable presences. Offerings and acknowledgment should be given to these ancestors and a harmonious partnership formed if possible. If you have not the skills or alignment to do this, certain places are best left alone for your own safety. Keep in mind that just because there are no physical dwellings in a place doesn't mean that no one lives there.

Your ancestors, be they who you came from or who, as you grow old, you are going toward, are part of your now. Your acceptance of them as mirrors, extensions of yourself, no more impinges on your integrity of being than do totems. Only ego fear can blind you or limit your freedom in using this inheritance. Spiritual destiny is led by consciousness, not genetic code.

During This Week

If you have photographs or objects belonging to your ancestors, set some in front of you, along with a mirror.

Look into the faces in the photographs with inquiring and compassionate interest. Discern the dreams behind those visages—the sufferings, the beliefs, the experiences. See the people as children, as youths, as adults, as elders. Feel how your ancestors were shaped by their families and times, and how their own choices made branchings in the ancestral current.

Speak lovingly, respectfully, to these ancestors—whatever needs to be said or asked. If you have no photographs, visualize them in your mind.

Then look in the mirror with the same inquiry and compassion. See what traces of ancestry have touched your face. See your own sufferings and experiences. See yourself as child, as youth, as adult, as elder. Look deeply and see the spirit within your eyes in its ever-becoming freedom and integrity. Speak lovingly to yourself—something spontaneous, not rehearsed. Smudge the photographs and the mirror.

Consider the inherited objects. Handle them. Feel their energy, their ways of connecting you to family and other times. What is the medicine of each of these objects? Is there any? Why? Why not? What is the best response to the keeping of these things?

Smudge the objects, remembering their origins and connections as you do so. Make a prayer within the circle of those before you and those yet to be born.

"WHAT IS A LEYLINE?" MY FRIEND'S DAUGHTER ASKED WHEN SHE HEARD that our mountain is crossed by one.

Imagine a globe, the Earth, covered with a spiderweb of luminosity, of glowing veins and arteries of moving energy; visualize the Earth as a being having meridians and chakras that guide the flows of its aura and body. That is sacred geography—the leys and places of power on the Earth.

There is a deep, strong leyline that moves through the mountain on which we live. Some people find living close to these currents uncomfortable. Perhaps it is a matter of some leys and some people being vibrationally dissonant. The one here has a smaller, close-to-the-surface tributary that runs past our house. At times the ley seems quite aware of our presence and activities. At other times it seems preoccupied with its own business.

Sometimes when I seek contact with the ley, I feel as if I'm dropping down a shaft—a sense of vertigo and rapid descent. Sometimes the ley speaks to me, or the area around where I sit becomes misty looking and strangely lit. I feel the oldness of the ley's current and the stories it carries. It is like a time river going to other ages and realms. Sometimes the vitality of the ley is clearly invigorating—making me almost giddy—and on other occasions it takes great stillness inside in order to sense the ley at all.

Ley currents fluctuate and can reverse direction. They can alter course and send out tributaries, or they can be altered by human intervention. Redirection by use of crystals, metal rods, or force of will should be done, if at all, with respect for both your own safety and the ramifications of tampering with these essential currents.

I have found when doing medicine work here on the mountain that the ley will add its energy to what I am doing, like an extra battery pack. I have also felt its presence in the sweat lodge. These experiences have led me to believe that ley energies are willing to ally themselves with human activities, like other totems and allies, in a reciprocity of relationship. Previously, I had thought of leylines as energy roads connecting sacred places—meridians having individual characteristics—but it did not occur to me to see them as entities interested in relationship.

In defining leylines, the semantics can be confusing. Some references consider the lines to be without energy in themselves—merely symbolic markings—and some feel that the leylines are like rivers of magnetic or ionized current. My own sense of them is that the line is a path and the ley is the emanation of localized energy embodied by sacred geography. Thus I see the ley where I live as a specific mountain energy whose manifestation is concentrated along a geographically and spiritually logical path that connects it with other leys. Positioned within this grid are the sacred places that have probably attracted interest since humans first walked this Earth.

Some years ago I visited Glastonbury Tor, an old magical place in England. Sitting on the hillside, I made my prayers and offerings of tobacco. I then asked the spirits of the Tor to share their teachings with me, if that seemed good to do.

I entered nonordinary consciousness and saw a dark, small being, who guided me into the center of the hill. To my surprise, it seemed hollow—a world within a world. In that place I was shown what was right for me to see and know; then I surfaced again to my body.

A few years later I read an account of Glastonbury's legends, one of which described the Tor as a hollow realm—as Mount Shasta is also said to be.

What is it that makes these places so special? Partly it is the geography—the way the Earth expresses its spirit-through-form in these places. This geography is the story of the Earth's ever-becomingness. For humans, it is also the story of our reconcilement to our geospiritual living context, our finding a sense of home here.

This establishment of relationship is another contribution to what makes certain places particularly significant to us. The human recognition of sacred geography amplifies what is already present there. Interaction in the form of ceremony, offerings, communion, and reverence encourages harmony between humans and the cosmos, bringing prosperity and balance through the realms. Humans need to abide in proximity to that which they experience as holy.

These two aspects then—what is there, and what is perceived and responded to—are the elements of sacred geography. Natural features of the land have characteristic qualities. In general, springs, great mountains, isolated hills, caves, and oddly shaped formations are gathering places for power and attention to power. Elemental forces tend to operate in distinct patterns, references to which can be found in such cultural systems as the Chinese art of geomancy, called *feng shui,* or in the European understanding of leylines.

These flows and concentrations of energy, like the meridians and chakras of the body, reflect the state of health of the planet, including its people. Involvement with sacred geography is one way well-being is maintained. The interface with spirit through place is one of the Earth's greatest gifts to you.

Certain places are highly charged with power, but an experience of sacred geography can be found anywhere in nature. Do not overlook the opportunities in your own backyard, in your attraction to the exotic promises of far-off spots like Stonehenge, Machu Pichu, or Delphi. Just as there are more erogenous zones than the genitals on the human body, there are more places to touch the sacred on the Earth than just the famed power centers. If you visit traditional ceremonial areas, consider these suggestions:

1. Before visiting, gain some background information about how this place has been traditionally regarded and used. Reassess the desire to go to this place; look at your intentions and what draws you there. Don't be a New Age tourist seeking phenomena or magical thrills.

2. Don't assume you will be welcome in a place just because you are a sensitive and spiritually minded person. Your presence may not be compatible with ancestral or guardian spirits. In simple terms, you may not know the right passwords. Move slowly and accept the possibility of withdrawal.

3. What you add to or subtract from a place changes it. Keep this in mind when making offerings or performing ceremonial actions. Don't invoke powers, move or remove natural objects, or leave crystals or other things unless you have permission to do so.

4. Protect the integrity of sacred places from destruction and commercialization. Be an advocate for respect of traditional grounds.

During This Week

Find your own special natural place of resonance, be it in a garden, forest clearing, or horse pasture, or on a stretch of beach. Let this relationship with place evolve in a gradual way. Feel its call to you, or its acceptance of you.

Experience the changing seasons in your special place. Feel the rhythms of the Earth's cycles and make ceremony there at the solstices and equinoxes and at the cross-quarter holy times that mark the midpoint between them. Be particular about whom you share this place with. Let it be a portal to other worlds of consciousness for you.

Visualize it in times of need as a sanctuary even when your body is elsewhere. The more you work with a place, the more focused and charged its atmosphere will be and the stronger your attunement will grow.

CELEBRATING THE SEASONS

IN THE WAY OF THE ANCESTORS, THE YEARLY CYCLE IS MADE UP OF VARYING degrees of light. During half the year, the days are longer than the nights; during the other half, the dark prevails. This cycle has not changed, but modern people's perception and attunement to it has. Whether we celebrate these seasonal shifts with the urgency of survival that our ancestors did or with a more metaphysical approach, there is something worthwhile in honoring the ancient round.

The seasonal holy days are an extended rhythm of growth and rest. Modern holidays have tried to usurp and absorb these pagan times of worship. Their power remains, however, enduring within whatever trappings we clothe them. At the times of these holy days, universal forces arrange themselves in potent configurations. This is when energy cycles culminate and shift to new cycles.

The year is divided into four fertility festivals and four harvest festivals. They can be pictured as a circle with the top half as the light part of the year and the bottom as the dark. The solstices would be at the highest and lowest points on the circle, and the equinoxes would be to the sides. In this way you can see the perfect balance in the cycle. The solstices and equinoxes are the quarters and the four festivals that alternate with them are the cross-quarters.

The cycle begins with October 31, called Samhain, Hallows, or Hallowmas. This holy day begins the season of sleep, rest, and dreams—the inward half of the year. It celebrates eternal life and honors the loved ones who have passed. The veil between the worlds is most thin at this point in the year. Black robes are worn; nuts, dried flowers, and autumn leaves are used for decoration in the home. It is the last of the four harvest festivals, dedicated to the remembrance of the eternal cycle of life, death, and rebirth.

On December 20–23 (depending on the year) is Yule, time of the Winter Solstice, the longest night of the year. The conception of the light is celebrated, and spiritual work concerning rebirth and renewal is appropriate. Evergreens, holly, and mistletoe are traditional representatives of this holy day. It is a time of profound faith in the rekindling of light and warmth and of appreciation for the deep fertility of darkness.

Candlemas or Imbolc comes next, on our modern Groundhog Day, February 2. Its energy is of quickening and clearing. It is when the increasing day length becomes noticeable and spring begins to stir. It is a good time to pay debts, clean house, and attend to health. Traditionally, Imbolc was the holy day for initiation, sacred to Brigid, patroness of smiths, poets, healers, and midwives.

The year moves next to Ostara, Spring Equinox, March 20–23. This is the third of the fertility festivals; it is dedicated to the trees. It is the time of perfect balance between light and dark, marking the emergence of Persephone from the Underworld. Its energy is of pause before crossing the threshold into spring. A good time to plan gardens, renew friendships, and hang prayer bundles in favorite trees.

Beltane, May 1, begins the flower season. It is the major fertility festival of the year and is an auspicious time for conceiving babies. Sexual energy seeks manifestation on this holy day that is traditionally represented by the Maypole dance and the wearing of flowers. In Beltane is the celebration of joy, freedom, possibility, beauty.

June 20–23 is when the Summer Solstice occurs and the sun is at its peak of light-giving. Alliances are formed and healings enacted. Herbs such as mugwort and wormwood are worn as garlands and thrown into the ceremonial fire for luck. The long light of Litha, Summer Solstice, gives opportunity for the powers of clarity, understanding, and actualization to express themselves.

Lammas or Lughnassad comes on August 1 and marks the second of the harvest festivals. It is a time for making goals and letting go of selfish motivations. It is a holy day for offering reciprocity for the gifts of the Earth. On Lammas we notice the waning of the daylight, just as on Imbolc we became aware of the growing solar influence.

As the wheel of the year reaches again into autumn, we have Mabon, Autumn Equinox, on September 20–23. It mirrors Ostara in its balance of light and dark. Mabon, in Libra, is a celebration of harmony and gratitude, the third harvest festival. At this time, we store what we need for the coming winter on all levels of need. Fruit, gourds, and squash represent our bounty from the Earth. It is an ideal time for reassessing relationships and balancing our inner natures.

As we bring ourselves in tune with the wheel, that inward and outward gathering and sowing, we find an integration of peace and strength, Earth and Sky, wheels within wheels.

During This Week

Think about your own ways of celebrating the seasons, and how much or little you correlate your festivities to the actual natural events and energies of your habitat. Do you follow a cultural tradition, or have you invented your own? Do you celebrate with family and friends or alone? What do these times mean to you?

SWEAT LODGE (Part 1)

THE SWEAT LODGE, WHEN USED IN A SACRED MANNER, IS A CEREMONY OF purification or rebirthing. You enter the Earth's womb, literally or symbolically naked as a babe, and allow the layers of suffering and superficiality to dissolve in the prayer-filled steam of the lodge. It is a singularly effective process for getting to the heart of things.

The sweat lodge is a primitive ceremony in that its elements cannot be broken into more basic forms. Earth, Air, Water, and Fire are present in highly charged states: the Earth of the lodge itself and the rocks bearing the heat of the Fire; the sacred Fire, power of life and transformation; the Water that is poured on the rocks and becomes steam; steam, the Air that cleanses and carries the prayers.

These elements, so charged and immediate, create a ceremonial environment that compels attention. This is not an experience you can just cruise along through or be unmindful within. You either struggle, and perhaps learn through struggling, or let go of barriers, limitations, and ego.

When you bring your intentions to the sweat lodge, it does not fulfill those intentions in an elusive way. It addresses you full-on, directly, totally. There aren't many modern experiences that can match the sweat lodge for multileveled intensity. Childbirth in its natural form is most similar.

In the non-Native community, there has been some backlash against the enactment of long or hot sweats—"warrior" sweats. The feeling is that these difficult sweats are elitist because they eliminate participation by people in ill health or of lesser stamina and that they are merely endurance contests that emphasize macho survival rather than focus on sincere prayer. My experience, which began in 1981 with Native-led sweats and has included many dozens of sweat lodge ceremonies, has not supported those objections.

In the traditional manner, sweats are often conducted specifically for people in ill health or of physical weakness, and these are not necessarily gentle sweats. The ceremony is not exclusive—belief is exclusive. Ideas about the sweat lodge and health are revealing of basic perspectives.

This is not to say that people with challenging health conditions should necessarily participate in sweats. It is to suggest that belief should be examined and deeper guidance looked to.

The endurance-contest concern has, in my observation, been a preoccupation for people who perceive physical discomfort to be a stimulus for emotional opposition. They equate discomfort with punishment or emotional suffering. In one tribe's traditional history, the sweat ceremony was brought to the people by a little boy; in another, it was brought by a holy woman. It is not a warrior ceremony. The valiant struggle to maintain a hero's stoic demeanor in the face of suffering is not the point of the sweat lodge ceremony. As in childbirth, the response to intense physical and spiritual forces needs to be one of acceptance and embrace, not opposition. These are not malevolent forces, and they are not uninvited. Your work with them needs to be cooperative, resonant, and transcendent of fear.

There is nothing wrong with mild sweats, but if you are willing to engage with a fullness of experience, or if you would give birth to new vision, it is self-defeating always to stop at the very threshold past which narrow concepts and ego demands lose authority.

Modern whites have a cultural prejudice against being disheveled, uncomfortable, and not in control of their habitat. This makes the sweat lodge a risky proposition—possibly liberating, probably undignified. With a mild sweat, you can keep your prayers well scripted and your pride of appearance relatively intact. With an intense sweat, all this will be lost—messiness will ensue, composure will topple, and then who knows what will happen?

I don't believe in the endurance-contest theory because it is usually the most macho types who cave in first in a hot sweat, and that takes the pressure off anyone else who was into that kind of competition. Hot sweats also discourage pretty-prayer contests. People tend to get right to the point and to what is truly heartfelt when they are in such intense conditions. A challenging sweat involves commitment of spirit but surrender of image and contest.

When I conduct sweats, it is not with the plan to make them as hot and long as possible. It is to be midwife to those in the lodge and in service to the medicine. Whatever is called for by the intentions present expresses itself and is worked with. In respect for the ancient fields of power and the spirits associated with the lodge, I do not seek to modernize this form. The sweat manifests to each participant in the way needed.

Sweat baths or sauna houses have been used worldwide for centuries as places of physical and spiritual renewal. In some areas, sauna houses were slept in, used for childbirth, or used as gathering places for socializing. The ceremonial use of a sweat lodge is a specific application of the renewal process, but it has links with these other forms.

In clarifying your own feelings about sweats, it may help to investigate what you are looking for in doing them. Is it physical cleansing, challenging your endurance, participation in something Native-like, group bonding, opportunity for prayer? These hopes can be fulfilled through sweating, but is the ceremonial lodge really the best context for them? Are they good reasons to be attending a ceremonial sweat?

Each of these desires could be carried through, perhaps more appropriately, in other activities such as saunas, powwows, prayer or drumming circles. The sweat lodge these days is being used to serve many purposes, and its ceremonial form is contorted to accommodate these needs. Amidst this, its original power is diminished or comes through in troubled ways. The more you make something resemble other things, the less its distinct impact.

There are many variations of traditional sweat lodge ceremonies for different occasions (sun dance, vision quest, healing, among others), for different tribes, and for different times in history. But in my understanding of this ceremony, several common denominators exist:

1. That the participant sweats, not just for the individual but for the good of all.

2. That unless it is a one-person sweat, there is a leader conducting the ceremony.

3. That it is a process of purification, renewal, and return to harmony.

For these conditions of ceremony to be met, there needs to be trust in the form, willingness to participate, and the capacity to align the personal will and sense of needs with the larger web of community.

The dimensions of such sweats extend far beyond the cosiness of group emotional intimacy or the physical and psychic high of a good-hearted ceremony. It is not an issue of intense heat, it is a matter of acceptance. Without that, no amount of heat or number of hours will be sufficient; with acceptance, whatever is present will be no more or less than is needed.

During This Week

Look into your thinking about the sweat lodge and about suffering, comfort, health, and control.

As was said in the previous lesson, sweat lodge ceremonies are of many varieties. The lodges themselves vary—some circular, some loaf-shaped, some facing East, some facing West or another Direction, some with the pit in the center, some with it off to one side. The number of rocks used varies with tribe and occasion, as does the number and dedication of the rounds.

These variations have meaning and purpose, and they are a fascinating aspect of medicine ways. They are the story of our perspectives from all parts of the medicine wheel.

Most sweats have a fire a little distance from the lodge, where stones are heated. The fire is tended by a ceremonial assistant who also brings the hot stones to the lodge. There is often a "road," either physically or spiritually delineated, between the fire and the lodge, with an Earthen altar mound rising from it just before the lodge's door. This road is a path of energy that during the ceremony, I was taught, should not be stepped across except by the fire tender.

The fire tender has an important job. The heat of the stones is the heart of the sweat, so the proper arrangement and heating of the stones is essential. The fire tender not only builds and cares for the fire, transports the stones to the lodge, keeps the stones hot that are needed for later in the sweat, and maintains the fire so that it lasts throughout the ceremony, but also is often responsible for other tasks as well.

The door flap needs to be opened and closed on request from the sweat leader. Medicine objects, water, or other items may need to be passed into or be received out of the lodge, and the sweat lodge area must be kept orderly and undisturbed.

To do all these things, the fire tender must be attuned to what is happening inside and outside the lodge and to the needs of the people before, during, and after the ceremony. It is work that requires more than campfire skills and a strong back. Good fire tenders are to be cherished.

Sometimes fire tenders will participate inside the lodge during the sweat, but this does not seem to be an optimal arrangement for the fire tender or the other participants. The fire tender remains concerned about what is happening outside with the fire and is thus distracted from the ceremony. It is also jarring to have one person going in and out of the lodge between rounds in sweats where everyone else remains inside for the entire ceremony, and it puts the fire tender out of sync with the rest of the group.

The style of lodge I have the most experience with is a round basket shape of about sixteen saplings—twelve planted in the ground, arched over, and lashed together to form a dome, with the others encircling the lodge parallel to the ground—with a single entrance/exit and a pit near the center for the rocks.

The lodge is covered with layers of blankets, canvas, or skins, and the ground inside with sage, cedar boughs, or other foliage. Prayer ties—pinches of tobacco tied in squares of cloth—may be hung inside, to be burned after the ceremony.

Outside the door is a mound of Earth from the rock pit. This altar may have an arrangement on it for a pipe to rest against. The mound's top should be kept clear for the sweat leader's medicine, but participants may want to place offerings on the altar's sides. It is best to ask first, if you are in an unfamiliar situation. Every leader has his or her own way.

What you contribute to a sweat has much to do with the experience you receive. Building the lodge and supplying firewood, stones, lodge coverings, and food for afterward are all part of what can make the ceremony strong for you and for others. Perhaps it will be what makes it happen at all. Do not forget the importance of mindfully offering tobacco and whatever else seems right to the sweat leader.

As with any ceremony, preparation has a definite bearing on what is experienced.

Physically prepare by drinking extra water, fasting in the hours beforehand, and abstaining from caffeine, alcohol, and other drugs for at least a day in advance.

Mentally and emotionally prepare by slowing down, meditating, making your intentions clear, and addressing your fears and concerns.

Spiritually prepare by praying, making tobacco ties or readying your offerings, clearing your chakras, and aligning with your guidance. Continue all these as you do the work necessary for the sweat and as you sit by the fire.

Inquire about how the ceremony will be conducted. Does the sweat leader adhere to certain taboos? Does the sweat leader expect you to wear (or not wear) clothing or to sit and behave in a certain manner in and around the lodge? Don't assume you know these things just because you've been to other sweats.

Some leaders conduct sweats during which drinking water is passed at intervals, some do not. There are sweats where you can go outside between rounds, and ceremonies where you remain within the lodge until the end. Most sweat leaders have no problem with a participant leaving the sweat before it is finished if the participant feels unable to stay with it.

There are things you can do if you feel overwhelmed in a sweat lodge, such as lying down (if there is room) or putting your head close to the ground, where the air is cooler. Places near the door are not as hot as those in the back of the lodge; breathing through a filter of sage leaves often clears your senses and helps you center yourself. For first-timers especially, endurance is mostly a matter of calming your panic and relaxing your resistance to the heat, steam, and close quarters. You will probably feel least overwhelmed when you are the one praying aloud. When you are sitting and listening to others pray, then the heat and humidity may seem suddenly unbearable. If you are with a sweat leader who is not strict about procedure, ask to pray aloud when you feel conditions become too much for you. Ask for support from others in the lodge—don't just suffer in silence until you are so overwhelmed you must bolt out.

Helping you may be what strengthens someone else, so together people can expand the sense of possibility and a capacity for compassion and support. You sweat for more than yourself. There is room for everything in the universe, in that small and humble lodge.

Extending beyond fear is not the same as recklessly disregarding what you know is physically too much. Respect your body's true needs but not its habits of comfort. As in vision questing, there is no success or failure—there is no test.

Conducting sweats requires particular skills and calling. It is not the same as leading prayer circles. Among egalitarian hippies, neo-pagans, and New Age folk, sweat leaders are often considered superfluous or a remnant of the hierarchical past. If a leader is present in these groups when they sweat, it is often a person of the "seen one, had one, done one," variety. Why is a skilled and experienced sweat leader important? For three reasons:

1. Because of the nature of the sweat lodge ceremony. Without a leader, people do as they wish: they have control of the habitat and happenings, and consequently there is not likely to be much stretching of limits. There is no trust needed, there is no courage needed, there is no unknown faced. They do not give themselves into Spirit's care. They do not become as babes. It is a therapeutic prayer sauna—nice, maybe very high, but not the same ceremony.

2. Because of the elements invoked by using an ancient traditional form. Each sweat lodge is spiritually connected to all other sweat lodges. It is an old and much-used form, and it has forces and resonances associated with it. Good sweat leaders begin working with these energies as soon as they agree to conduct a sweat. They have certain songs to help them during the sweat and an alliance with the spirits present at sweats. It is a matter of service and destiny, not hierarchy.

3. Because it takes training, experience, and suitability to conduct a ceremonial form with as much power as a sweat lodge. Balances within the physical, emotional, and spiritual levels of being are changed in the course of a sweat lodge ceremony. People have died in sweat lodges; people have shifted into severe and extended altered realities. There are real consequences that stem from the enactment of such transformations; it is not a precinct for experimentation.

The leader keeps track of the coming and going of spirit forces in and around the lodge, keeps track of each person's state of being and needs, is alert and focused—not lost in private experience. He or she knows how to deal with difficult situations, how to help the people within an intense, life-altering ceremony. The sweat leader's connections reach through the realms and through time. In this way the medicine of the sweat is served.

During This Week

Consider making yourself a one-person lodge for sweating in. Keep your sweats simple—times for prayer and renewal. Use them as ritual preparation for other ceremonies or for clearing yourself when you feel out of harmony with the cosmos. If possible, have someone tend the fire and keep vigil while you sweat, then switch places. Don't, however, consider these as training for sweat leading. If you feel that calling, seek competent guidance.

BACK IN WEEK 11, PART 1 SUGGESTIONS WERE GIVEN FOR USING YOUR developing psychic and intuitive abilities to help others. In this lesson are suggestions relating to ethics. They are applicable to any sort of spiritual practice with others, whether that of healing, divination, aura work, shamanic services, or other assistance. These thoughts, like all else in this book, come from what I was taught, what I have experienced, and what I understand and believe at present.

1. *Permission and trust.* These must always be present and honored. It is not enough to know you can do something. You also need to ask "May I?" and "Should I?" These questions are addressed to the person you are working with and to the Spirit that guides you. They need to be asked at each step of the way. Don't presume. Permission for one thing does not imply permission for other things.

2. *Timing.* This is knowing how not to interfere with people's own processes of insight, discovery, and healing. It is knowing what to let be and knowing when to do or say what is needed for you to do or say. This is wisdom's core.

3. *Responsibility.* Who has it, for what? Obsession with responsibility is an ego-trip, whether you use it to blame yourself or to be the savior. Avoiding responsibility is also unethical. A clarity in this comes with understanding what you are accountable to—then you know what you are accountable for. If you are acting out of neediness or in response to the pressures of expectations, you will keep bumping into problems with responsibility. The pressure to perform will lead you into deceptions, reliance on razzle-dazzle, shortcuts, and avoidance of important follow-up. It can lead to misjudgments. Work this one out—if you are clear you will be a wise and unassailable practitioner. Outcomes are not your responsibility—the present moment is.

4. *Credit.* Give credit to your teachers, guides, associates, and resources. Continuity gives a momentum to power—let it flow. Don't be a name-dropper; be part of the web of relations. Honor alliance.

5. *Naming.* Be honest and careful in what you name yourself and your work. Don't seek glamor through association or misuse the names of traditional callings. Be accurate in spirit as well as word. Understand the implica-

tions and obligations of names. Never misrepresent your extent of training, experience, skills, and knowledge.

6. *Karma.* To the extent possible, have mutual understanding with whomever you are working with about the probable effects on all levels of what is being done—not just the direct results for the person you are assisting but the consequences for yourself and the interconnecting network. Step back from the tunnel vision of attending to the specific and see the ripples moving outward from it.

7. *Influence.* Trust gives space for acceptance. Be very mindful of this. Identify your beliefs and opinions as such, and don't impose them under the guise of psychic knowledge. Someone who observes your spiritual competence in one aspect of practice will tend to assume it is all-encompassing, and that you are an all-around enlightened and advanced soul. In reality, most people are strong in some areas and neglectful in others—wise in some ways, immature in others. Be as trustworthy as you can, but be honest in your missteps, foibles, and personal opinions. Resist the urge to pontificate, convert, air your gripes, or influence someone else's life path. Have a light touch.

8. *Confidentiality.* This is a much-abused cornerstone of ethical practice. Think of something else to talk about. Don't use your intimate knowledge of someone as a topic of conversation with someone else, whether it is from need to pump up your self-image, impress someone, or be entertaining. If there is actual need to discuss the work you are doing, ask permission to do so, and be discriminating in what you say.

9. *Re-examination.* Look regularly at your beliefs and working modes and techniques. Reassess them from a perspective informed by Spirit's guidance and input from your allies. Don't be attached to what you have believed or have done in the past. As your understanding and experience deepen, your beliefs and working modes will naturally change. This is a vital process, and nothing should be immune from it. Be prepared to let go of things you thought were a permanent basis for your work. Truth is much more subtle than its expressions. Just because you're good at something doesn't mean you should necessarily continue doing it or that you won't do it again at some other time. Your commitment is to Spirit's guidance, not to your skills or spiritual career.

10. *Payment.* This issue will be addressed in the next lesson also. In terms of ethics, mutual fairness needs to be present, based on what you feel is right, not on the market's perspective. Don't go by cultural habit or New Age doctrine. Examine your own feelings about this. Be creative. Live your wisdom, whether that is barter, gifting, capitalism, sliding scales, or

a vow of poverty. Belief about money is not separate from the other aspects of your work and path.

If you are engaged in work as a spiritual practitioner, these suggestions are offered for perspective. If you are one who may someday become involved in some form of community practice, these suggestions may contribute to your preparation for that. If your path is one that will not take you into the fields of public practice, these suggestions may be useful when you seek assistance from others. Even in personal rather than professional relationships, they have application.

During This Week

Think back on the caregivers and practitioners of all sorts you have encountered in your life—doctors, therapists, healers, medicine people, counselors—and their modes of practice.

Which ones did you especially appreciate? Which ones were most effective in their work? Which ones seemed most ethical? Look at the opposite end of the scale also. What are the elements that contribute to these feelings and evaluations?

CONNECTION AND SERVICE TO COMMUNITY

THE EAST-WEST AXIS OF THE MEDICINE WHEEL IS THE PATH OF SELF. IT IS the journey of realization and acceptance, the path of being. The South-North axis of the wheel is the road of Spirit brought into manifestation. It is the path of community, of alliance, of doing.

In the North of the wheel, you stand not only in relation to community but in service to it. Never are you separate from the web of community, except in illusion, but in the North your work within that web becomes explicit. Many books about metaphysics talk at length about personal power, but at some point, for power to be more than therapy or an ego game, the personal must grow up. North is the precinct for this—the embodiment of the sacred.

What is community but the web of life? What is the web of life but an expression of the Mystery? You serve the Mystery through the community; you serve the community through the Mystery. Nothing is separate. The way of your service is not for others to define, but the impact of your work touches all. That is why the North is the elder, the wise one.

The hermit and solitary practitioner are not separate from community—theirs is only another vantage, like the vision quester alone in the wilderness, crying for the lives of all. The urban dweller may have immediate access to human interaction but must reach further and deeper for the truth of relationship with Sequoia, with Rattlesnake. Such reaching can bring crucially needed perspective to a population that often lives and consumes in forgetfulness of what is outside city experience. Each person with a spark of medicine moves in a realm, in a habitat, in an aspect of realization that is part of our wheel of community. There is infinite opportunity for service—the Mystery ever-present, the universe alive with beauty.

The teaching of community experience is compassion. In love, you respect each living form. You are touched by it in awareness of connectedness—you are able to align with the sacred. Without compassion, power will be misused. Explicit work in community is the opportunity to develop and express compassion. Love, patience, good humor, wisdom, strength, all are linked with compassion—the teachings of parenthood brought into the larger realm of application.

Wholeness is not an individual affair—it is not the personal Humpty Dumpty put back together again. It is the remembering of the cosmos, which is not a thing of which you are a fragment; it is the sacred dream, in ever-transforming completeness, in which you are awakening, remembering.

Community is not just a collection of people gossiping, jockeying for position, posing as this or that, crying into their pillows, having passionate, predictable bouts of romance, anger, jealousy, ambition, and religious fervor. It is full of drama but also of emergence, and in its emergence it reaches out and encounters a stately tree, a swooping bird, a child's giggle, a kindly touch. Sometimes the life within community gets burned, slapped, or trod upon, but still it reaches because it must, like a hatching chick.

The desire of life to manifest itself, to express form, is intrinsic to community. It becomes a dance of relationship of many expressions, distinctive and particular. Then the wheel turns and the tree decays to soil, the crone becomes ancestor, the cloud drops as rain. Where are the borders then? There are none, and the ego shivers and fears death. Know the web of life, know the dream, and self will expand and community be understood.

Learn to listen. Hear adults as you would children. Listen without condescension; listen with sympathy, in stillness, uninterrupting. Hear the suffering and hopes behind the words. Hear the vulnerability and loneliness, the need to connect and be understood. Listen. Listen to birds, crickets, wind, flowing water. Listen to the stars. As your listening deepens, your capacity for wise counsel grows. You'll know when to be silent, when to offer advice, and when to simply repeat what has been expressed.

Let go of your need for equal time. Listen, not from inhibition or fear of speaking, not from arrogance or a withholding that is cruelty, but from love. Ask for listening from others when needed—ask at the right time, of the right people.

In your giving, develop also the capacity to ask for and allow help. Honor the flow within the web. Do not set yourself apart in a cage of service. In your giving, don't be bullied or coerced. Follow the guidance of your medicine. Do what needs to be done—what is right for you to do. Remember to what you are accountable. Deal with truth, not shadow projections, not needy expectations.

When discussing spiritual service and interaction within community, the subject of money always arises. You may think I'm going to rant about how California urban New Age yuppies and pseudoshamans have exploited traditional medicine ways and commercialized spirituality. I could go on about all those goddess knickknacks and pricey pilgrimages. But what I want to address here is the other side of the coin, if you'll pardon the pun.

Sincere, spiritually minded people have told me, "I would never take money for spirituality" or "I could never take payment for healing work" or "It's not right to involve money in spirituality." I do not dispute these convictions about individual conscience and guidance. I do dispute it as a judgment applied to all.

We must each come to our own terms about right livelihood. It seems to me too pat an answer, however, to say that spirit and matter are separate realms of endeavor. I ask, What is right livelihood if it is not a reflection of Spirit? To divide the realms is to create a duality that is foreign to my experience of the sacred.

How does this world ever regain integrity of interrelationship if Spirit is not part of the means for prosperity?

If the community does not support spiritual contributions, where is the circle of giving and receiving? Where is the connection to spiritual reality in daily life? Where is the recognition of value?

Spirituality is not a commodity. It is a living, moving power of truth. Its application is inseparable from life. Spirituality has to be lived, expressed in every act, every relationship, every aspect of life's embodiment. The virtuous intention that keeps spirituality on a pedestal in some pristine corner has secluded it from the very places it is most needed.

In tribal times, spirituality was the center of community, permeating all beliefs and activities. Spiritual specialists were materially supported—paid, as it were— and considered vital to community function and health. There is no inherent denigration of spirituality in its being materially supported.

You get on very shaky ground when you try to sort out what work is spiritual and what is not, how that relates to payment, and how payment relates to right livelihood. Should our spiritual practitioners be out tracking down dollars in the marketplace instead of being available to the people who need their services? Do you think the Sage totem objects to being involved in helping contribute to someone's prosperity through the sale of sage leaves for people to smudge with?

Modern communities need to take care of their metaphysical specialists just as they need to support their other workers, and the practitioners need to clarify their relationships to community so that there is neither exploitation nor neglect on either side.

Money is a transitional tool. The gift system is better, with each person giving from his or her skills to whoever needs them. This system is part of an integrated perspective of community that allows everyone to be cared for and to care for. It is right for people to give and to receive—it is not good for it to be always unidirectional. In mutual support, given and accepted in the particular ways that are needed, is abundant nourishment for all.

If all livelihoods were seen as sacred possibilities, people would begin to understand what is truly valuable.

During This Week

Practice your listening skills. Practice not interrupting, even in your mind by preparing what you're going to say next. Practice understanding instead of debating or giving advice or expressing opinions. Ponder your own feelings about money, right livelihood, and spirituality.

THE JOURNEY OF THE MEDICINE WHEEL IS AN ELEMENTAL EXPERIENCE. You can attempt to overlay it with all manner of belief systems, but if the journey is taken with intention to see and experience yourself anew, then those belief systems become transparently absurd. It makes no difference if you place the Winds in the East or the North, if you find Snake in the West or the South, if you smudge with cedar or sage, face your lodge to the rising or setting sun. Ultimately, you discover that all ways are true ways if they are Spirit-directed and followed with tolerance for the ways of others.

Medicine is a living force bringing change and growth. Its continuity is not in a sameness of form but in transformative reliability. The seed and the fruiting tree are one but not the same. This book has given some forms and practices for the medicine, but they are living forms and simple practices, seeds ready for the sun and waters of creative experience.

After encouraging your participation in the web of relationship, I will now track coyote prints across your clear path by saying that this is one way of opening and awakening and expanding, but it is not the final answer to the spiritual imperative that calls you.

Knowledge is a wondrous path, encompassing and interweaving much, deepening and enriching us as a people. But what you seek in a Spirit-directed path are ways to discover truth, not just knowledge.

The peoples of the world whose cultures were elementally attuned tended to use natural patterns as focal points. These were visual, such as tea leaves, crystal balls, and animal entrails, or auditory, such as drum or rattle sounds, mantras, chants, and bells.

The more mentally oriented cultures tended to use symbolic systems through which to access spiritual consciousness, such as runes, tarot, alchemy, scripture, and the I Ching. Physical movement, such as dance, martial arts, and yoga, has been used for centuries by various cultures as ways to attain powerful states. Techniques that use the portals of smell (aromatherapy), taste (psychotropic plants), and touch (tantric sex) have been widely experimented with and refined in the search for spiritual awareness.

Any or all of these can be valid and appropriate practices for the seeker on the journey. Any or all of them, including totem medicine, can be traps, distractions, or dead-end roads if you do not realize that you are capable of direct experience of Spirit. To be beguiled by the elegant complexities of knowledge is to many a satisfying life. Others find fulfillment in attuning to Spirit through the "primitive" experience of the sweat lodge, trance drumming, and vision fasting.

No way nourishes for long unless you understand that no system, tool, technique, or intermediary is required to reach spiritual consciousness. Each person is of Spirit. Putting that realization into daily practice releases you from reliance on other resources. These resources can be profound teachers and guides, initiating much important work. But you must not become complacent, must not try to fit everything into a system, must not forget that your purpose is beyond collecting knowledge, skillfully using intuition, or defining your beliefs. Your purpose is in wholeness.

The wisdom of wholeness does not deny what has been learned. Observe the crone gathering herbs. She knows all their names and virtues. She knows when to gather, how to preserve, and how to bring out their medicine gifts. Yet it is not this knowledge that is her power. She could gather any plant at all, in any stage of its growth, and use it to heal. Actually, she could just call upon the medicine of the plant's spirit to be present, without any material form at all, and heal. In fact, she can heal just by seeing a person's wholeness with such strength and clarity that they see it too and are healed. Yet she gathers herbs. She honors life that way and teaches the young.

In the North all knowledge comes into its full application and is exhausted—emptied—and truth flies free from the egg. Knowledge is a community of information, an attempt to comprehend reality through complexity. Truth is an essence that is realized when an abiding simplicity reveals itself. Like spirit within religion, like love within marriage, truth is where things begin. It is what endures despite complexity and what in wisdom is found when knowledge is seen as a fruit of intelligence, not a destination of spirit. Knowledge is a pattern, and truth is what transcends it.

All patterns have keys, and when you release yourself from conditioned opinions you can find those keys and participate in life from a place of freedom. This is only a beginning, which is also a continuity, as each dawn is a newness and yet familiar. Again you go forth, and I wish you all beauty on your path.

On the land where I lived we had sweat lodge ceremonies regularly, and people in the area and people passing through often came to sweat together. Visiting medicine people were invited to attend or lead sweats, and each had his or her own way of doing it. I always asked people how they did their lodge, how many stones they used, how they laid their fire, how many rounds they dedicated and in what way. It is all of great interest to me—each bit of information is part of how we make peace with diversity, of how we enact the recognition of the sacred and pass that understanding to those who follow us.

The people who came to sweat often sat by the fire as the rocks heated, looking at the altar mound and listening to the singing and the drums, and sometimes they'd say, "You seem to be doing things in a good way here."

I would smile because it was a good way, but I don't know what way it was anymore. It is just the fire and the rocks, the steam and the singing, the smell of sage and the prayers of the people.

During This Week

Prepare your North/Winter bundle.

STONE CEREMONY

TAKE YOUR BUNDLE TO A PLACE WHERE THE EARTH'S POWERS ARE strongly felt. Go there at night, at a time when there is no wind. Bring seven candles and holders, your offerings, a special cleared stone or crystal, and your bundles for the North, South, East, and West.

Set four candles in the Directions, and put another one in the center. Set the other two near, in whatever pattern seems good. Put your bundles in their respective Directions, with the candles. Smudge yourself, your space, your bundles, the stone, and the candles.

Stand and call to the Directions to hear your prayers. Call to Earth and Sky, and to the Mystery. Invite the spirits of place and of ancestors. Invite your guides and allies.

Go to the East, light that candle, and speak your gratitude for the teachings and blessings received there. Make your offering and stand for a few moments, listening for messages from that realm.

Go to the South and do likewise, and to the West. In the North do the same. Then take your stone and, facing North, make a prayer. Ask the Stone nation and the powers of the North to recognize your stone as an emissary of good relationship between you and their realm. Ask that the stone speak to them for you and to you for them. Ask that this stone be a presence of peace wherever it goes, so that harmony will be facilitated between you and the places of Earth.

Charge the stone in this way, for purposes of communication and peace. (Be sure in advance that the stone is agreeable to this work.) Then touch the stone to your North bundle and set them together.

Light the candle of Earth and give thanks for the blessings of protection, nourishment, and change. Light the candle of Sky and express gratitude for light, expansion, and spiritual destiny. Light the center candle and pray to the Mystery in the way that is truth to you.

Bless your North bundle in the light of all the candles. Sit awhile and reflect on the past year and all the teachings and experiences that have touched you. Meditate or enter trance for a while, opening to guidance from the spirits, from the Mystery. Then extinguish the candles and bless your bundle with the night.

Say to the universe: All my relations.

I came to the wheel of stones
empty-handed, agitated in all directions,
sat in the west,
the afternoon sun was warm there.
Slowly Spring came,
I heard the birds—
chickadee, gull, crow, wren,
heard the breeze in the cedars—
began to awaken, breathe.

Summer moved in, spider's web was there
between sweat lodge rocks,
why did it take so long for me to see?
Nettle's green led eyes stone to stone,
each patterned with stories
too old for knowing,
their circle beginning again the
remembering that contains the fire.
Thank you nettles, thank you stones.

I sat in Autumn, a shell of water,
amethyst heart, moss dreaming upon
the trees; I wondered what good
I do upon this Earth. The light
on the tree's curving trunk is alive,
feeding life, at twilight
poised for magic
and I cannot sing, but did
breathe it in the heart.

The deer came through in Winter,
knocking stones free of their order,
I was watching everything then,
drawing in, expanding to become.
There is only being gratitude.
Small stones will scatter
transforming the child's design.
What holds there will be truth,
the altar of intention, prayers
in the wind-shaken trees,
bird call opalescent in the surface
of a rain-filled shell,
small spider threading the air.

I stood, moved up the path,
a branch snapped loudly underfoot.
I have not yet learned how
to walk this land.

CONCLUSION

THE QUEST FOR SPIRITUAL FOUNDATION AND DIRECTION STEMS FROM the natural desire of life to unfold in a purposeful manner within transformative manifestation. When consciousness awakens to purposefulness, there is awareness within participation.

Awareness is true human nature. Awareness is the ever-available teacher. What have been offered in these lessons are doorways that open into participatory awareness: doorways of the senses, doorways of practice, doorways of natural rhythms and patterns of consciousness. Learning to discern what is motivating and guiding perception and experience, you learn clarity of participation. With understanding comes the potential for freedom, and with freedom, wholeness and joy.

To seek fixity in spiritual knowledge is to stifle truth. Such a quest is an expression of fear, a constriction that would deny life's essential movement. Each knowing dissolves within a subsequent transcendence or transmutation or mirroring of perspective. The ego balks at such lack of permanence, fearing loss, instability, obliteration, the unknown, yet the ego is also dissatisfied with the status quo.

In striving for spiritual perfection as if it were a destination, all failures to arrive are judged wasteful, if not sinful. But the truth is, the path is created with each step, is lived in each moment, is the blessing of awareness—not of measured achievement.

Looking into the face of personal belief, you see your self-image, your teachers, your constructions of experience, perception, and assimilation. To do this looking wisely, deeply, and with compassion, you need tools that support clarity and offer recourse. Using the model of the medicine wheel, awareness is the dawning into which understanding and intention are invited. From there you engage with alliance and resource—you move, you choose action and response. But for mind and will to proceed effectively on this path of participation, you need the dimensions of consciousness to be infused with love, the medium of life's wholesomeness.

Love comes through acceptance and understanding of self and through familiarity with the spiritual universe that underlies the embodied realms, the heart of being.

Listening with attentiveness is carried into your expression of doing, calling on the wisdom and strength that affirms the beauty of participation. This, then, is the medicine wheel, which makes available all that is needed for the nourishment of awareness.

In words it may seem dense and complicated, but in practice it is as simple as kindness, as lucent as a butterfly's wings, as ever-present as the breath. Regardless of where you enter, everything is interconnected, so everything is present. This is true on a practical, daily basis. Alliance with a tree opens understanding of sky, clouds, sun, rain, Earth, air. Nothing is separate once the mind expands its horizons.

Loneliness, insecurity, greed, hatred, despair, fear, jealousy, adversariness—all are experiences of isolation, a misunderstanding of self.

Opening to relationship with a tree, you loosen the boundaries of self-image, you expand to include more, you let a few beliefs unclench their fisted certainties. The natural curiosity of the mind reaches out to explore, to look within the tree's mirror. The heart reaches toward resonance, the senses awaken to the language of beauty. There is peace in this and a deepening of resource that diminishes isolation. This is how healing begins.

As you explore the web of embodied life, you find common ground—diversity leads to the realization of what is shared, and you find that the center of the wheel can be reached from any direction. The center, the core of Mystery, becomes your sacred alignment, your reference for belief and action.

The intention of these teachings, then, is to use the particular to open the mind to the infinite. In tending to the specific, to the moment, to the daily round, to the breath you are right now given, you participate in life fully. This is where power abides; this is where conscious change is possible.

Fragmentation and alienation are at the root of all struggle for happiness. You are taught to divide body from mind, success from failure, human from animal, male from female, real from ideal, and on and on, with little integration or meaningful communication across the gaps.

The little chimp raised by humans and taught sign language was terrified and hysterical when brought to her natural jungle habitat to meet her own species. "Black bugs" she called the other chimps and would have nothing to do with them. Have we become unrecognizable to ourselves also? Is the human self-image askew? Have we been looking into distorted mirrors?

Taking your orientation back to the simple and profound grounding in natural cycles and core realities, the confusion begins to fall away. It doesn't matter if you are Buddhist, Christian, New Age, Native, agnostic, or neo-pagan; there is something basic in living mindfully, in relating respectfully and compassionately, and in being grateful for the gifts of each day. Teachers and teachings that embody these precepts go beyond dogma to a spiritual terrain that has room for all to be blessed and to find their paths home.

TOTEM REFERENCE GUIDE

TOTEMS AND ALLIES FROM THE BIRD, ANIMAL, PLANT, AND MINERAL realms are listed here with notes concerning both their physical and metaphysical attributes.

The lists and accompanying notes are of course incomplete—the web of life is vast and diverse. The brevity of description will give much space for your own insights and study.

Categorization of the totems is done in several ways in this guide—by Direction, by planets of influence, and in the stone and plant sections, by alphabetical order. These categories are flexible and suggestive of some of the possible approaches to organization and perspective.

Totems and allies are referred to as "it" throughout this book in order to avoid gender bias. This word choice is not meant to objectify the totems.

The information in the guide is descriptive of the first three levels of totem knowledge—the physical, emotional, and mental. Spiritual understanding and relationship is something that must evolve from personal commitment and experience. Through that reality, the knowledge given here will come to life or your own realizations and truths will be revealed. Each person's journey into alliance creates the medicine wheel anew. May you be guided by love every step of the way. All my relations.

BIRDS

Sun Birds

Baltimore oriole.   Making new friends, finding home

Flicker.   Illumination, mental striving, finding the way, guidance

Goldfinch.   Sending small bright messages, modest wealth and luck

Hawk.   Message carrier, fierce, protective, independent, having keen senses, journeying bird, business success, counting coup, decisive action

Kingbird.   Defending personal space, crossing lines, assertion

Meadowlark.   Giving praise, harmony with open spaces, glad-heartedness, generosity

Scarlet tanager.   Letting your light shine, sexual clarity

Credit for input on some of the totem listings goes to Medicine Hawk Wilburn. Many thanks.

Moon Birds

Nighthawk.   Watchfulness, benign hunter, being at home in the dark, quickness

Owl.   Occult power, wisdom, vision, prophecy, night seeing, transmutation, escape, transformation, dying to the past

Snowy egret.   Stature, dignity, purity, grace, rarity

Owl

Earth Birds

Brown creeper.   Finding direction, grounded flexibility

Brown thrasher.   Being grounded, unselfconscious, task concentration

Grouse.   Childlike trust, responsiveness, being oneself while blending in, drumming

Kinglet.   Household blessing, release from fear

Pheasant.   Aristocratic, risk taking

Phoebe.   Seeker, tenacity, keeping busy

Quail.   Clan harmony, group success, modest gains

Robin.   Message of change, integration, relatedness

Whippoorwill.   Forest spirit messages, voice of conscience, call of mysteries.

Woodcock.   Simplicity, faith, unpretentiousness, clairaudience

Woodpecker.   Attention to detail, straightforwardness, purposefulness, removal of obstacles

Wren.   Love of home, luck, charm, pregnancy, good cheer

Mercury Birds

Hummingbird.   Quickness, confidence, brilliance, feistiness, ecstasy

Killdeer.   Vulnerability, linear goals, sacrifice

Swallow.   Joy, freedom, playfulness

Tern.   Peerless flier, fearlessness

Venus Birds

Bluebird.   Good fortune, contentedness, well-being

Dove.   Treaties, nonviolence, promises kept

Indigo bunting.   Special gifts, peace, inspiration

Macaw.   The favored of the Goddess, balance, medicine, healing

Mourning dove.   Hidden virtue, artistic ability, sensitivity

Pigeon.   City prosperity, friendship, message carrier

Roseate spoonbill.   Shy love, fragility, undemanding friendship

Rose-breasted grosbeak.   Sexuality, attraction, discrimination

Sparrow.   Diversity, cherishing of all life, cyclical voices

Stork.   Fertility, birth, courtship, home building

Swan.   Spiritual power, righteousness, beauty

Thrush.   Inner beauty, solitude, serenity

Townsend's solitaire.   Elegance, singleness, quiet style

Waxwing.   Reassurance, uplifting of the ordinary, balance

Jupiter Birds

Chickadee.   Intrepidness, intelligence, maturity of heart, positive attitudes

Eagle.   Strength, majesty, high aspirations, courage, pride, large perspective, farseeing, sun messages, leadership, spiritual power

Osprey.   Success, respect, incisive action, working the interfaces

Pelican.   Sustenance, providence, clan prosperity

Snow goose.   Organization, leadership, group attunement, abundance

Mars Birds

Cardinal.   Standing out, ceremony, fire energy, awakening

Evening grosbeak. Comfortable in crowds, hierarchy, hiding behind masks

Nuthatch.   Contention, self-reliance, lack of gullibility, temperance

Red-winged blackbird.   Claiming boundaries, participation in life, displaying

Towhee.   Youthful energy, sticking up for yourself

Saturn Birds

Crow.   Omens, rowdiness, opportunism, laughter, mimicry, decoding archetypes

Junco.   Seeing things through, being where you need to be

Starling.   Making a pest of yourself, mirroring societal imbalance, consequences

Vulture. Patience, justice, karma, keeping time, impartiality, healing, protection

Uranus Birds

Blue jay.   Speaking warnings, being hard to fool, communication, dapperness

Catbird.   Solitary waiting, twilight times, clairaudience, shape-shifting

Magpie.   Telling tales, dreams of home, knowing names

Neptune Birds

Blue heron.   Truth, judgment, intuitive knowledge, patience, accuracy, focus

Canada goose. Togetherness, future hope, seasonal cycles, safe travels, monogamy

Cormorant.   Looking beneath the surface, fulfilling emotional needs

Cuckoo.   Shy curiosity, rain foretelling, listening

Duck.   Working things out communally, conversation, family matters

Kingfisher.   Self-expression, finding things, individual success, focus

Loon.   Introspection, feeling like a misfit, protection in water

Sandpiper.   Romance, dexterity, knowing your gifts

Water oozel.   Pluckiness, understanding the flow, freedom from strife, ability to move naturally upstream without loss of energy

Blue Heron

Pluto Bird

Raven.   Hidden self, transformations, knowing what is sought, facing shadows

MAMMALS

Mountain Goat (East)
Clarity of vision, climbing prowess, aspiration, balance

Mountain goats like high terrain with plenty of grass and browsing for their vegetarian habits. They live in flocks, with males ranging separately except during breeding season.

When alarmed these agile animals bound away over rugged terrain of rock and ledges. They seem to delight in standing perched on precipitous drop-offs—a dizzying sight.

At breeding time the males have butting contests for territory and mates. These are mainly for show and don't seem to create lasting animosity or result in injury.

The life expectancy of mountain goats is about fifteen years.

Comments: The Mountain Goat teaches sure-footedness in the high places of the inner and outer worlds. It helps us be nimble in our relationships and in our

Mountain Goat

movement through our environment. This totem leads us to places where our vision is clear and with wide perspective, while we still have our feet firmly grounded and steady. This ability to balance Earth and Sky is essential to the medicine path and makes the Mountain Goat a special teacher.

Mouse (East)
Seeker of visions, attention to detail, innocence

Mouse

Mice, in their myriad varieties, are found almost everywhere. Many are nocturnal. They are the prey of nearly all the carnivores and must live carefully if they are to live at all.

Mice have territorial ranges that often overlap the areas of other mice, but the immediate vicinities of nests are rigorously defended. Within the home range, mice have many refuges besides the home burrows. Mice prefer to clean their fur rather than their homes and will move to new quarters when the nest becomes too soiled.

Many different foods make up the diet of mice, including fruit, seeds, grasses, insects, snails, and carrion. Mice that are nesting indoors often nibble on whatever goodies they can find and will take pieces of clothing, books, and upholstery for nest linings, winning them much human animosity.

Sometimes mice form permanent pairs, but usually the male just moves into the female's nest for a short time. Most mice live only a few years, having busy but short existences.

Comments: The Mouse totem is the archetype of the vision quester. The Mouse brings the power of the seeker, the innocent, the harmless one. The Mouse totem is alert and has a close-up perspective of life, seeing the small things, the details, in a childlike way. Mouse totem's strength is the vulnerability that is necessary for opening the heart. Things will come to the Mouse because it is small and without dangerous defenses.

Wolf (East)
Reconnaissance, forward vision, intelligence, communication, sensitivity

Wolf

Wolves are courageous, intelligent, and ferocious hunters. These facts have been distorted to create intense fear and loathing of wolves in many human societies. Wolves don't look for trouble with people and are not running about pulling down vast numbers of deer, cattle, sheep, moose, or other large mammals, as claimed.

Wolves live in open country and forests, hunting by day and resting at night in rocky areas, under fallen trees, or in holes in the ground. They sometimes hunt alone or in pairs but more often will range in family groups or larger packs. Wolves have great endurance and can run all night if necessary. There is evidence of a wolf traveling 125 miles in two weeks, covering four mountain ranges. Wolves need lots of space. They are good swimmers, too.

Most of their diet is mice, rabbits, and squirrels, though packs will sometimes bring down caribou, musk oxen, deer, and horses. There are intricate cooperative maneuvers used by wolves in hunting large prey. Wolves mate for life, and both parents teach the young to hunt and forage. Wolf packs have complex systems of social order and communication, which incorporate scent, posture, vocalization, and behavioral signals.

Comments: The Wolf totem has traditionally been used by only the best warriors in a tribe. Its powers of hunting and pathfinding are legendary. The Wolf totem helps us find our way through the world using uncanny sight to follow the right trail. The Wolf is protector and faithful companion but is no tame pet. Wolf medicine is fierce, tempered with keen intelligence, great emotional sensitivity, and a sense of appropriate place in the group.

Badger (South)
Fierce courage, self-sufficiency, tenacity

Badgers are nocturnal, often staying inside the burrow, or sett, even on nights of bright moonlight. Badgers are especially clean animals, frequently changing their bedding and building latrines twenty or so yards away from their setts.

Badgers probably mate for life. They are carnivores with strong teeth and claws, but they eat a wide variety of food, from earthworms, wasps, snails, and frogs to mice, moles, bulbs, berries, fungi, and grass.

Badgers can dig rapidly, which helps for making burrows and for going after rabbits and other rodents.

Their only enemy is humankind, since they are extremely fierce when pestered, though not aggressive otherwise. Their reaction to danger is to make a violent snorting noise, then make all their hairs stand up, making them look twice their normal size. It is an impressive display even to larger animals. Nobody badgers the badger.

Badger

Comments: Badger medicine works best for people at home in the dark. It is more a protective than a hunting medicine and is a good aid for loners. Along with a totem bag, use face painting or a mask—marked with the strong black-and-white striping that is so predominant on the Badger's face—to amplify the Badgerness of the medicine. It is good for use in situations where it is important not to be backed down.

Boar (South)
Strength, power, speed, ferocity

European wild boars were brought to this country for hunting purposes. Domestic pigs were bred from the European boars and Chinese wild pigs that were imported to this continent. Many wild boars that are running around these days are actually feral pigs that escaped from barnyards and reverted, over generations, to being boarish.

Boars have foot-long curved tusks that they use for digging up the roots they

Boar

like to eat. These tusks also make formidable weapons. The strength and speed of boars should not be underestimated.

These beasts spend their days lying in thickets and feed in the open at night. They are mainly solitary by nature.

Comments: The Boar totem is fierce and aggressive if disturbed. It is not a totem for nice people. It is, however, an intelligent and canny ally, often found around warrior types and backwoods loners. The Boar minds its own business but won't brook being harried.

Coyote (South)
Trickster, creator, survivor, fool, teacher

Despite being heavily hunted year after year, the coyotes are still with us in large numbers and over wide-ranging territories. Coyotes have a knack for survival, which lies in their legendary sense of wariness and in their gift for adaptation.

Coyotes are blamed for many livestock kills, while the facts are that most of these animals die of other causes. Then coyotes feed on their carcasses and are blamed for the deaths. Such is the life of the opportunist.

Coyotes feed mainly on rabbits, mice, moles, and other small rodents, though with the huge reduction in the wolf population, coyotes have begun to fill that ecological vacuum by preying on larger animals. They also eat vegetable matter, insects, and fish—in other words, whatever is available. It's been said that they are particularly enamored of watermelons.

Coyote

Coyotes hunt alone or in pairs, lacking the pack social system of wolves. They usually live in burrows that once belonged to woodchucks or foxes, and they mate for life.

Coyotes like to sing together. Two or three coyotes might get together each evening to have a good howl session.

Comments: The Coyote totem is the great Heyoka teacher in many traditions. In Coyote are all the so-called paradoxes of life; stories show this totem as both wise hero and silly fool. Coyote brings growth, transformation, reaching, testing—lessons we are often reluctant to face. Coyote teaches by humor, by example, by mirroring and reversal. This medicine brings rapid changes and expanded perception, which can be painful to the personal ego. Coyote is purposeful chaos.

Deer (South)
Quickness, magical secrets, purity, grace, life force

North America has several kinds of deer, found in all the regions of the continent. They all have the characteristic speed and lightness that make them so special to watch.

Some kinds of deer live in herds, others in smaller groups or alone. All of them are browsers, eating leaves, bark, shrubs, lichens, nuts, and some grasses.

Deer are heavily hunted by humans, who have killed off most of the deer's natural predators such as bears, wolves, bobcats, pumas, and coyotes.

In autumn the usually timid male deer enter into their breeding season. For many kinds of deer this includes forming "harem" groups with as many females as they can collect. Fawns are born in the spring and are immediately able to walk, which is important for their survival. The young deer are on their own within a year or two of birth.

Comments: The Deer totem helps keep you from harm's way through quickness, acute hearing, and camouflage. The Deer brings secrets of healing and magic to those of pure intention. Deer medicine is graceful and light and carries the fertile power of the forest. This is a good totem to learn to dance; especially effective at sunrise and sunset. The Deer has knowledge and power gained through silent observation rather than force of presence. The Deer's antlers are like psychically sensitive antennae. Deer medicine has a refined beauty. It is a great blessing. Elk, the Thunder Deer of the West, is associated with sexual power.

Deer

Fox (South)
Clan medicine, cunning, secrets, clairaudience, quickness

Foxes are widely found in our world because of their adaptability. Like the coyotes, foxes are considered fair game because of their fondness for poultry. Foxes prefer wooded or brushy areas but will live almost anywhere. They have been known to climb trees—even sleep in them—but are usually found in ground cavities or burrows.

Foxes are nocturnal for the most part. They eat rabbits, rats, mice, voles, squirrels, frogs, snails, and beetles as well as a lot of vegetable matter. They are actually not particularly prone to henhouse raids, being more likely to scavenge than plunder.

Fox pups are cared for by both parents, who feed, play with, and teach the young for the first two months of life.

Foxes use a great variety of calls, including barking and screaming. They are naturally playful beings, often drawing prey to them, deliberately or not, by their wild antics.

Fox

Comments: The Fox has a quick, secretive, unexpected energy. Smaller than Wolf or Coyote, the Fox is good at elusiveness, but the brightness of the fur's color lights up the Fox's aura. Fox totems are good for families living off by themselves, and they are often found near children. Fox is an effective hunter but will run and hide rather than fight an aggressor. Fox will help you make smart decisions and adapt to difficult situations and environments. There is magic in Fox totem's wildness. No fool, Fox misses few details, and this totem's sense of play fits perfectly with goals of prosperity and victory in a way uniquely Foxish.

Porcupine

Porcupine (South)
Defense, sabotage

The main thing that porcupines have going for them is their quills. With protection like that, who needs speed, dexterity, cunning, or quick thinking? Porcupines are slow, cumbersome, armored rodents. They are found throughout most of North America, living mainly in forested areas. They eat bark and other vegetation and are good climbers. Anywhere you find a pile of wood chips and leaves on the ground, look up and you'll probably see a porcupine. They are easy to come up on since they don't move quickly and aren't as vigilant as most animals.

Porcupines have few natural enemies. Bobcats, mountain lions, and fishers prey on them. On the whole, their defensive measures keep most predators at a distance. When threatened, porcupines raise their quills and flail their tails at potential attackers. They don't throw the quills, as is commonly thought, but the quills are so loosely attached that they are easily transferred from the porcupine to the tender nose of the attacker.

Porcupines love salt and will chew on anything salty, including shovel or ax handles, wheelbarrow handles, tractor tires, door sills, and brake lines of cars in areas where the roads are salted in winter.

Comments: Porcupine sets a clear barrier against predation on all levels. It is a defense that does not require any conscious action other than awareness of danger, so it is useful for people who need that kind of automatic protection. They are also a totem that can sabotage the tools of humankind, making them totemic Earth Firsters!

Rabbit

Rabbit (South)
Adaptation, proliferation, moon magic, trickster

Rabbits live in open grasslands or open woodlands in burrows that are often complex systems of bolt holes, stop runs, and emergency exits. Rabbits like the social life of these warrens, being gregarious by nature.

Rabbits are mainly nocturnal and will rest on the bare soil inside their burrows during the day. In the evening they come out to search for food, which is almost exclusively vegetarian, though rabbits will occasionally eat snails or earthworms.

Rabbits are not promiscuous but are polygamous, one buck mating with several does. Each doe has her own territory within the warren. The mother rabbits defend their young using their hind feet against weasels, male rabbits, and other dangers, but otherwise rabbits prefer to use their speed and erratic escape movements to elude predators. Their alarm signal to other rabbits is a thumping on the ground with both hind feet. The chief predators of rabbits are the weasel family, humans, owls, hawks, rats, ravens, gulls, badgers, foxes, dogs, and cats.

Rabbits are normally silent unless terrified, when they will scream. Mother rabbits will sometimes utter low sounds while nursing their young.

Comments: Rabbit is the Cherokee trickster totem. Rabbit is a messenger for the other totems for councils, and it leads the dances. Rabbit medicine gives alert vigilance and is the bringer of light and new life. Rabbit medicine is used for invoking fertility and sexual magic and is strongly responsive to the power of the Moon. Rabbit is both mischief maker and luck bringer.

Raccoon (South)
Ingenuity, fastidiousness, disguise, curiosity

Raccoons are found only in North America, but they range all over the continent. They live mostly on the wooded shores of lakes and streams but have adapted well to suburban neighborhoods, too.

They like to nest in hollow trees close to water and are good climbers. They are nocturnal, hunting for clams, crayfish, turtles, frogs, nuts, fruit, eggs, birds, and vegetables (preferably corn), and denning up in really cold weather. They are often seen rinsing their food before eating it.

Raccoon mothers keep their young with them for a year after birth, teaching them how to find food and keep away from predators, including humans with a fondness for coonskin caps.

Raccoons are known for their quick intelligence and curiosity. They are sometimes made pets of, though their propensity for creating havoc in a household is legendary. These are not animals that are content with lying about and waiting for handouts.

Comments: Raccoon messes with things until it understands or grows bored with them. This is a dexterous and clever totem; it is the totem of the guide on the vision quest who is smart and savvy but keeps anonymity. Raccoon helps but will not readily give answers. It is a clean totem with orderly processes but one that is never really tame or predictable. Raccoon's intelligence is active.

Raccoon

Rat (South)
Survival, tenacity, adaptation, infiltration

Rats and humans are closely bonded in life despite human lack of appreciation of the fact. The biggest enemy of rats is also the rat's finest benefactor, providing food and shelter in abundance. Rats eat almost anything without ill effects and can survive being flushed down toilets, falling from great heights, and being relentlessly hunted by disgusted humans.

Rats will migrate en masse when living conditions become too crowded, chirring and whistling to each other as they travel. When not on the move rats live in family groups that will not tolerate strangers. They inhabit runs that are used regularly as the rats forage for food. Rats are excellent swimmers and inveterate egg stealers.

Rats are prolific breeders but usually live only about a year. They are hunted by cats, weasels, owls, and foxes, though a full-grown rat is no easy prey.

Rat

Comments: Rat medicine is powerful stuff—giving prosperity and survival in the face of stiff resistance. Rat totem is ideal for finding objects and information and for getting past barriers, whether physical or subtle. The Rat totem is street-smart and has a sardonic sense of humor, being nearly immune to hostility.

Wolverine (South)
Raiding, invulnerability, appetite, individuality

Wolverine

Wolverines, forty-four inches and thirty-five pounds of ferocity, are nevertheless scarce these days. Having no natural enemies has not protected them from decimation by hunting and by habitat loss.

This largest member of the weasel family lives mostly in Canada and the northernmost areas of the the United States. They are one of the strongest animals in the world relative to their size and are totally fearless, driving bears and wolves away from food. Left alone, they will live up to sixteen surly years in the forests, bushlands, and tundras of the north.

Wolverines have prodigious appetites owing to their high metabolic rate. They eat rabbits, mice, gophers, rats, birds, eggs, and carrion. Usually they hunt by stealth, but the advent of human trappers altered their routine behavior and turned them into trap raiders. Wolverines became the trapper's bane as they followed trap lines, taking the animals in them, springing and sometimes burying traps, and evading being trapped themselves. To add insult to injury (in the trapper's view), wolverines also became fond of breaking into trapper's cabins, eating everything (including canned goods), making monumental messes, and then spraying a noxious musk onto everything. This spraying is used by the wolverine to keep other animals from eating its kills.

These solitary animals use a home range of hundreds of miles, sleeping in whatever den is available. They are strong; they are good climbers and swimmers. Wolverines walk on the soles of their feet like bears and humans do. Their motto is, If anything can be eaten, it should be eaten.

Comments: This is quite an astonishing totem, when you consider all the things it is good at doing. It is not friendly or sociable though. It is a fierce, strong, hungry, smart, and intimidating spirit who does not respond well to civilization.

Bat (West)
Clairaudience, elusiveness, working between the worlds

Bat

Bats live in a wide variety of places, singly or in colonies that can number into the hundreds. They like drainpipes, caves, hollow trees, and rock crevices; in the colder parts of their range they will hibernate for a short period.

Bats hunt for food in early evening (this varies with different species), flying between six and forty feet above the ground and emitting shrill squeaks as they catch insects on the wing.

Bats rely heavily on echolocation to catch their food, though they aren't blind. They are intelligent animals and have no trouble keying in to human expectations if they live with human companions. Most fearful myths about bats are

TOTEM REFERENCE GUIDE 185

false—they are not dirty, aggressive pests, but neither are they passive when handled, so respect the bat's feisty temper.

Comments: Because Bat totem is neither a ground animal nor a bird, it is unique medicine. Its betweenness is also expressed in its using the twilight times for taking nourishment and doing its work. Bat is helpful for being present but uninvolved with a situation, and for times when you need to be elusive or be receptive to someone else's signal of elusiveness. Bats have sometimes been called the thought forms of sorcerers. Bat medicine boosts psychic hearing and aids in movement between the realms.

Bear (West)
Healing, dreamkeeper, strength, rites of passage

Bears need a lot of room to range; they are big animals with big territorial needs. Their sense of sight is poor, but their senses of smell and hearing are acute. Bears are not normally aggressive, but when provoked, injured, or with cubs they are ferocious.

Brown bears, which include grizzlies and Kodiaks, live singly or in family groups in wild mountainous country as well as forests. They are wanderers, averaging a home radius of more than twenty miles in their search for food, which varies greatly with the individual bear. Some are wholly vegetarian, some eat only meat, but most eat a mixture of plant and animal foods.

Bears usually den up during part of the winter in natural shelters such as large hollow trees or among rocks. Cubs are born during this winter rest and stay with their mothers for at least a year. Bears live for as long as thirty-four years.

Brown bears can kill a bison with a single powerful blow, making bears one of the Earth's strongest creatures. Many species of bear, however, have been hunted to extinction. With the reduction of ranging area, bears such as the grizzly are now on the edge also.

Bear

Comments: The different kinds of Bears have different medicines. Black Bear totem is more playful, less fierce, and more communal. Brown Bear is suited to people who can accommodate that kind of bigness, and Polar Bear is specific for work that requires camouflage, extreme adaptation, solitariness, raw strength, and cunning. Bear is for healing work—Brown Bear is good for this. It is a totem protective of the young, as bears are fierce mothers. Bear, the hibernator, is the dreamer's totem. Call on Bear for help clarifying, remembering, and working with your dreams.

Cat (West)
Hunting, aggressive protection, finding lost objects, independence

The Cat totem encompasses all feline species from domesticated to wild. All cats are basically primal; they are independent whether they live with people or not. Cat expresses joy in movement: the grace and power of primal energy.

Mountain Lion

Tiger

Creek legend tells of Mountain Lion having a giant wheel, which was used for finding lost objects, and the Cherokee consider Panther to be invulnerable. Cat totem is alive with mysterious powers, and its paradoxical ways are epitomized by Cougar's twin virtues of being both a hunter and a healer totem. Cat's dual nature is manifested also through its being related to the sun and the moon. Cat easily crosses the portals between realms and can move in all time simultaneously, so it is a totem of foretelling and divination. Hunting is not always a stalk for food, it can also be hunting for enlightenment or knowledge. Cat is for any type of stalking.

Snow Leopard is the North aspect of Cat; African Lion is in the East; Wildcat carries the South aspect; and Jaguar or Leopard stands in the West. Tiger often guards power places and is lunar. Mountain Lion is solar. All cats are totems of protection, manifested in the form of aggressive defense.

Cats purr too, and the Cat totem can be a comforting companion, especially to those on solitary paths. Cat is a sensual Venusian being.

Domestic cats can help alert you to spirit presences and are good readers of human nature. Cats often like to participate in medicine work, though this involvement often takes the form of a snooze in the center of the altar.

Comments: Because of the number of different kinds of cats, the physical description is generalized and integrated with the discussion of totem aspects.

Dolphin (West)
Communication, intelligence, group mind, telepathy, play

Dolphin

Dolphins, although they are mammals, are as well-suited to their water environment as any fish. Their horizontal flukes move them powerfully and make them capable of killing even sharks if necessary.

Dolphins live in groups, breaking off into small units when food is scarce. They pack together in time of danger and help any injured companions by lifting them to the surface to breathe. Dolphins can stay submerged for as long as fifteen minutes at a time.

Hearing is the keenest sense in dolphins. Their sight is not particularly good, though they do have partially stereoscopic vision, and their sense of smell is almost nonexistent. Dolphins hear very high tones and communicate verbally with a language of grunts, whistles, clicks, and cracks. They eat fish and shrimp.

Baby dolphins are born tail first, their mothers helping them immediately to the surface to breathe. Two midwife dolphins swim on either side to protect the mother and birthing baby from sharks. While the young are growing, the mother is very protective. Dolphins become sexually mature at age five or six.

Comments: The Dolphin totem is one of exceptional consciousness with a great deal to teach us. Dolphin can lead us to an understanding of how to live in harmony with the twin needs of individuality and cooperation. Dolphin carries balance, peace, joy, compassion, love, and power. This is a networking totem often attractive to those working for global changes. Dolphin is freedom within the group context and finds happiness through service and communication.

Fisher (West)
Hermit, swiftness, assurance, timing, frugality, reproductive success

Fishers are almost extinct because of trapping and habitat destruction. They are fifteen-pound members of the weasel clan, having twelve-inch tails and living eight to ten years. Fishers eat fish, rodents, weasels, mink, martins, muskrats, porcupines, birds, frogs, insects, and nuts. They have no natural enemies and are the fastest tree climbers known to humans.

Fishers live on the ground, roaming large areas in search of food and using a different sleeping place each day. The female will mate whenever she can but has the remarkable ability to delay implantation, timing the birth to occur in spring. She has a thirty-five day gestation, which culminates in a litter of three babies. She stays in one den until the babies are weaned and then goes back to roaming.

Fishers live in deep coniferous forests and are nocturnal. They are excellent runners with beautiful fluid movements. Fishers are very effective predators but will never waste food; anything they don't eat at one meal they will stash for later.

Comments: Fisher is a solitary totem from the deep wilds. It has incredible swiftness in climbing after what it needs and doesn't squander what it has obtained—valuable attributes. Combined with unusual reproductive adaptations and a lack of predatory worries, this totem is one with great gifts. It is not adaptable to civilized ways, however, so it is not a totem suitable for most.

Fisher

Manatee (West)
Satisfaction, accord, dreams

Manatees are large sea mammals living in the warm waters of the south Florida coast. They weigh up to two thousand pounds, are thoroughly adapted to water life, and are peaceful vegetarians.

Manatees have valvelike nostrils that close as they feed on aquatic grasses and open when they come up for air every five or six minutes.

They prefer the calm areas of estuaries and lagoons and thus are often injured by motorboat propellers. They are also very sensitive to cold and suffer badly during the occasional plunges in temperature that occur in their area.

When nursing their young, mother manatees will rise to the surface, holding their heads and shoulders out of the water, cradling their nurslings to their breasts with their flippers. Manatees were mistaken by many sailors for mermaids.

Comments: Manatee is gentle but fearless, a totem of group consensus based on common goals, lack of aggression, and inner balance. It is an ocean totem and

Manatee

thus is connected with the world of spirit dreams, especially dreams that drift and move slowly in the fertile part of the subconscious.

River Otter (West)
Freedom, play, confidence, fluid movement, secretiveness

River Otter

Otters, except during the mating season, are usually solitary creatures. They are exceptionally elusive and will disappear into the water with hardly a ripple at any sign of danger. They have an uncanny ability to merge with their environment, whether in water or vegetation, owing to the "boneless" movements of their bodies and the shifting colors of their coats.

Otters are masterful swimmers and don't hibernate in winter. Instead, they catch fish under the ice, with periodic visits to a breathing hole. Their undulating movements, which appear similar to a dolphin's, are fascinating to watch. They take great pleasure in their swimming skills and will slide, dive, and play for hours.

Otters are nomadic, traveling along lakes, rivers, and large streams catching fish, crayfish, mussels, frogs, eels, birds, and small mammals, and eating some vegetation.

Mating takes place in water, year-round; there are usually two or three cubs in a litter, which stay with the mother until she mates again.

Comments: Otter medicine suits the solitary roamer who is deeply entwined with the natural environment, especially the water. Otter gives elusiveness, fluid movement, and camouflage. It is of help passing through fluid media, on any level. Otter aids the individual in search of joyful expression in life and promotes a harmony between pure play and skillful provision.

Seal (West)
Individual provision, water adaptation

Seal

Seals spend most of their lives in water, but they haul up onto beaches to rest, breed, and bear young. Seals eat mostly fish but also catch squid and krill. They can dive deeply in their pursuit of food.

Bull seals during breeding season claim territorial areas on beaches and try to gather females to mate with. It is a difficult task, requiring them to patrol their little kingdoms and herd females into their boundaries as well as to scuffle with other males.

Orcas are the main predators of seals, besides humans (more people have seen seal coats than have seen live seals.) If undisturbed, seals live about thirty years, though they don't breed past their twentieth year.

Cumbersome looking on land, seals move with quick, strong grace through the water, their fur and blubber making them comfortable and healthy in even the coldest climates.

Comments: Seal carries its own abundance, storing in the body what is needed for a good life. Their medicine is for moving through difficult relationships—the cold water times. Seal helps us in learning skills, especially those things that require quickness of reflex.

Skunk (West)
Keeper of the scent, repelling danger, balance

The bold black-and-white fur pattern on skunks warns all would-be predators that this beast is not to be messed with. Skunks live in woods, on plains, and in deserts, in burrows where they lie up during the day and come out to forage during the night. Skunks in the northern regions sleep a great deal during the winter. Occasionally several skunks will den together.

Skunk

Insects, mice, frogs, eggs, birds, and crayfish are the staples of the skunk's diet. Some skunks eat snakes—hog-nosed and spotted skunks are thought to be resistant to the venom of pit vipers and rattlesnakes respectively.

Skunks are generally left alone by predators, though pumas and bobcats will occasionally make meals of them. The great horned owl is the only reliable preyer upon skunks. Cars often run over skunks, who stand their ground and spray at the cars as though the automobile were simply a large animal.

When attacked, skunks lower their heads, raise their tails, and stamp a warning with their front paws. If that fails to get the point across, the skunk turns and sprays a noxious fluid from glands at the anus, with remarkable accuracy up to twelve feet. If the fluid touches the eyes, it can cause temporary blindness, though some may assert that the clinging smell is more to be feared than the loss of sight.

Comments: Skunk totem keeps you from being bothered and penalizes those who invade your space against your wishes. Of all the senses, the sense of smell is the most closely tied to the unconscious, making Skunk a direct gateway to the deeper realms of the psyche. The distinctive black-and-white striping holds the polar opposites, promoting balance and wholeness.

Weasel (West)
Guide to the underworld, hunter, fearlessness

Weasels hunt mainly by scent, and with their snakelike bodies are swift and agile predators. They are good climbers and swimmers. They pounce on their prey, usually killing with a bite on the back of the head. Weasels hunt alone, in pairs, or in family groups.

Weasel

Weasels occupy territories, living in all kinds of terrain and marking their areas with scent. They are exceedingly courageous and will attack animals much larger than themselves. In winter, in the colder parts of their range, weasels undergo a color change to white.

Weasels don't like eating carrion, preferring to hunt small rodents, birds, fish, and eggs. In turn, weasels are sought by owls, foxes, cats, large hawks, and humans. It is unfortunate that farmers don't realize that each weasel can kill at least five hundred small rodents a year, something most would consider a boon.

Despite their cunning and hunting prowess, weasels have a life span of only about six years.

Comments: Weasel is often used by shamans as a guide to the underworld realms. Weasel's primal energy and fierce courage make it a formidable ally. It is said that a weasel can pass through a wedding ring, and indeed its skull is small enough to allow it access through narrow cracks, a fact that adds to the stalking and infiltrating powers of this totem. Weasel is not always an easy totem to work with, but it is a valuable ally for the experienced shaman.

Whale (West)
Love, immensity, depth, collective memory, communion

Whales are of many different kinds, though they are grouped simply in two categories—toothed and baleen. The toothed whales include the orcas, which eat seals, but the other toothed whales eat fish; baleen whales are filter-feeders, eating plankton and other microscopic creatures.

Whales are the largest mammals on the planet. They travel all the oceans, following the feeding grounds, periodically surfacing to blow out warm moist air through their blowholes.

Whales communicate in various whale languages, in snorts, clicks, whistles, wails, and indescribable songs. The humpback whales are the virtuosos of song in the whale world; the beauty of their haunting melodies is unlike anything else.

These huge creatures have been hunted relentlessly for their blubber and bone. Despite all the activist gains in banning whaling it still continues, often in the guise of scientific research. Whales, with their calm intelligence, must wonder when the madness will end.

Comments: Whale totem holds a vastness of knowing, feeling, and remembering. It is a totem of unconditional love and of communication. Whale holds the keys to the deep subconscious and to ancestral spiritual memories. With the whale you learn equanimity of the soul.

Whale

Beaver (North)
Building, plans, industriousness, lodgekeeping

Beavers, the second largest member of the rodent family, live in the northern parts of America, though in far smaller numbers than previously. They have been trapped remorselessly for their fur.

Beavers live in loose colonies, each made up of up to twelve members. The parents mate for life. They live either in burrows along the bank or in lodges in ponds that have been created by the beavers' damming of streams.

Beaver

The engineering of these lodges and dams is ingenious, and beavers are very interesting animals to observe. They eat bark and sapwood, and the beaver ponds are rich habitats for birds, plants, fish, and other creatures.

Beavers rely on escape and hiding for protection from predators; they use their teeth and claws for building activities rather than for fighting.

Beavers live up to twenty years, and the young stay with the parents for two years, learning the ins and outs of beaverness.

Comments: Beaver is a perfect example of a way of living that intrinsically enriches the environment at the same time that it benefits the individual or tribe. Beaver totem helps with long-range plans and changes that build security in positive ways. It is a good family totem, especially for the choices of monogamy and raising children. It is a builder's totem also, with strong and wise engineering of structures and backup systems. Beaver will also warn of approaching danger in no uncertain terms. A lawyer friend uses Beaver medicine to make strong court cases on behalf of battered women and abused children.

Buffalo (North)
Strength, prosperity, power, provision,
steady progress, renewal

Buffalo

The two North American buffalos, the prairie bison and the mountain bison, roamed in vast numbers before the coming of the whites to the West. Living in herds, they foraged their way across the plains, digging for grasses under the snow with their sharp hooves in winter and calving in spring.

Buffalos provided the western tribes with almost all their needs—food, shelter, clothing, tools, and utensils—and were greatly honored for their giveaway. No part of a killed buffalo went to waste, and buffalo were never killed for idle sport. Some fifty million buffalo once lived on this continent, but they were carelessly hunted by the whites to near extinction within an incredibly short span of time.

Bison feed mainly on grass and make seasonal migrations of hundreds of miles to find feeding grounds.

The females leave the herd to drop their calves, but the whole herd helps defend the babies, whose main danger is from wolves. The calves stay with the mother for three years, at which time they become sexually mature.

Comments: The strength of Buffalo totem comes from its purity of purpose. Buffalo is the spirit keeper of the North and represents all the North qualities. Buffalo's power is steady movement toward a positive goal rather than impulsive, erratic, or confused action. Buffalo shields the vision seeker and brings the spring; it brings renewal and abundance to the people. Buffalo is prosperity and practical gifts to those who put good heart into the mundane efforts of livelihood and understand the importance of the giveaway in keeping the circle powerful. Spiritual purity and care for the people are Buffalo's medicines.

Dog

Dog (North)
Friend, urban scout, companion, watchful protector

Dogs were probably the first domesticated animals. The wild ancestors of today's dog are extinct. Dogs come in an array of sizes, colors, coats, and behaviors, but their role in modern life is mainly as companions to people.

Dogs enjoy their relationship with us, for the most part, and bring youthful enthusiasm, devotion, and intensity to our lives. With all domestication, juvenile characteristics tend to be retained in the adults.

Dogs are promiscuous breeders. The pups are born blind and deaf and remain so for the first week to ten days. The babies are weaned at four to six weeks, making for a short dependency period on the mother.

Dogs are not solitary by nature and will readily attach themselves to their human companions; they get lonely if left on their own.

Dogs are generally classified by groups: sporting dogs, hounds, working dogs, terriers, toy dogs, and nonsporting dogs (bad sports?). Dogs have also been used in war and, more positively, as guides for the blind.

Comments: Dog will often appear in physical form in one's life, this being easy in our society. Dog totem helps the town or city dweller to find a safe path in the urban environment. For the urbanite, dogs and other companions can be an important daily link with the natural web. Dog is a protector in some instances, keeping watch and warning of danger. It is a sociable totem and a faithful one. Dog's qualities of playfulness, endurance, keen senses, willingness to participate, and acceptance make it a totem that is called upon often.

Horse

Horse (North)
Speed, endurance, travel, vision powers, wealth

Horses, domesticated more than four thousand years ago, still have no trouble surviving when returned to their natural wild state. Unfortunately, there is little wilderness left for them to roam in—cows have replaced them on public lands.

Horses like to live in herds, which usually consist of a group of mares, their young, and an adult male. Horses live twenty to forty years, the record age being sixty-two.

Domestication of horses has made changes in human society. They were and are status symbols; they have been used for transport, war, and as work animals. The many breeds of horses each have unique characteristics that lend themselves to specific uses. Looking at modern horses, it is hard to believe that their ancestors were the size of rabbits.

The coming of horses to the Plains Natives radically improved their lives. There are few riders on this continent who match the grace, ferocity, and skill of those Native equestrians.

Comments: Horse totem is hard to sneak up on and will leave pursuers in the dust. The strength, speed, and peripheral vision of Horse are valuable medicine powers. Horse is also adept at adjusting to changes in environment and situation. Horse is a vision totem with a high degree of psychic empathy. Horse dreams are good vehicles for travel in the spirit realms, and a Horse ridden into conflict during trance states will help keep you safe and victorious.

Mole (North)
Steals hearts, sensitive to subsurface

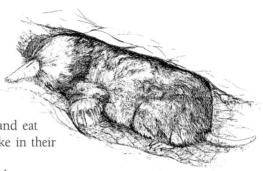

Moles are masterful tunnelers. They can dig a foot deep in three minutes or a hundred yards in one night. Their wedge-shaped heads and enlarged forelegs with long, broad nails are ideal for moving soft earth.

Moles catch insects, worms, and small animals in their tunnels and eat them. People don't like the earth ridges and mounds that moles make in their yards, so they often kill the moles despite their insect-eating habits.

The ears of moles are small, and moles don't see very well, but they are remarkably sensitive to sound vibrations in the ground and very sensitive to touch on their noses and tails.

Mole

Comments: This totem concentrates on the realm of experience that runs just beneath the surface of things. Information from this area can be very helpful. Moles steal the hearts of those who try to hoard or withhold love, teaching emotional generosity and the joys of giving love to others.

Opossum (North)
New life cloaked in death, rapid growth cloaked in rest

Opossums are the only marsupials living outside of Australia. Their resilient survival in the face of competition from placental mammals may be partly a result of humans, hunting off the opossum's main predators.

Opossums live in wooded areas, where they forage on the ground for insects, voles, snakes, mice, plants, and small birds. They do not hibernate in winter but remain inactive during long periods of cold weather.

The tiny baby opossums, when born, crawl into the mother's pouch, where they remain for ten weeks. Then they huddle in a nest or ride on the mother's back until they are about fourteen weeks old.

When frightened or attacked, opossums, if they can't escape, will play dead, suddenly going limp, with their tongue lolling out and their eyes shut. Animals that do not eat carrion consider this disgusting enough that they will go off, leaving the opossums to gradually come back to life. Electroencephalograph recordings show that the opossums are not in trance or catalepsy during this behavior but are fully awake and alert.

Oppossum

Comments: Opossum totem brings medicine of renewal and information about changes. In situations where things seem stagnant or stalled, consult Opossum for truth about what is going on. Opossum is good in situations where you are left hanging; it brings hope and resurrection to stale relationships. Opossum also teaches lying low and quiet when you're not sure about what to do. The medicine of the female Opossum has the additional power of caring diligently for early-born vulnerable projects or babies.

Prairie Dog

Prairie Dog (North)
Sociability, community, activity

Prairie dogs are a kind of ground squirrel whose barking gives them the dog appellation. They are the size of small woodchucks and live in holes in towns that can stretch for miles. One unusual example is a town that was 250 miles wide by 100 miles long, containing four hundred million prairie dogs! These critters like companionship.

Prairie dogs are bright and active during the day, visiting each other, digging holes, and foraging for grasshoppers, roots, grass, and other vegetation. They are preyed upon by eagles, badgers, coyotes, and other carnivores. In danger they run to their holes, stand on their hind legs beside the burrows until the last second, then pop inside.

Comments: The emphasis of this totem is on conversation, sociability, and town life. They are not idle gossipers though; they are engaged in useful activity. Prairie Dog is a totem with news to tell, and though small, this totem will not cower or cringe in the face of danger—it is a spirited, last-word totem.

Squirrel

Squirrel (North)
Gathering provisions, sports, escape, interrelationships

Squirrels are found around human habitation often, so they are easy to observe in their busy daily routines. Tree squirrels forage on the ground mainly but use trees for nesting and escape. The grey squirrel is especially acrobatic. All the squirrels are great climbers and jumpers, using their wonderful tails for balance and steering.

Squirrels are primarily vegetarian, eating nuts, berries, buds, fungi, and fruits, but they will also steal birds' eggs and feed on nestlings and carrion. Traditional hoarders, they bury nuts, acorns, and berries in shallow holes for later retrieval. Squirrel incisors grow continually and quickly, being worn down with the heavy chewing.

When squirrels are disturbed they scold and hide in trees, peering down at intruders in an irate manner. Natural predators of squirrels are hawks, owls, snakes, foxes, bobcats, and pine martens.

Comments: Squirrel is a totem of husbandry and provision. Squirrel becomes an indirect instrument in spreading the seeds of spirit and nature. Squirrel is a great talker with boundless energy; it can leap from place to place almost instantly—an escape artist. Use this totem for developing conversational skills and for making rapid assessments. Squirrel is especially helpful to those living in harsh climates, where storing and gathering provisions is essential to survival.

Woodchuck (North)
Guardian of crystal magic, weather foreteller

Woodchuck

Woodchucks like to make their compartmented burrows at the wooded edges of meadows; waste is regularly removed and buried outside the burrows. Woodchucks seldom wander far from home. They hibernate in winter, waking in spring hungry for grass, flowers, fruits, and the like.

These animals are diurnal, feeding in the morning and late afternoon. They can swim well and, unlike most big members of the rodent family, will also climb trees in search of food.

Woodchucks feed many predators, including bears, coyotes, wolves, eagles, hawks, dogs, mountain lions, and people. Woodchucks are alert for danger and will usually bolt for their burrows when threatened. Occasionally a woodchuck will stand its ground and fight.

Legend has it that if the woodchuck (groundhog) emerges from the burrow on February second and sees its shadow, it will return to sleep for another six weeks. If no shadow is seen that means winter is over.

Comments: Woodchuck with its underground dwelling and long hibernation period is a keeper of Earth secrets, especially those of quartz crystals. This totem stays close to home, alert for danger and protective of its young. It is a good householder's totem for keeping a clean orderly home and is very grounding for those with airy tendencies.

REPTILES

Alligator
Swamp medicine, deceptive speed, concealment of power

Alligators, whose name comes from the mispronunciation of *el largato* (the lizard), are long-lived reptiles who spend most of their time basking on sunny riverbanks in the southeastern United States.

With intense hunting of these creatures for their skins, the average size of alligators has dropped, and the record measurement of nineteen feet will probably not be seen again.

Young alligators feed on insects and freshwater shrimp, and as they grow older they eat frogs, fish, and snakes. Mature alligators live mainly on fish but will also catch small mammals and birds. Really big 'gators have been known to pull deer and cows into the water and drown them.

During breeding season the males roar and quarrel a lot and the females take an active role in courtship and territorial defense. Alligator eggs are laid in a large nest mound made of rotting vegetation, and when the babies are hatching, the mother often assists their emergence. At all their early stages of growth the young alligators are preyed upon by birds, fish, and mammals, as well as larger alligators.

Comments: The Gator totem is not just an awesome predatory power but also a totem of creation—the alligator makes lagoon habitats with the thrashing of its body, which are then homes for many other creatures. Alligator is not aggressive unless disturbed or looking for food. This totem, despite its large size, can travel in the water almost invisibly, can sit still for long periods, and can move with great speed when necessary.

Lizard
Divination, prophecy

Lizards are found mainly in the warm areas of the world. There are more than twenty-five hundred species, grouped in about twenty families. Nine of those families are found in America, accounting for approximately ninety species.

Lizards are scaly, four-footed, five-toed creatures with movable eyelids. They have ear openings on the sides of their heads. Most lay eggs, although a few bear their young alive.

They eat insects, plants, and larvae, catching their meals by virtue of being very fast when they move and very still when they don't. Other than the Gila monster, North American lizards are not poisonous.

Comments: Lizard is a totem for conjuring and learning secrets. It knows a lot but doesn't usually volunteer this information without being asked in the right way. Lizard is a survivor of adverse conditions in the wilds but doesn't tolerate life in captivity well. Lizard is good at future-telling and often speaks in riddles.

Snake
Fertility, wisdom, healing, knowledge, kundalini

Snakes evoke strong reactions in most people, though most snakes are non-poisonous and beneficial to human endeavors. Even the thirty-six species of North American snakes that produce poison are not aggressive under ordinary conditions.

Snakes lack limbs, ear openings, and movable eyelids. They are scaled. The lower jaws on snakes move separately, enabling them to swallow large prey. Their teeth are small and hooked; their tongues work as sensing devices. The whole body of a snake picks up vibrations from the ground, telling it when something is on the move around it.

Snakes eat rodents, insects, frogs, and worms. Some see quite well at night, and some catch prey in the water. After eating, snakes spend a lot of time lying around digesting their meals. They don't eat carrion. Some snakes need to eat only twice a year!

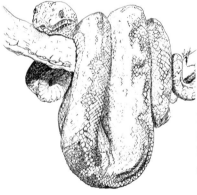

Snake

Like lizards, most snakes lay eggs, but a few kinds give birth to live young. The parents do not give the babies any care, but the young grow quickly and are full-grown within two to three years. They shed their skin at least once a year.

Comments: Rattlesnake is associated with the Thunder Beings and rain medicine. Blacksnake is a rain bringer too, and a totem of seeking and climbing. Copperhead is a snake of transformation, and King Snake is a defense against all types of poison. Snakes are traditionally the totems of healers and wise folk.

Turtle
Home, stability, focus, the Earth we live on

Turtles are many in variety, but all are known for carrying their homes upon their backs. They are very ancient in design, as are many reptiles, which first appeared some two hundred million years ago.

Turtle

Turtle bodies have not changed much through all those years. The top shell is formed from widened ribs, and the legs are attached within the ribs. Turtles don't have teeth, but their tough bills can rip into plants or animal food. Turtles feed mainly on fish, insects, grubs, and plants.

In the north, turtles hibernate under soil or mud and females lay eggs that are hatched in due time by the warming of the sun.

There are seven families of turtles, one of which is the land tortoise, the only true tortoise. Sea turtles have had a hard time despite their inherent longevity because of human predation for their shells and meat.

Comments: Turtle Island is what the Natives call North America, and stories about Turtle are many. This totem stays steady for the long haul and does not act on impulse. Turtle carries us to safety and gives us a place to stand. If you see a turtle trying to cross a highway, take a moment to help it over. Turtle has been here a long, long time and should be honored. Meditate on Turtle for stability and grounding.

AMPHIBIANS

Frog

Amphibians are animals that spend at least part of their lives in water. They are different from reptiles in not having scales or clawed feet. Amphibians lay jellylike eggs in clumps or strings, which hatch into larvae or tadpoles that live in the water. As adults, amphibians live mainly on insect diets and return to the water to mate and lay eggs. In the colder areas they hibernate.

Comments: Frog is of the West. It is keeper of the medicine waters. Frog is weather magic. Tree Frog is the voice of cheer and gratitude for spring—sort of an amphibious chickadee. Salamander is a dream totem of the deep mind. Salamander's messages are often inscrutable and usually have to do with spiritual group matters.

FISH

Fish

In general, fish have to do with moving through fluid realms, with intuition, dreams, primal memories. A few of the many Fish totems:

Bass.   Participation, scrappiness, parenting skills

Catfish.   Creation of positivity and prosperity from raw materials

Salmon.   Cycles, abundance, mysticism, spiritual strength, purposeful surrender

Sturgeon.   Patience, wisdom, endurance, depth

Trout.   Purity, aspiration, elusiveness, spirit world

OTHER SMALL CRITTERS

Snail

Crab.   Protection at sea, oblique energy

Long-legged spider.   Master of illusion

Scorpion.   Predatory skill, aggression

Shrimp.   Supply, abundance

Snail.   Keeper of the life path

Spider.   Web builder, creator of environment, hunter

INSECTS

Ant

Butterfly

Insects are everywhere and have been here a long, long time. They live varied and fascinating existences, come in fantastical colors and configurations, and have much to teach us about survival, adaptation, and life cycles.

Insects are related to lobsters and crabs owing to skeletal similarities. Their bodies are in three parts: head, thorax, and abdomen. Most have six legs. Many insects also have wings. Some insects have two sets of jaws, two kinds of eyes, and one pair of antennae. Spiders are insect relatives, as are centipedes and millipedes. More than nine hundred thousand species of insects have been named, though some say this is only 10 percent of the insects in the world! Too often we ignore or demean these planetary companions who may out-survive us by a long shot.

Ant.   Builder of bridges between the worlds, totem of Earth magic

Beetle.   Creation and exploration

Butterfly.   Spiritual progress and enlightenment, blessings, transformation

Cicada.   Renewal

Cricket.   Joy in being, weather changes, household luck

Dragonfly.   Fire energy, seeing through the dimensions, messenger

Firefly.   Light-bringer, soul messages

Grasshopper.   Community matters, jumping ahead

June bug.   Cyclic changes

Katydid.   Warning, news

Moth.   Spiritual realization and attraction

Roach.   Urban survival

Scarab.   Ancient power and good fortune

Termite.   Breakdown of institutional structures

Woolly bear.   Weather prediction

Dragonfly

Bee
Love, heart sustenance, cooperation

Honeybees live in colonies in human-built hives or wild in hollow trees. They differ from many other bees by being able to live through winters on their stored food. A typical strong colony will have a queen, fifty thousand to sixty thousand workers, and a few hundred males (drones).

Honeybees collect nectar, pollen, and resin from plants and in the process do the invaluable service of pollinating many plant and tree species.

The worker bees are guided by scent and sight to the flowers, keeping track of their whereabouts by solar angles, polarized light, and a time sense that enables them to make compensations for the movement of the sun.

Bee

Queens stay in the hive, mating with the drones and laying as many as fifteen hundred eggs a day—a prodigious task.

Workers communicate where nectar is to be found by dancing. Their bodies are specialized for the work they do. Honeybees are not interested in stinging unless severely disturbed; the sting is usually fatal to the bee, who has better things to do than seek suicide.

Bees are eaten by birds, dragonflies, and some moths, but their greatest danger is from disease and starvation in this age of chemical agricultural sprays and general pollution.

Comments: Honeybee carries sweetness to those in need of love. Its work is large-scale fertilization of the life-sustaining beauty of the planet. Sit beside a field of blossoming clover and listen to the humming mantra of love's fertility. Next time Honeybee comes to you, regard it as a valentine. Bumblebee is a totem of vibratory sensitivities, particularly for use in literally feeling out the energy of a place through chakra centers in the hands. Bumblebee increases the ability to tune in to different energy levels.

PLANTS

Alfalfa (Medicago sativa)
buffalo herb
North/Venus: Prosperity

Alfalfa is a plant rich in nutrients. Its roots go very deep into the Earth. It is a gentle diuretic and a mild beverage tea good for improving the appetite.

Comments: This is a money totem with powers to keep away hunger and bring prosperity.

Aloe (Aloe vera)
burn plant
West/Moon: Protection

Aloe is the herb for first-aid treatment of burns, including sunburns. It is sometimes used internally as a purgative or for ulcers, though for these it should be combined with buffering herbs.

Comments: Aloe is hung over doorways for protection and planted on graves for peaceful passage.

Angelica (Angelica archangelica)
archangel, masterwort
East/Sun: Exorcism, protection

A valuable herb for preventing infection—angelica is burned in sickrooms to guard against contagion. Used by midwives to expel placentas, it is also a good lung strengthener. Not to be used by diabetics or those with high blood pressure.

Comments: Angelica is a protector, especially against evil intentions. It not only wards off negativity but also attracts goodness to the aura. Its qualities are of understanding of inner realms, visions, and wisdom. It is often connected with Atlantis or the archangel Michael. It is smoked, burned as incense, carried, or placed about the house; it is a stately totem.

Anise (Pimpinella anisum)
aniseed
East/Jupiter: Youthfulness, purification

Anise seeds are an excellent decongestant and also good for expelling gas and calming the stomach. They promote lactation and soothe colic.

Comments: Anise is used to preserve youthfulness and for gentle dreams. It is a good companion to the astral realm and helps those in search of happiness. Anise combines well with amber, and star anise is especially appropriate for psychic work.

Apple (Pyrus spp.)
West/Venus: Love, immortality

Apples treat diarrhea and rheumatism.

Comments: Cut an apple in half crosswise, and the seeds make a star pattern. Apple is the sacred tree of immortality and the symbol of love. Its wood is used for wands, and it is associated with unicorns.

Ash (Fraxinus americana)
South/Sun: Prosperity, sea magic

Ash is the Druidic world tree, the Celtic equivalent of the medicine wheel, encompassing all realms. Protective, especially for sailors, it is not a tree to stand under during electrical storms.

Balm (Melissa officinalis)
lemon balm, sweet balm, sweet melissa
West/Moon: Love, healing, success

Lemon balm is for nervous problems, cramps, and insomnia. It is often put in baths or sleep pillows. It is given for mild fevers, too, being diaphoretic.

Comments: Balm attracts love as sweet flowers attract bees. It is a healing totem and is used for ensuring success. It strengthens the solar plexus.

Basil (Ocimum basilicum)
sweet basil
South/Mars: Love, flying, protection, courage

Basil is widely used in cooking. Its medicinal value is mainly associated with the stomach. It is soothing to headaches and is sometimes put into remedies for whooping cough.

Comments: Basil protects from fears, especially those relating to initiation and spiritual growth. It promotes courage and is connected with dragons. Basil is for love divination and attracting right relationships. It is both a fertility and a fidelity totem; it is a bringer of prosperity (dragon's hoard?).

Bayberry (Myrica cerifa)
candleberry, wax myrtle
West/Venus: Love, fertility, youth, prosperity

This herb is a good gargle for sore throats and a stomach healer. It is always used in small doses and is for treating dysentery and diarrhea.

Comments: Bayberry preserves youthfulness in love and spirit. Bayberry candles are used for attracting money.

Beech (Fagus sylvatica)
East/Saturn: Creativity, companionship, peace

Beech, with its smooth gray bark, is a fine tree to sit in. Upon its kind branches the Muse will perch, bringing creative energies along peaceful channels. Beech has a grace and modesty of spirit yet is strong and enduring.

Belladonna (Atropa belladonna)
banewort, deadly nightshade, witch's berry
West/Saturn: Astral projection, visions

This plant is highly toxic and is not to be used in its physical form. It is a valuable homeopathy remedy for nervous system disorders and for pain.

Comments: Belladonna is a powerful companion in the psychic realms, bringing visions and journeys. It must be approached with caution and respect.

Birch (Betula alba)
North/Venus: Healing, protection, enlightenment, beauty, purification

Birch leaves are used for gallstones, kidney stones, and for skin problems. An oil of infused birch leaves makes a good rub for sore muscles.

Comments: Birch, the lady of the woods, is an elegant totem known for qualities of cleansing and protection. Cradles were often made of this lovely strong wood. Meditation beside a birch will attune you to woodland spirits. Its bark is sometimes used for magical writings or for kindling sweat lodge fires.

Blessed Thistle (Carduus benedictus)
West/Mars: Protection, invocation

This herb is a strong emetic, so it is avoided in large doses. It is for inducing vomiting of toxic substances; in small doses it will stimulate appetite after a period of illness. It also promotes milk production after birth.

Comments: Blessed thistle has long association with the god Pan and is used to invoke him or related aspects. It is a spiritual protector, especially for mothers, and helps bring dreams into manifestation in positive ways.

Borage (Borago officinalis)
bugloss
West/Jupiter: Courage, gladness, psychic powers

Borage is for lactation and restores vitality. It is calmative and anti-inflammatory and a good addition to baths for sore muscles.

Comments: Borage is for courage and was traditionally worn in the shoes of travelers. It brings joy and cheer during difficult times. It promotes psychic abilities when used as a tea, smoke, or amulet for that purpose. The sight of its blue, star-like flower is gladdening to the spirit.

Burdock (Arctium lappa)
burrseed, cocklebur, great burdock
West/Venus: Protection, healing, perseverance

The root is used to neutralize and eliminate toxins. The leaves are applied fresh to poison ivy or poison oak; they are taken internally for liver problems. Burdock root is a blood nourisher, kidney tonic, skin healer, and jaundice remedy.

Comments: Burdock teaches about hanging in when things get tough and guards against negativity. It is an ally for keeping track of where someone is going.

Cactus (Cactaceae)

Cacti are ancient allies of the shaman. They are very protective in the defensive sense, warding off aggression. Some cacti, such as peyote, are central totems to tribal cultures and should be approached with knowledge and respect for those traditions and relationships.

Catnip (Nepeta cataria)
catmint
West/Venus: Cat magic, love, beauty

Catnip is a wonderful children's herb, soothing colic, upset stomachs, and nerves. Good for fevers, headaches, and menstrual cramps also.

Comments: Catnip links the Cat totem, the plant world, and the human. A friendship and love totem, drawing love, beauty, joy. For shape-shifting and night prowls.

Cedar (Thuja occidentalis)
South/Sun: Purification, offering, protection, new life

Cedar is used as a smudge herb to clear negativity and to call in blessings. Cedar oil is used to anoint people and ceremonial tools. Cedar is old, wise, strong.

Chamomile (Anthemis nobilis or Matricaria chamomilla)
ground apple
East/Sun: Prosperity, sleep, purification

This herb has many uses—for cramps, stomach ills, flatulence, nerves, and pain. Externally, it is a wash for wounds or an oil for swellings. It is a mild tea, appropriate for colic or for intestinal ulcers in adults.

Comments: Chamomile is the gambler's ally: it attracts money and luck. It is a healing totem, with the Sun's beneficent blessings of health and success.

Cherry (Prunus avium)
West/Venus: Divination, menstrual ceremonies

Cherry is a lovely, sweet totem associated with love and divinations of love. It is used in conjunction with puberty rituals for girls.

Chicory (Cichorium intybus)
succory, wild succory
East/Sun: Invisibility, psychic awakening, removing obstacles

Used medicinally for jaundice, spleen illness, and the glandular aspects of digestion. Applied externally for inflammations.

Comments: The beautiful blue chicory flowers are used for opening the third eye. It is a totem of invisibility and is carried to clear the path of obstacles. This totem requires pure intention and can be a potent ally.

Cinquefoil (Potentilla anserina)
silverweed, five fingers
South/Jupiter: Prophetic dreams, flying, protection

A fever herb useful during flu bouts. Treats skin problems and bacterial infections.

Comments: Helps movement through the astral and dream realms. The five petals correspond to love, money, health, power, and wisdom, making it a broad-ranged totem. Used to protect the household or as a wash for exorcising negativity.

Clover (Trifolium spp.)
shamrock, trefoil, trifoil
South/Mercury: Protection, money, love

An herb for clearing the blood and lymph, often used in treating cancer. It is beneficial for the digestive and respiratory systems and is a tasty tea.

Comments: Clover is well known for good luck. It is for consecrating ritual tools, insuring fidelity, and seeing fairies. It is used for all kinds of divination. Sometimes a whimsical totem, in its serious mode it can promote success in all endeavors.

Comfrey (Symphytum official)
knit bone, healing herb, bruisewort
West/Saturn: Safe travel, healing

Comfrey is full of nourishing vitamins, minerals, and protein. One of the greatest of healing herbs, used for respiratory, digestive, and skeletal systems, both internally and externally.

Comments: Guardian to the traveler, a strong and robust totem with powers for regenerative healing. Adversity seems to encourage comfrey.

Corn (Zea mays)
maize, sacred mother, giver of life
South/Venus: Divination, harmony with cycles, life force,
blessings, protection

The Corn Mother is the provider of abundance and fertility. Corn, beans, and squash are the three sacred sisters bringing us our daily sustenance upon the Earth. Blue corn is used to bless and is given as an offering during some ceremonies. Corn hung in the doorway confers luck and protection. Corn pollen is a blessing to any medicine bag or totem pouch. Humbly invoke Corn Mother for growth and bounty.

Daisy (Chrysanthemum leucanthemum)
eye of the day
East/Venus: Love

Daisy is the flower of the fairies and is used for divinations of love. The sight of a field of daisies bobbing in the wind, shining in the sun, makes the heart young and free. The Daisy totem has the eyes of a child.

Damiana (Turnera diffusa or T. aphrodisiaca)
Mexican damiana
South/Mars: Visions, sex magic

Damiana is used medicinally as a female herb and to stimulate sex drive.

Comments: This is a lusty totem used for sex magic and for inducing dreams and visions. It is smoked to increase psychic sensitivity, particularly clairvoyance. It is used as a booster for other workings, as it brings more intense energy to quieter totems. Damiana works well with quartz.

Dandelion (Taraxacum officinal)
lion's tooth, puffball, piss-a-bed
East/Jupiter: Calling spirits, divination, wishes, weather magic

Dandelions are laden with minerals—a good spring tonic or a cure for anemia or jaundice. They tone all the organs and passages of the body and are helpful externally for boils and other skin disorders.

Comments: Dandelion is associated with the Sun as well as Jupiter, so it brings expansive energies to bear. The tea is used to call spirits and develop psychic ability. Dandelion totem is mighty but very benign and playful.

Datura (Datura spp.)
jimsonweed, thorn apple
West/Saturn: Protection, visions, journeying

Datura is a shaman's totem plant. The Mexican variety is stronger than the American, though both are considered poisonous. It is smoked or ingested for shamanic journeying and trancework and is not recommended for use by the layperson.

Elder (Sambucus canadensis)
old lady, pipe tree, eldrum, sweet elder
West/Venus: Exorcism, protection, healing

Elder flowers are excellent for treating fevers, especially children's. They are used externally as a wash for wounds, and taken cold internally, they have diuretic properties. (Black or blue elder and red elder are poisonous.)

Comments: The spirit of the elder, the Elder Mother, is a very powerful being who won't respond kindly to being tampered with without permission. Elder is protection and blessing; it is often used for wand or pipestem making. Spending midsummer's night in an elder grove is a traditional way to see fairies.

Elecampane (Inula helenium)
elfwort, elfdock, wild sunflower
East/Mercury: Psychic power, love, protection

Used for chest congestion, chronic lung problems, and bronchial infections. Externally, elecampane is used for its astringent and antiseptic qualities.

Comments: Elecampane has long been associated with the magic of elves. It is used in rites of initiation, for love sachets, and for divination. It is a vitalizing energy, though it carries the unpredictability of elfish ways.

Eyebright (Euphrasia officinalis)
red eyebright
East/Sun: Psychic vision, joy, wonder, clarity of mind

Eyebright is a remedy for almost all eye ailments, from inflammations to poor sight. It is also used for treating hay fever and lung problems.

Comments: This totem is clear of spirit, full of joy and life. It is used over time as an infusion applied to the eyelids to increase psychic vision. It helps us perceive right direction and to see the truth of situations. Eyebright aids memory and thought. It is used as a fluid condenser for clearing magic mirrors and other scrying devices.

Fennel (Foeniculum vulgare)
sweet fennel, wild fennel
South/Mercury: Healing, purification, strength in adversity

Fennel is an aromatic herb. It is helpful for digestion, cramps in the stomach or bowel, or mucous congestion. It is also a promoter of lactation.

Comments: Fennel's energy is one of warding off unhappiness and facing down fears. It purifies on a deep level of the spirit, making it possible for one to digest life's lessons and to live long and courageously.

Fern (Filicineae)
East/Mercury: Invisibility, rainmaking, youth

Ferns, in their many varieties, are used in the spore form for invisibility or for being unnoticed in your movements through the world. They are associated with Puck and the fairies, with divination, luck, and protection. They can be burned to bring rain. Fern magic is of the deep woods and sandy hillsides, hiding activity beneath their spreading fronds.

Frankincense (Boswellia carterii)
incense, olibans
South/Sun: Protection, invocation, exorcisms, prayer

Frankincense has long been used as a religious incense to purify places for spiritual purposes. It was used by Catholics, Chaldeans, Hebrews, Babylonians, and Egyptians, among others, usually to call forth the male aspect of spirit. It is a powerful totem of protection, driving all negative vibrations from a place and aiding meditational focusing. It is a disciplined totem but with a strong energy. It works well with topaz.

Garlic (Allium sativum)
stinkweed
South/Mars: Protection, healing, purification

For treating all kinds of infection and for prevention of illness, garlic is most helpful. It is antiseptic, making it useful for cleaning wounds, and is good for problems of digestion also. Garlic is employed for treating intestinal worms, for curing colds, and for regulating blood pressure.

Comments: A famed protective herb, especially against fearful manifestations, it has been used for ages to guard the home and was often carried by soldiers and sailors as protection and to give courage. Garlic carries sexual energies also, though it is more often associated with the crone aspect.

Ginger (Zingiber officinalis)
South/Mars: Success, power

Ginger alleviates nausea, particularly morning sickness and motion distress. It is used for colds and often added to herb combinations as a catalyst.

Comments: Ginger has a hot energy, stimulating and adding intensity. It is used to attract love, money, and success and is connected with the first chakra.

Ginseng (Panax quinquefolius)
sang, wonder of the world
South/Sun: Healing, protection, sexual potency, luck

Ginseng has been used to treat almost all illnesses and has been particularly venerated by the Chinese over the centuries. It is best used in small doses over extended periods of time. There are many varieties of ginseng having varying properties.

Comments: The root, with its distinctive shape, gives this totem special significance in healing and magic. It is potently sexual in energy and can be a bearer of wishes and a protector against negativity.

Hawthorn (Crataegus oxacantha)
May tree, whitethorn
South/Mars: Chastity, joy, beginnings

The berries, leaves, and flowers of this tree are wonderful cardiac tonics, appropriate for all kinds of heart problems. Hawthorn is also used for its astringency.

Comments: Hawthorn heals the heart, bringing joy and strength. Sacred to the fairies, hawthorn shelters from storms. The leaves are used as chastity sachets.

Horehound (Marrubium vulgare)
white horehound, bull's blood
East/Mercury: Creativity, clarity, protection

Well-known remedy for lung congestion, sore throat, and smoker's cough, horehound is gently laxative as well and has been given to those preparing to fast as a cleansing tonic.

Comments: Associated with the Egyptian god Horus, it frees the mind for clear thought, creativity, and centeredness. Good for the aura.

Lavender (Lavendula officinalis)
elf leaf
East/Mercury: Purification, blessing, birth ally, peace, sleep

Lavender is often used in oil form for headaches, insomnia, and skin disturbances. It is antiseptic and can be used internally and externally.

Comments: Lavender is a strong ally at births, bringing peace and clearing the way for only the best to occur. It can be used as a wash, hung in a room, or applied as an oil. Lavender attracts love, joy, and long life. It is a calm, beautiful totem that opens the heart, clears the mind, and blesses those near.

Mandrake (Mandragora officinarum)
Indian apple, wild lemon, Alraun
South/Mercury: Fertility, money, protection

The European mandrake is not related to the American mandrake (*Podophyllum peltatum*). European mandrake is used as an emetic and purgative and is often applied in homeopathic form.

Comments: Mandrake, like ginseng, is a human-shaped root, giving it particular significance. It is used to increase power of ceremony and psychic work; it is a potent totem to be related to with care.

Maple (Acer spp.)
East/Jupiter: Longevity, abundance, happiness

Maple is a totem of prosperity, a kind and happy spirit. It is a good totem tree for children especially, though it is not the best one to use for meditation—the harder woods are better. It teaches the ways of the forest and of joy in cycles. Maple's sweetness is nourishment, and its fall colors are inspiration.

Marigold (Calendula officinalis)
Marygold, calendula
South/Sun: Psychic dreams, legal matters, consecration

The flowers are used for their antifungal and healing properties and for vaginal douching. Also excellent for cleansing wounds and for skin problems.

Comments: The glorious brilliance of this totem, like sparks of sunfire, brings brightness to the mind and heart. They open the way for positive events, confer luck in legal matters, and strengthen the inner sight.

Mints (Mentha)
East/Mercury: Money, stimulation, travel

All the mints are soothing to the stomach, ease headaches, and relieve colds and fevers. They are often added to other herbs because of their good taste and fragrance.

Comments: Mints are associated with making money and bringing pleasure. They are lively spirits, protective to the traveler.

Mistletoe, American (Phorandendron flavescens)
holy wood
East/Sun: Fertility, hunting, protection

This herb has been used for epilepsy, convulsions, heart problems, and nerves, but it is a plant to be taken with caution; its berries are highly poisonous.

Comments: Mistletoe is a totem of sexuality and rebirth. It protects the home and is worn for good hunting (visions, dreams, love). It has long been associated with the religion of the Druids and was cut by them with a golden sickle on the Summer Solstice and not allowed to touch the ground.

Mugwort (Artemisia vulgaris)
artemisia, sailor's tobacco, muggons
West/Venus: Psychic dreams, strength, astral travel

Mugwort is an aid to the bladder, liver, and digestion. Effective as an oil for massage of sore muscles or as a bath herb.

Comments: A robust totem sacred to Artemis, the Moon Goddess. It is a visionary for clear dreaming and prophecy. It can be used as a fluid condenser for cleaning scrying devices. Mugwort gives strength to travelers.

Mullein (Verbascum thapsus)
Aaron's rod, flannel flower, velvet dock, candlewick plant
South/Saturn: Healing, protection

A fine herb for respiratory ills and relief of pain and inflammation. It is a treatment, in oil form, for hemorrhoids.

Comments: The tall stately mullein with its spear of yellow blossoms is a reassuring sight, standing guard, ready to offer its soft leaves for the healing of wounds and illness. It was used as a torch in the past. Mullein offers a steady, pure energy.

Myrrh (Commiphora myrrha)
gum myrrh tree
West/Moon: Exorcisms, spirituality, consecration, invocation

Myrrh is antiseptic and astringent, widely used as a disinfectant or wash for wounds. A good gargle for gum infections, mouth sores, or tooth problems.

Comments: Myrrh is ancient, burned as incense to purify and uplift. It has a high vibration and is often in the company of frankincense. It helps us attain meditative states and is appropriate for consecrating ritual tools or as an offering incense, bringing peace of mind and soul.

Nettle (Urtica dioica)
South/Mars: Protection, vitality, action

Nettles are rich in minerals such as iron and make excellent spring tonics for the blood. They stimulate digestion and promote lactation.

Comments: Nettle is a warrior totem protecting the Earth in disrupted places. Nettle offers purification and, with it, vitality—a totem of upright action and strong blood. Approach nettle with respect for its service of protection to the Earth.

Oak (Quercus alba and related species)
South/Sun: Potency, strength, fertility, power

Oak, with its noted astringency, is used medicinally. Oaks have ancient connection with Druids and were also venerated by the Romans. Oak is powerful, giving strength of body and promoting fertility. An excellent tree to meditate beside and to consult with.

Parsley (Petroselinum staivum)
persil, rock parsley
East/Mercury: Honor, purification

Parsley is full of nutrients, making it a very nourishing tonic. It is ued for gall-stones, and is a good bladder remedy, but it should be avoided by those with kidney ills.

Comments: Parsley is a paradoxical totem sitting on the borders of karma. Its presence in a woman's garden used to be considered a sign of witchcraft. It is an herb of magic given to confer honor to the recipient and to promote sobriety. Parsley baths are appropriate for those wanting contact with the Great Mother.

Pine (Pinus spp.)
East/Mars: Peace of mind, protection, knowledge, fertility

Pine bark relieves headache and treats colds. Pine needles in baths will stimulate circulation.

Comments: Pine is burned as a cleansing incense. The pine never sleeps, being evergreen, so it is a good watcher over the home. The whisper of its branches is soothing and brings peaceful messages. Pine cones are fertility symbols, especially those gathered at solstice, and the pine totem is linked with the god Pan.

Poplar (Populus tremuloides)
West/Saturn: Flying, prosperity

Poplar buds are for fevers and sore throats, or as a wash for inflammations.

Comments: Poplars attract money, but this totem is more often involved with astral travel and trancework. Poplar is for journeys and gathering perspective.

Rose (Rosa spp.)
West/Venus: Love, psychic powers, divination, beauty

Rose petals are a common ingredient of sachets, potpourris, and baths. Used medicinally for heart, nerves, and for the vitamin C in the rose hips.

Comments: Rose is selfless beauty, joy in giving, and love. The thorns teach that these things are not to be carelessly grabbed for, not without pain. Rose is a totem of the heart, a gift of the Mother Goddess.

Rosemary (Rosmarinus officinalis)
sea dew
East/Sun: Cleansing, youth, memory

The astringency of rosemary heals wounds and sores. Internally it is used in small amounts to stimulate digestion and liver function.

Comments: Rosemary is a traditional incense for purification and is very powerful in this role. A totem of remembrance, it is associated with staying young in body and heart, though it is not a very playful totem. It has direct energies that strengthen rather than coddle.

Rowan (Sorbus aucuparia)
South/Sun: Psychic abilities, protection, healing

The rowan or mountain ash is astringent, diuretic, and mildly laxative.

Comments: Totem for Aquarians, with a long history as a wood for wands, rowan promotes psychic abilities and guards the night traveler as well as watching over the home and maintaining its integrity.

Rue (Ruta graveolens)
herb of grace
South/Mars: Mental powers, protection, judgment

Rue is used with discretion for relieving rheumatic pains, treating hot flashes during menopause, eliminating intestinal worms, and promoting menstruation.

Comments: Rue clears the mind and is protective. It is a good totem for trancework and for keeping things in a positive focused flow. The totem has a calming blue-green aura that brings balance and peace to the mind.

Sage (Salvia officinalis)
garden sage
East/Jupiter: Wisdom, long life, purification

Sage is an herb for throat problems, is antiseptic, and is an expectorant. Used as a gargle for mouth sores and tonsillitis, it is a drying herb, thus reducing lactation and perspiration. It is also put into baths and douches.

Comments: Garden sage is a different totem from prairie sage but is still a purifying and clarifying energy. It is associated with long life and wisdom. The smell of sage is calming and clean, aiding clear perspective.

Sandalwood (Santalum album)
santal, white sandalwood
West/Moon: Meditation, peace, spirituality, protection

Sandalwood oil is used for bacterial infections, and the tea is a fever remedy.

Comments: This is a totem of tranquillity with a very high vibration that calls to Spirit as it wards off negativity and confusion. The oil or incense forms are good for meditation and maintaining calm. It works well with turquoise and emerald, and is burned with cedar and juniper in scrying fires.

Sassafras (Sassafras albidum)
saxifrage, ague tree, cinnamon wood
South/Jupiter: Health, love, wealth

Sassafras is a blood purifier and tonic; it is used to bring down fevers and to treat arthritis and rheumatism. The oil is potent for pain relief and is antiseptic.

Comments: Sassafras promotes positive events on the physical plane, attracting health and money. It is for making choices and clearing karma.

Sunflower (Helianthus annuus)
South/Sun: Fertility, abundance, health, positivity

Sunflower seeds are highly nutritious and benefit the bladder.

Comments: Big sunflower has an expansive energy of looking toward the bright side and basking in the rays of health and happiness. Sunflower brings luck and prosperity to those who cultivate its friendship.

Thistle (Carduus, Cirsium, Onopordon)
South/Mars: Protection, strength, healing

Thistles of all kinds are totems of the warrior, the protector of life. They promote vitality and recovery from ills.

Thyme (Thymus vulgaris)
garden thyme
West/Venus: Courage, patience, purity, consecration, psychic strength

Antiseptic, expectorant, and carminative, thyme is used for whooping cough, washing wounds, and lung congestion. It is also used in the bath to increase circulation.

Comments: For development of psychic powers, courage, and energy. Put thyme into the bath for ritual cleansing or for clearing magical spaces for work. Thyme teaches patience and the release of cares and woes, and helps us see other realms.

Tobacco (Nicotiana spp.)
East/Mars: Offering, purification, healing

Tobacco is used by Native people for spiritual offerings and to honor the giving of teachings. It is given in thanks to the spirits or to medicine people for their work. It is carried in totem bags, some medicine bundles, or in pipe bags.

Uva Ursi (Arctostaphulos uva-ursi)
bearberry, kinnikinnick
South/Mars: Psychic work, prophecy

Uva ursi is often used in douches or sitz baths for its astringent and healing properties. It is a specific for urinary tract infections and is diuretic.

Comments: This totem is mainly used in its smoke form for shamanic purposes.

Valerian (Valeriana officinalis)
fragrant valerian, garden heliotrope
West/Venus: Sleep, protection

Valerian is strongly sedative, used for headache, insomnia, and other nerve disorders. It promotes menstruation while relieving cramps but should be used in small amounts, infrequently, to avoid side effects.

Comments: A totem to drive away evil, purify a space, and attract love. It will help bring deep sleep to those who need an uninterrupted space for fears and stresses to subside.

Violet (Viola odorata)
West/Venus: Fairy magic, love, luck, sexuality, peace, simplicity

Violet flowers are rich in vitamin C, and the leaves are used for cancer and in treating cysts.

Comments: Violet is queen of the fairy totems, granting peace, bringing love, and promoting lively sexuality. Violets are for knowing self and being in the path of positive energy through the acceptance of that knowing.

Willow (Salix alba)
West/Moon: Love, mystery, divination, healing

Well-known herb of the healer for relieving pain and disinfecting wounds.

Comments: Willow wands are for magic and immortality. Willow is totem of the underworld and the unconscious. It works deep magic but must be used with knowledge. Willow weaves, bends, and hides secrets beneath her branches. Willow saplings are favored for the making of sweat lodges and shield frames.

Wormwood (Artemisia absinthium)
South/Mars: Protection, dreams, moon magic, psychic energy

Wormwood is used medicinally with discretion, as a vermifuge and an aid to the stomach and liver.

Comments: Wormwood is sacred to the Moon and brings the energies of psychic consciousness, dreams, and risk. It is beautiful yet secretive, available to those who are adept at calling to the spiritual realms. It invokes peace among nations.

Yarrow (Achillea millefolium)
milfoil, old man's pepper
West/Venus: Divination, courage

Yarrow is an excellent fever remedy and good for breaking up colds. Used for some urinary illnesses and as a douche ingredient for leukorrhea.

Comments: Yarrow stalks are the traditional I Ching diviners. Yarrow draws the attention of the spirits. It is a good totem to invite to weddings and brings courage to those in need.

STONES

The brief notes given here describe some of the minerals widely known and used for metaphysical work. Each individual stone is unique—what is presented here are generalizations. Remember that nongemstones are just as powerful as the stones we call precious. In working with stone totems, be keenly aware that most minerals are mined from the Earth with a greedy violence that cannot be disregarded within your right spiritual relationship with these totems. This applies to the use of quartz crystals also.

Agate

Ruled by Mercury. For insomnia relief and pleasant dreams. Helps in understanding visions and activates the sixth chakra. Brings harmony and practicality, gives sexual balance. Moss agates are Earth stones, cooling, grounding, restoring energy. They increase the ability to ward off self-induced negativity. Blue lace agates give tranquillity and clarity of mind. Other agates are energizing, giving the strength, receptivity, and attunement needed for balance.

Alexandrite

Ruled by Gemini. Increases the body's energy field. Attracts and concentrates energy, so should not be used by those in fragile states of health.

Amazonite

Activates the solar plexus and stimulates nerve and brain activity. Gives strength for action and decision making. Good for shy people.

Amber

Ruled by Cancer. Not a stone but classified as such for totem purposes. Heals asthma, headaches, jaundice, deafness, gum problems, digestive upsets, hysteria, infection. A low intensity vibration, warm and sensual, nourishing to the younger self. Amber takes a charge well and absorbs the wearer's energy, thus protecting health. It strengthens the electromagnetic field and improves memory. Good for tuning in to nature spirits. Keep amber away from intense heat, alcohol, and caustic perfume. It also scratches easily.

Amethyst

Ruled by Jupiter. Very high vibration stone that counters negativity, sobers passions, quickens intelligence, gives calmness in danger, protects from infection and evil, and soothes nervousness. It increases spiritual awareness and is a good dreaming stone. Warmed and placed on the forehead, amethyst is helpful in easing headaches. It purifies and amplifies healing rays. This stone works well with copper or silver. It is often given for love or worn for metaphysical advancement. It is a powerful totem.

Apatite

Ruled by Mercury. Clears confusion from the mind and promotes communication. Place on the sixth chakra when using for mental clarity.

Aquamarine

Ruled by the Moon. A water stone, soothing and inspiring. It raises hope and gives safe travel across water. A good stone for seekers and seers, it calms nerves, cleanses the body, reduces fear, and brings understanding.

Aventurine

Ruled by Venus. Activates independent thinking and creativity. It stimulates opportunity, motivation, and insight, and aids in creative visualization.

Azurite

Improves psychic abilities, opening the sixth chakra and invoking spirit guidance. Good dreaming stone and a healer's ally.

Beryl

Protects from negativity, reduces laziness, relieves anxiety, and activates the intellect.

Bloodstone

Ruled by Mars. Gives courage and endurance, heals wounds, protects longevity. It is used in weather working and in bringing success. This stone removes blockages to the heart (emotional flow) and stops hemorrhages. It helps the spirit to strive for balance—a stone for good health.

Carnelian

An Earth stone. Grounds, clears thoughts, cools the blood, soothes the stomach, quells discord. Good for courage in childbirth. Banishes sorrow. It is a symbol of spiritual love and a talisman for fertility.

Chalcedony

Ruled by Aquarius. Drives away nightmares and phantoms. It promotes maternal instincts, eases fear, gives enthusiasm and goodwill.

Chrysocolla

Helps with throat problems, promotes musical and singing abilities, and enhances speaking. Reduces guilt and tension.

Chrysoprase

An Earth stone. Refined energy that is healing, balancing, and soothing. Attunes to nature, promotes generosity, and gives protection during sea voyages. This stone makes conscious that which was previously unconscious, thus aiding problem solving and insight. It is used to prevent congestion, ulcers, and cancers that are karma-related.

Citrine

Opens the mind, aids digestion, encourages healing, and helps unblock subconscious fears. Should not be used by sufferers of toxemia or of heart or liver problems. A strong energy stone.

Coral

White coral is ruled by the Moon and clears negativity coming from outside. Red coral is ruled by Venus and dispels anger. Coral is used for safety, wisdom, sanity, fertility, and for warding off danger and fear. It is a good totem for children. In healing it is used for spleen and intestinal disorders.

Diamond

Black diamond is ruled by Capricorn, yellow diamond by the Sun. They are for peace, wealth, fidelity, protection, innocence, joy, serenity, and success. Master healers and light-bringers.

Dinosaur Bone

Low-intensity fossils symbolizing atavistic power. For making contact with the energy of antiquity, for protection, and for tapping deep Earth magic.

Emerald

Ruled by Venus. High vibration stone used to heal and cleanse the aura and to balance the chakras. A poison antidote in olden times. It attracts beauty, heals the eyes, sharpens the wit, and gives prophetic dreams. Good in childbirth and for sailors.

Fluorite

Increases the clarity of the dream state. Also strengthens the bones and teeth and reduces sexual tension and hyperactivity.

Garnet

Ruled by Mars. Averts nightmares. For friendship, health, cheer, constancy, and to heal blood and inflammatory diseases. A hormone balancer, garnet improves emotional balance, enhances self-esteem, and gives success in business matters. Good for developing the will and seeing into past incarnations.

Hematite

Brings strength and calm. Used as a grounding totem for balance and attunement.

Herkimer Diamond

A good stone for the aura. Radiates energy, releases stress, increases healing abilities. It quickly takes a charge and can easily confer it to fluids for medicine work. Stores thought forms and can act as a beacon. This is a good pendulum stone.

Jade

An Earth stone. Healer of kidneys, stone of sages and seers. Brings psychic power, serenity, wisdom, blessings, clarity. Provides a link between the spiritual and the mundane. For justice, mercy, and longevity. Good connector to the ancestors.

Jaspar

An Earth stone. Brings rain, protects, balances, gives courage. This stone increases the life force and activates insight, sympathy, and telepathy.

Kunzite

For a light heart. Gives self-esteem and brings joy. A good blood tonic and memory improver.

Lapis Lazuli

Ruled by Jupiter. A high-vibration stone emanating strong spiritual energy while grounding. Used for wisdom and love and for increasing psychic abilities. It aids self-expression, heals, and strengthens. Good for artists.

Malachite

An Earth stone. Compatible with copper. Brings peaceful sleep to babies, protects against lightning, nightmares, colic, falling, and other misfortune. Gives inner security, insight, and abundance.

Moonstone

Ruled by the Moon (of course!). Pure vibration, helps raise consciousness and develop psychic capabilities. Protects travelers by night, reconciles lovers, and is used for divination. Good stone for mothers—it promotes an open heart and eases childbirth and menstruation.

Nephrite

Used for making magical weapons. Protective charm. Promotes tissue regeneration and aids kidney function.

Obsidian

An Earth stone. Draws the aura close to the body, attracts energy, dissipates negativity. Used for divination. Aids the stomach in the absorption of nutrients.

Onyx

Ruled by Saturn. For stability, strength, and balance. A stone of letting go and separation. It will not attract negativity, and it retains the user's physical story the way moonstone retains the etheric story.

Opal

Ruled by Mercury. Attracts energy; it is not for nervous people. Good for improving sight and memory, opening the third eye, clarifying the mind, and giving confidence. Opal gives psychic vision and understanding.

Pearl

Ruled by the Moon. Emanates purity and reason. Calms tempers, brings tranquillity. A gentle totem, giving faith, charity, creativity, and love.

Peridot

Ruled by Virgo. A medium-vibration stone, it is good set in gold. Protects from night terrors and can balance energy centers if of high quality. It affects mainly the three upper chakras. Frees the mind from envy and anger. Enhances sight.

Rhodocrosite

Heals emotional trauma, activates forgiveness, cleanses the subconscious. A stone for friendship and affection. Use of it leads to higher realms of thought.

Ruby

Ruled by Mars. A highly charged stone, good for rulers or others interested in power. Brings energy, protection, and health. Stimulating, promotes courage. Ruby increases vigor and vitality, removes obstacles, and strengthens the blood. It frees the imagination and brings boldness.

Sapphire

Ruled by Jupiter. A very high-vibration stone that attracts divine favor. It brings peace, devotion, and enlightenment. It stimulates the upper chakras and may be too much for some people. Star sapphire is ruled by Saturn and is protective—it will continue to protect even after passing into other hands. Used as a totem for hearing and understanding oracles.

Tiger Eye

An Earth and Sun stone. For enhancing clairvoyance while grounding. Should be used altruistically. Good for clarity of thought. A strong guardian.

Topaz

Yellow topaz is ruled by the Sun, red topaz is ruled by Mars, and Orange topaz is ruled by Taurus. This is a high-energy stone that purifies and uplifts. Blue Topaz stimulates idealism. All topaz banishes fear and is for friendship and love. It calms and guards against outside stresses. It restores energy.

Tourmaline

Ruled by Gemini. A high-vibration stone promoting optimism, helpfulness, and perserverance. A gentle totem, bringing peace and inspiration as well as flexibility, understanding, and objectivity. It has electric and magnetic properties and is not usually worn as jewelry.

Turquoise

Ruled by Venus. Radiates courage, wisdom, and peace. It confers protection on horseback and is sensitive to the health of the user. Eases tensions in relationships. A healer, it also guards against environmental pollution. In turn, you need to protect turquoise from harsh soaps, caustics, perspiration, grease, perfume, dirt, and heat. A stone for meditation and love.

Zircon

Yellow zircon is ruled by the Sun, blue by Sagittarius, red by Mars, and white by Venus. A high-vibration stone bringing self-assurance and well-being. Attracts money, protects travelers, and stimulates appetites. Used for safety from accidents and to calm jealousy and restlessness. The blue and white zircons are preferred.

GLOSSARY

Allies.   Beings from the plant, mineral, animal, and other realms who have helping and teaching relationships with a human for a specific range of purposes.

Altar.   A space, indoors or out, consecrated and maintained as a short- or long-term sacred place for medicine objects and ceremonial tools in specific spiritually significant arrangements.

Aura.   A general term for the subtle energy bodies surrounding and interacting with the physical forms of living beings.

Centering.   Quieting one's thoughts and emotions and gathering one's attention to a peaceful and actual here-and-now awareness focused through breath.

Chakras.   The major vortices in the human aura where energy moves to, from, and within the aura, and where the aura intersects the physical body.

Charging.   Imbuing a receptive crystal, stone, or object with an intentional energy message.

Clearing.   Smudging, washing, grounding, or burning away with light all undesirable influences from a person, place, or object.

Directions.   The six major pervasive realms of manifested power in our world: East, North, West, South, Earth, Sky. The medicine wheel orientations.

Energy.   A general term given to various expressions of life force, including those formed by thought, emotion, physical processes, or spiritual directive.

Great Spirit.   Great Mystery, that which creates, maintains, recycles all life and is expressed in the diversity and relatedness of all life. Genderless, nonpersonified, and omnipresent. The breath, power, intelligence, and beauty of being are the languages by which we commune with the Mystery.

Grounding.   The act of making conscious and functional a connectedness to the Earth's balancing, rooted, and orienting aspects.

Guides.   Benevolent disembodied beings willing to offer perspective and help to the spiritual seeker.

Heyoka.   Medicine of the trickster-fool that teaches by reversal, mirroring, and unpredictability. Often totemized by Coyote, Raven, or Rabbit in some Native traditions.

Leylines.   Natural, interconnected energy pathways in and on the Earth.

Medicine.　The manifestation of spirit power in distinctively sacred forms. The particular truth of each expression of Spirit in relation to all.

Medicine person.　Two-legged destined for, trained in, experienced in, committed to, and in harmony with the spirit power of the Earth, who uses that skill and knowledge in conscious daily healing practices in service to the Great Mystery.

Medicine wheel.　The mandala of consciousness awakening to relationship in all realms of sacred expression. The map of being, the hoop of power, the elements of existence and their corresponding aspects in a harmonious, living dance.

Offerings.　Tobacco or other appropriate tangible recognitions honoring something being given on the medicine path. Offerings help keep us from arrogance, presumption, and dangerous carelessness.

Power.　Concentrated, focused energy in intentional motion, creating specific patterns of flow and effect, owned by no one, neither good nor bad.

Prayer.　Participation in life through reconnecting with all relations. Articulation of gratitude, remembrance, right intention, and respect, which then reveals the state of grace and possibility that is our true world. Affirmation of spiritual reality.

Realms.　Dimensions, perspectives, and aspects of our multilayered, diversified, and vast world of being.

Relations.　Our kin in all realms, the web of life, interconnected, interdependent.

Sacred.　That which is addressed on the basis of its spiritual identity.

Shaman.　Two-legged natural magician of elemental medicine whose service is directed by the Great Mystery in aid of the people. One who lives in many realms of nonordinary reality and uses that for healing work.

Smudge.　To clear a person, place, or object with smoke from a burning plant, usually sage, copal, cedar, or sweetgrass, rubbed over the body or directed with a feather. Spiritual housecleaning.

Spirit.　Essential consciousness.

Totems.　Beings from the plant, mineral, animal, or other realms who have long-term and wide-ranging medicine relationships with a two-legged to mutually further their growth and well-being.

Trance.　A state of consciousness characterized by attunement to nonordinary realms of reality.

Vision quest.　Traditional Native process for personal revelation on behalf of the whole. An experience that deliberately breaks habituated or mundane patterns to bring into awareness transformative truths, insights, or alliances. A way of discovering one's medicine.